ON CALIFORNIA

TO STEVEN SPURRIER

Our inspiration, our mentor
and, importantly, our friend

ON CALIFORNIA

From Napa
to Nebbiolo...
Wine Tales from
The Golden State

EDITED BY SUSAN KEEVIL
FOREWORD BY KAREN MacNEIL
INTRODUCTION BY WARREN WINIARSKI

ACADEMIE DU VIN LIBRARY

Published 2021 by Académie du Vin Library Ltd
academieduvinlibrary.com
Founders: Steven Spurrier and Simon McMurtrie

Publishers: Simon McMurtrie and Hermione Ireland
Editor: Susan Keevil
Art Director: Tim Foster
Index: Hilary Bird
Text © 2021
ISBN: 978-1-913141-20-2
Printed and bound in the EU
© 2021 Académie du Vin Library Ltd

JULY 2022

CONTENTS

FOREWORD

KAREN MacNEIL

I fell into California in a ballgown. Every New York woman had one back then. I got mine from a thrift store on the Upper East Side (the best place for pre-owned black tie). I was wearing it that night because a wine importer with deep stocks of Bordeaux and burgundy was throwing itself an anniversary party at the newly reopened Rainbow Room on the top of the Rockefeller Center. The renovation had cost an astounding $26 million. In 1986, no one spent that kind of money on a restaurant – even if it did have a 360-degree view of New York and a dance floor bigger than my apartment.

Everyone in wine was at the event, including the five men I'd come to think of as the wine-writing mafia. Between them, they got every writing assignment and every wine column in every magazine – even publications like *Ladies' Home Journal*, *Vogue* and *Good Housekeeping* – magazines which a little old-fashioned good form might have dictated they leave to us, the three New York women who wrote about wine in those days.

In the middle of the soirée that night, the wine that would make me a Californian was served. It was a Puligny-Montrachet with a golden flavour so spellbinding I couldn't help it: I opened my evening bag, took out a tiny notebook, and started scribbling a tasting note.

And then it was if I'd been struck. A wave of shame washed over me. Here I was in a fancy New York restaurant, in a ballgown no less, and in the course of a few minutes, was passing judgement on a wine that its maker had agonized over for a year. This was all wrong somehow. What did I really know about wine?

I got up and went to the bank of phone booths near the ladies' room. In those days, expensive restaurants had phone booths with glass doors you could close so that your conversation would be private.

I called Jack Cakebread, who owned Cakebread Cellars in Napa Valley.

'Jack,' I said. 'I've just had a crisis of conscience. I realize I know nothing – nothing important – about wine. Can I come out and work the harvest at Cakebread?' 'Where are you?' he demanded. 'At the Rainbow Room. I just had this white burgundy, and...' 'Take an aspirin and go to bed,' he advised. 'It's an admirable thought. But, really, you don't have to work the harvest.'

'Jack, Jack...' I protested. 'You don't even own a pair of jeans,' he pointed out. 'I'll buy some.' After a bit more wheedling, Jack relented, with a few conditions.

His 'deal' was that I had to work an entire week – no copping out after a day or two. He would assign me to Miguel, the foreman of a Mexican crew. I'd stay by myself in a one-room barrack in the middle of the vineyard. Three days later, I was on my way to Napa.

The next night at two in the morning, someone banged loudly on the door of my room. I stumbled into the jeans and threw open the door. In front of me was a stern-looking Mexican man and behind him an idling pickup with 10 men in the truck bed. 'Ready, lady?' he barked. 'Yeah,' was all I could think of to say.

That night, and only that one night, Miguel let me ride with him up front in the cab of the truck. I could tell from his vibe that he hated the idea of a woman working with his crew. We bumped along on dirt roads in the dark for a while, and then all of a sudden the pitch-black night sky was filled with blinding white lights. In every direction, there were other crews of pickers already slashing at the vines. Miguel slowed the truck, and reached onto the dash for the orange-handled, claw-like knife that was sitting there. He handed it to me.

'Lady, one advice,' he said. 'Yes, Mr Miguel?' He held up his left hand. It was missing a thumb. 'Got it,' I murmured.

I did, in fact, last the week. We picked for what seemed like 10 hours a day. I lost all track of time. Each day around noon Miguel yelled stop, and we all dragged our last lug box of grapes to the truck. By the end of the day, I was so tired I fell into bed with my clothes on.

At the end of the last day, I went up to Miguel. 'When you were a picker, how many grapes could you pick a day?' I asked. 'Three tons – no problem.' And for the first time, I saw him smile.

A year later, I moved to California. I could no longer go to the Four Seasons or Le Cirque, or the 21 Club or any other place New York wine tastings were held without feeling a little dishonest. By that time, I was convinced being near vines would somehow, through some weird osmosis, make me a better writer.

California has taught me how to write about wine. But California has also taught me about natural beauty so grand I have found myself weeping just driving over the Golden Gate Bridge.

It's a beauty that's also bittersweet. From my backyard I look up at the vineyards, giant firs and old oak trees on Howell Mountain. Much of the land has been left scarred, broken and charred black by wildfires last year.

But this year, spring came again. And the tiny white flowers on the vines fertilized themselves. Now it's summer and miraculously the vines have small perfect clusters that peek out from under green leaves.

California, a kind of Camelot, knows how to endure. California will always give us – as it has given us in this book – many stories to write.

INTRODUCTION

WARREN WINIARSKI

I am delighted to have been asked to offer a few thoughts of introduction to *On California*: a thought-provoking and diverse collection of essays on the story of California and wine. A plethora of words on California's wine story already abound, but this book is unique. It is not a chronological narrative on the development of California's wine endeavour. Instead, *On California* offers a display of the singular elements behind California's modern wine potential and success, and how that success was achieved in such an extraordinarily short period of time. It also proffers some informed speculations about current challenges facing the state's wine industry, as well as some we have yet to face.

I want to congratulate the editors who cast their net so wisely and well to assemble such a lyrical array of different voices and perspectives. Through them, we journey back and forth through time, discovering as we go the pillars of California's success: the people, their goals and dreams, the methodical post-Prohibition pursuit of empirical knowledge, the state's natural resources, and its viticulturally blessed locations. There are also accounts of the uncontrollable circumstances (phylloxera twice, Prohibition and World War II) and the unforeseen god-sends (the Paris tasting) that shaped, moulded, and forged a modern viticultural endeavour in an untried land.

One might pause at first, to question why no more was made of the generally accepted beginning – the importation of *Vitis vinifera* by the Spanish missionaries. Rather, the plentiful but unkempt character of Agoston Haraszthy is presented as an alternative starting point. From there, another narrative is quickly established and the essays show that those woolly beginnings were followed by an undishevelled nerve of purpose and outcome. This is a fresh approach that will make *On California* a must-read, then re-read, addition to any wine lover's library.

As I read through the anthology, I was struck by how clearly my friend Steven Spurrier's spirit must have been a guiding light for the publishers and editors at the Académie du Vin Library. Steven's love for wine, and his ever-enthusiastic hope to rouse a similar appreciation in others, shines through these pages. In the early days, Steven spread the word of wine through classes and tastings. Later came the writing for *Decanter* and other publications, and the numerous speaking engagements. Now, through the Académie du Vin Library's words on wine, so handsomely printed and bound, a tactile pleasure is added to the joy of learning.

In the broad spectrum of topics covered in the book, one sees Steven's penchant for championing the broader, more universal story of wine at the same time as he valued the qualities of particular wines. To this thoughtful bent of mind *On California* stays true. Each essay reveals some critical facet in the plotline of the California wine story and answers questions about the elements essential to a good story. Who were the compelling characters? What were their motives and driving goals? What were their challenges and obstacles? Where was the story set? How did the setting affect the outcome? Who and what might star in the sequel?

The answers to these questions and many others, dear wine-loving readers, lie within these pages. Some articles explain the vital roles played by California's natural resources. 'Without the Pacific We're Nothing' describes how California's temperate climate is due to the moderating influence of the cold Pacific Ocean. Similarly, 'A Volcanic Tour of California's North Coast' explains how California's prehistoric volcanic past, left imprinted in the soils, accounts for much of the immense diversity of wines that can be grown here.

As for the main characters, the 'Brains, Boffins, Whizz-kids and Scholars' section is full of them. The history of the amazing research and sheer dogged persistence of Professors Hilgard, Amerine, Winkler et al, is both important and fascinating. And California wine has had its share of colourful storytellers too – not least Harry Waugh who, as the editors note, was perhaps the first British champion of Napa wines. I met him in 1964, in my first year of apprenticeship at Souverain. I recall that he was so impressed with our Souverain 1961 Cabernet Sauvignon that he 'bought and paid for a case of it, there and then'. In his 1972 *Diary of a Winetaster*, he explained that he wanted to send it back to the UK to offer 'yet another proof of the possibilities of the great wines of this district'.

California is my home now after almost three lifetimes of my family forbears residing in the middle of this great country. My surname suggests that it and wines and vines have a tethering further back in time. Only in California, with its 'many forms of viticultural gold', did the fullness of that tether come to pass.

I did not think of that when I first heard of the results of the Paris tasting. I knew nothing beforehand of the wines or the tasters, and for a very new winery, good results in a tasting are always 'nice news'. Only later, with fuller knowledge, would I realize the 'Copernican' implications of the Paris tasting on the international wine universe. '*Eppur si muove*.'

The 2021 harvest will mark my 57th, and I often get the question: 'How have things changed?' Henceforth, I will simply recommend inquirers to this book, *On California*. It will give them more comprehensive answers than I can provide and possibly provoke some thoughts on how the next chapters of the California wine story might unfold.

PREFACE

SUSAN KEEVIL

California has an extraordinary wine story to tell. No other region has come so far, so fast, with quite so many dramas played out along the way. The villains of the piece tend to reach in from the physical environment – namely fire, fog, phylloxera and seismic disruption – while its heroes undoubtedly take human form: Agoston Haraszthy, Robert Mondavi, Warren Winiarski and Steven Spurrier have starring roles. As in the films, the good in California always triumph.

At first sight, California's stage players – the grapes themselves – make wine identification easy: we've met most of them already; they're as clearly signed as any roll call of Hollywood actors. But California wine is far more complex. The interplay of ocean, sky, geology and man make knowing this outwardly modern winescape more difficult than its early adventurers – even those kick-starting its wine scene after Prohibition – ever supposed. The factors of terroir seem to be writ larger here than anywhere else, and to manifest themselves more fiercely, paving a way for wines that are equally bold – in tune with the American landscape and character – but not always.

This book sets out to explain the human part in the California wine adventure. It is a history of sorts (though not chronological), and a portrait of the pioneers and philosophers who made it happen. But more importantly, it is a description of the challenges thrown by this rugged Pacific hotzone and the way winemakers work with them to create wines that fascinate those of us who live far beyond the state boundary – and awake pride in the wine lovers within it.

The first step in knowing any wine region, of course, is to identify what happens where. The map opposite shows California's four most important regions for quality wine: the North Coast, Central Coast, Central Valley and South Coast. It also shows the state's 58 counties – 49 of which produce wine grapes. While California's counties are often used to explain a location, it is its 139 AVAs (American Viticultural Areas) that receive special attention here: these are delimited geographical areas selected for the distinctive quality of the wine they produce. California's most distinguished AVAs are numbered 1–43 on the map.

The North Coast (red) is dominated by the Napa Valley and Sonoma County. Napa, at just 48 kilometres (30 miles) long, and sandwiched between the Mayacamas and Vaca mountain ranges, has a jumbled mixture of volcanic and quake-prone terroirs that yield some of the most complex, expensive wines on the planet,

CALIFORNIA WINE REGIONS

OREGON

NORTH COAST

CENTRAL VALLEY

CENTRAL COAST

Pacific Ocean

SOUTH COAST

MEXICO

NEVADA

ARIZONA

See inset

Napa Valley AVAs

28 Calistoga
29 Howell Mountain
30 Diamond Mountain
31 Spring Mountain
32 St Helena
33 Chiles Valley
34 Rutherford
35 Oakville
36 Mount Veeder
37 Yountville
38 Stags Leap District
39 Atlas Peak
40 Oak Knoll
41 Los Carneros
42 Coombsville
43 Wild Horse Valley

Napa Valley

Coast Ranges

Lake Berryessa

NAPA

SONOMA

Sonoma

Napa

0   10 miles
0   15 kilometres

AVAs on main map

North Coast
1 Mendocino
2 Anderson Valley
3 Dry Creek Valley
4 Alexander Valley
5 Sonoma Coast
6 Northern Sonoma
7 Russian River Valley
8 Green Valley
9 Napa Valley
10 Sonoma Valley
11 Los Carneros
12 Petaluma Gap

Central Coast
13 Livermore
14 Santa Clara Valley
15 Santa Cruz
16 Monterey
17 Santa Lucia Highlands
18 Arroyo Seco
19 Paso Robles
20 Edna Valley
21 Santa Rita Hills
22 Santa Ynez

South Coast
23 Temecula

Central Valley
24 El Dorado
25 Clarksburg
26 Lodi
27 Sierra Foothills

○ Major city
○ Other city
—300— Contours (heights in metres)

0   50   100 miles
0   50   100 kilometres

N

notably from Cabernet Sauvignon grapes. Over in Sonoma, it's hot and it's cold: Sonoma County's multiple AVAs sit to the west of Napa and include pockets of coast-cooled terroir suitable for growing more delicate Pinot Noir and Chardonnay fruit, but there are bold, intense Cabernets from its warmer vineyards too. Mendocino and Anderson Valley, to the north, are cooler again: here you'll find sparkling wine, Riesling, and much more.

On the Central Coast (purple), in between the whale-watching sites (Monterey), stands of tall redwood trees (Santa Cruz) and the beachside vines of the Urban Wine Trail (Santa Barbara), the AVAs are a hotbed of unpredictability, experimentation and brand new quality – to be watched for exquisite Chardonnay, Rhône varieties and even Nebbiolo.

The South Coast (green) is dry and warm – a little too warm for quality wine, but one AVA, Temecula, makes very decent Syrah.

The Central Valley (gold), at 650 kilometres (400 miles) long is by far California's largest wine region and grows 75 percent of California's wine grapes. While most of this is bulk-made jug or box wine, Lodi and the Sierra Foothills are both AVAs to watch for quality – not least for their majestic old-vine Zinfandels.

The wine regions are explored far more extensively in the chapters that follow where our team of authors, journalists and California specialists shed light on the wines and their ever-deepening connection to the land they come from.

For help in bringing this company together, my thanks go to Hugh Johnson, John Cullimore, Clare Tooley MW, Elaine Chukan Brown, Norm Roby and Brian St Pierre, and I thank Hugh, too, for setting out the compelling set of California themes that we've all enjoyed following. Steven Spurrier, whose enthusiasm for these wines is now legendary, was there for the start of this project and had a clear vision for its finale. I hope we have done him proud.

I'd especially like to thank Karen MacNeil, Elin McCoy and Kelli White who were in the midst of major life projects but who still found time to set pen to paper for *On California*. And our trio of winemaking royalty – Warren Winiarski, Paul Draper and Randall Grahm – who have been at the very forefront of shaping California wine; they have helped us shape this book too.

It has been a great pleasure to be swept along by the tide of enthusiasm that carries this great wine state forwards.

1

ON THE CUSP OF DISCOVERY...

Who paved the way for wine in California? Who then found the grapes that defined it and made it great? And which of its 'terroirs' would come to parallel the great vineyards of France; any of them? The last 200 years have seen California wine burst to life, and the discoveries in its vineyards still continue...

HUGH JOHNSON (1989/2020)
The Madness of Agoston Haraszthy

JANE ANSON (2021)
The Arrival of King Cabernet

HARRY WAUGH (1971)
The New Napa

ELIN McCOY (2021)
Hearing the Wake-Up Call

THE MADNESS OF AGOSTON HARASZTHY

Hugh Johnson introduces the Hungarian count and 'all-purpose adventurer' who revolutionized California wine growing at a time when gold miners had ready thirsts to slake.

HUGH JOHNSON (1989/2020)

There are many parallels between Agoston Haraszthy and Australia's James Busby. Each is known as the 'father of wine growing' in his respective adopted land. Both introduced many of the vines that were to shape the flavours of the future. Both travelled to Europe to investigate and report, in most readable journals, on the regions that every ambitious wine grower would want to emulate. They were both quixotic men who left schemes half finished because something else caught their fancy. The principal difference is that Busby, the young Scot, set his heart on wine growing from the start, while Haraszthy, a nobleman (so he claimed) from a part of Hungary which is now in Yugoslavia, was an all-purpose adventurer who happened to pick on wine growing to absorb the energies of his middle years.

Haraszthy arrives on the scene (and departs from it, too) in an aureole of legend. He was (it says) educated in law, served in the Austrian Imperial Guard at the age of 18 and acquired the rank of colonel, became private secretary to the Viceroy of Hungary under the Austrians, left to grow wine and silkworms on his country estate, married a Polish countess, the beautiful Eleanora de Dedinski, and became embroiled in the Magyar independence movement. Political exile was the reason he gave for suddenly taking ship from Hamburg to New York in 1840, at the age of 28. A young cousin who went with him said it was just wanderlust.

The count – or colonel, he answered to either – made straight for Wisconsin, where he formed a partnership with an Englishman named Bryant to found the town that is now Sauk City. (He called it Town Haraszthy.) America was buzzing with such entrepreneurs at the time. They operated steamboats and stores, farms and construction companies. Haraszthy also found time to travel round the States and write a book encouraging his fellow-Hungarians to emigrate to this bountiful land. Indeed, he went home and fetched his family and his parents himself.

Agoston Haraszthy, already a legend in his own mind, took a ship from Hamburg to New York in 1840, his eventual destination California. Wine was one of his many motivations.

News of the gold-strike in California was bound to attract Haraszthy. He had been sadly disappointed that wine was not a proposition in icy Wisconsin. The whole family and a number of friends joined the '49ers in the gruelling slog by ox-wagon down the Santa Fe trail, losing only one member, his 15-year-old son Gaza, who decided to enlist with a cavalry unit in New Mexico.

Their goal was the new town of San Diego, just developing from the little mission pueblo and with a population of 650. Haraszthy was soon (instantly, rather) speculating in real estate, running a livery stable and even a butcher's shop, and also running for election. In 1850 he became the town's first sheriff. The jailhouse he built fell down, but the gallows did its work. Then in 1854 he tired of San Diego, and went to serve on the state assembly in California's new capital, Sacramento, where he backed a move to divide the state in two. At the same time he bought land between San Francisco and the ocean: 200-odd acres near the old Mission Dolores. Was he about to settle down? If he had enquired about the mission he would have learned that its vineyard was never a success.

Haraszthy nonetheless had a bundle of vines just arived from Hungary, and he planted them. According to his son Arpad, writing years later, they included the first plants of the vine that is inextricably associated with his name: the Zinfandel, and also the Muscat of Alexandria.

There was a brisk market in San Francisco, Haraszthy discovered, for eating grapes. What he could not supply he bought in Los Angeles – the Mission grape was good to eat. Perhaps by buying different varieties from 'Don Luis' in Los Angeles he realized the possibilities (and the need) for more varieties in much larger numbers in North California. In any case he rapidly abandoned his foggy property and moved down the San Francisco peninsula about 40 kilometres (25 miles) to Crystal Springs, where by 1856 he had managed to acquire some 1,000 acres. Cattle, fruit trees, strawberries, grain, grapes; he raised them all. He also went into the gold-assaying business which was frantically overstretched by the flow of gold from the mines, and in no time was made the US government's smelter and refiner: the head of the San Francisco mint.

No novelist could have invented Haraszthy. There is a surprise around every corner of his life – and how many lives have had so many corners? After two years of supervising the blazing furnaces of the mint, which ran day and night, he was charged with embezzling $151,000 worth of gold. What had happened, as the jury discovered, was that the rooftops of San Francisco were liberally gilded with the specks of gold that had flown up the overheated chimney.

While the mint was too hot, Crystal Springs, Haraszthy found, was too cold. Even down the peninsula he had a fog problem: his grapes were failing to ripen. In his mind's eye he had an earthly paradise north of the Bay, where he had called on General Vallejo. Sitting on the porch of Lachryma Montis, the legend runs, he had sipped his host's wine and delivered the deathless line: 'General, this stuff ain't bad!' In January 1857 he bought 560 acres almost next door to Vallejo and set his son Attila to planting cuttings from Crystal Springs, while he projected a sort of Pompeian villa to be called Buena Vista.

This is where his contribution to California's wine growing really began. In contrast to the General and everyone else, he planted dry slopes with no possibility of irrigation. Most of his vines were still the faithful old Mission, but there was no mistaking the difference in quality that dry-farming made. Furthermore he persuaded a dozen prominent San Franciscans to invest with him in the new experiment. Charles Krug, shortly to become the virtual founder of the Napa Valley wine industry and the deadly rival of Sonoma, was among them.

For the moment the competition was between Haraszthy and Vallejo. A newspaper reported in 1860 that 'there is still an active rivalry [between them] as to who shall have the neatest-looking vine-fields and make the best wine. Dr Faure, a French gentleman, has charge of the General's wine department. His last year's make of white wine is of excellent quality.'

Meanwhile Haraszthy, at the request of the Californian State Agricultural Society, wrote a *Report* on *Grapes and Wines in California*, a manual on planting and winemaking, urging experimentation of all kinds, particularly with different vines on different soils – but also a polemic urging the government to spend money on collecting cuttings in Europe using the consulate service, and distribute them in California. At Buena Vista he propagated vines by the hundred thousand. And he dug deep tunnels in the hillside to store their produce.

Haraszthy was still not ready to pause for breath. He urged that more research was needed. In 1861 the state governor commissioned him to visit Europe to learn all he could in the best wine areas and to bring back vines. His journey from San Francisco via New York to Southampton took six weeks. From late July to October he stormed round Europe, from Paris to the Rhine, to Switzerland, to Piedmont and Genoa, to the Languedoc, to Bordeaux, round Spain, to Montpellier and Burgundy, and back to Liverpool. Within six months he was back in Sonoma, finishing his book on the whole experience and awaiting the arrival of 100,000 vines of 300 different varieties, which the Wells Fargo Company delivered in January.

Most writers agree that this collection was the Hungarian's most important contribution to California's viticulture. It (theoretically) made possible all the experiments that were so necessary to match vines with soils and climates. That they were largely frustrated by the legislature, who declined to distribute the cuttings, or even to pay him for them, was partly perhaps due to the Civil War in the distant east (Haraszthy, as you might expect, supported the rebel South), but largely to the stinginess and apathy of civil servants. Nothing (or not greatly) daunted, Haraszthy did his best to distribute them himself.

Just how essential his imports were is shown in the plantings that, even two years later, he and Vallejo had in Sonoma, the most go-ahead district in the state. Both were still planting the Mission massively. Haraszthy had 120,000 Mission vines established, plus 140,000 newly planted, as against 6,000 'foreign' vines established, and 40,000 new-set. Vallejo had 40,000 old Mission and 15,000 new, with 3,000 established foreign vines and 12,000 new.

It was only from the mid-1860s that superior vines were available in any numbers in California, with Sonoma enormously in the lead. The next few years saw the apotheosis of Buena Vista, and its collapse. The final act of Haraszthy's frantic story should be told here, before we survey the rest of the awakening state. In 1868, disillusioned with California, he decided the future lay in Nicaragua, rum and sawmills. In 1869 he fell into a stream where there were alligators.

This excerpt is from *The Story of Wine – From Noah to Now* by Hugh Johnson, Chapter 35 'East Coast, West Coast', Académie du Vin Library (London) 2020. Reproduced here with kind permission of the author.

THE ARRIVAL OF
KING CABERNET

How did Cabernet Sauvignon make it to California in the first place? Following the footsteps of seven celebrated wine pioneers, Jane Anson traces the likely routes of California's greatest grape from Europe.

JANE ANSON (2021)

Let's imagine a dinner party where around the table you have seated Sir Joseph Banks, Thomas Jefferson, Jean-Louis Vignes, Antoine Delmas, William Lee, Peter Legaux and Agoston Haraszthy. They were all – give or take a few decades – contemporaries in the late 18th and early 19th centuries with nationalities ranging from British (Banks), French (Legaux, Vignes, Delmas), Hungarian (Haraszthy) and American (Jefferson, Lee). All larger-than-life explorers with an eye on what history would say about them. And all united by their impact on the growth of Cabernet Sauvignon in California.

They shared a love of science, exploration and travel, so we could expect the conversation to be lively. And the food copious, as they all seem to have had serious appetites; so let's serve them up beef tenderloin, braised lamb, veal tongue, turtle soup, venison chops and soufflés, all typical foods for the wealthy at this time.

Conversation might start out with Sir Joseph Banks being peppered with questions. I certainly have a few. This is a man who had a front seat in Captain Cook's 1768 expedition on the *Endeavour* to South America, Tahiti, New Zealand and Australia. He might not have directly set foot in California (he died 30 years before the state joined the Union), but he is in many ways the grandfather of the modern wine industry right across the so-called New World.

Banks spent his career importing and exporting botanical samples, including countless vine cuttings, building up 11,000 cultivated species in London's Kew Gardens and sending a further 20,000 samples around the world. We have records of numerous letters being exchanged via various mutual friends discussing the work of both Banks and Jefferson, almost always filled with botanical queries over anything from dry rice seeds to geranium bulbs, but they don't seem to have met directly. As a diplomat, then president, Jefferson only visited Kew once, in 1786, and there is no record of Banks being there to receive him, so our dinner party would serve as an excellent opportunity for these two men to exchange ideas directly. What is certain is that both were polymaths – their interests mirroring each other on far sides of the world – both wine lovers and gourmets, and both provided inspiration for the world of botany and viticulture for centuries to come.

Jefferson had more direct contact with two other men around our dining table: Peter Legaux and William Lee. Each one played a key role in getting us closer to landing Cabernet Sauvignon in California. Lee, who was born in Boston, began his career aged 18 as a commission merchant – a trader who bought and sold a variety of goods on behalf of others, taking a fee each time. He travelled to Europe, moving through Great Britain and Holland before ending up in Bordeaux in 1796, where he settled and was appointed American Consul in 1801 by the newly-sworn-in President Jefferson. This was a time when Bordeaux was the most important port for transatlantic trade, with 173 American ships registered in the local docks in 1801 alone.

A consul's job was essentially to be a shipping agent, overseeing transatlantic trade, assisting captains and their crew, and sending intelligence to Washington about the local political situation – with war between France and England ever threatening, this task would dominate Lee's time as consul from 1801 until 1816. Lee was, by all accounts, the most successful of the consuls who worked in France during those years, described as orderly and efficient, writing regular updates and above all extremely loyal to Jefferson (a book of his letters is entitled *A Yankee Jeffersonian*, a phrase he used to describe himself on many occasions).

You can picture him at the dining table dressed, as all consuls were, in the uniform of the American navy: a deep blue coat with red facings, linings and cuffs, blue breeches with yellow buttons, black cockades and a small ceremonial sword. I'm hoping someone is pouring him a large glass of wine in recognition of the role he played, in 1805, in spreading the fame of Cabernet Sauvignon in the young nation of the United States of America. He did this by sending 4,500 vine cuttings from Châteaux Lafite, Margaux and Haut-Brion to the Pennsylvania Vine Company in an attempt to ensure its new planting project was a success.

This was half a century before the 1855 Classification anointed these châteaux as the First Growths of Bordeaux, but they were already the most prestigious properties in the region, and choosing them as donors of vines was a clear vote of confidence in the project. We don't, as is often the case, have a record of exactly which varieties he sent, but plantings in those châteaux in the early 19th century would have been dominated by Malbec along with Cabernet Sauvignon (also known as Petite Verdure or sometimes Petit Cabernet), Cabernet Franc, traces of Merlot and a host of now rare names such as Castets and Sainte-Macaire. There were white varieties too; lots of them. Most importantly for this story, of

Clockwise from left: Joseph Banks, Thomas Jefferson, Jean-Louis Vignes, Agoston Haraszthy and William Lee. 'All larger-than-life explorers with an eye on what history would say about them. And all united by their impact on the growth of Cabernet Sauvignon in California.'

course, there was Sauvignon Blanc – which, a century earlier, had been one half of a spontaneous crossing with Cabernet Franc to produce Cabernet Sauvignon.

The recipient of the vines was Peter Legaux. Born in Metz, northeastern France, Legaux had emigrated to the United States in 1786 after what seems to have been a colourful and slightly shady life as a local politician in both France and the French West Indies. He seems to have annoyed several of his new neighbours in America too, but he is also the first of the men at our dining table to have genuinely focused his life on bringing viticulture to the United States.

On arrival in Philadelphia, he bought a 206-acre estate at Spring Mill, Montgomery County, where he began planting European vines and building vaults for storage of wine. In 1793 the Pennsylvania General Assembly authorized the incorporation of a company to promote Legaux's vineyard by subscription – making clear that he was looking for investors.

Legaux was nothing if not ambitious, writing to Jefferson in March 1801 to congratulate him on the presidency and offering to send him thousands of vines to plant in Virginia. When Jefferson politely declined, Legaux tried again, writing to him about the difficulties in establishing his vineyard and inviting the president to become an investor. He apparently was not able to coax any money from him (in fact, let's assume Jefferson would not want to be seated next to Legaux at our dinner), but nonetheless, he did send vines to Jefferson's Monticello estate in 1802.

A few years later, the Bordeaux vines arrive from Lee. Legaux's diary entry for April 15th 1805, held by the American Philosophy Society, records: '*This day at ½ past 10 o'clock at Night, I received a letter from Mr McMahon with 3 boxes of Grapevines, sended by Mr Lee Consul Americain from Bordeaux, all in very good order and good plantes of Châteaux Margeaux, Lafitte and Haut Brion. 4,500 plantes for 230# . . . and order to send in Town for more etc.*'

We don't know if any of these vines ended up in California in the following decades, but we do know that Legaux's vineyard went a long way to establishing an industry that was slowly but inexorably heading west, and we know that early vines in California came from two sources: European imports and shipments from these earlier-established vineyards in New England, Connecticut and Pennsylvania.

Twenty years later, and we finally have near-certainty of Cabernet Sauvignon making its way west. It came care of Jean-Louis Vignes (or Don Luis Vignes as he was known locally in a region that was heavily Spanish-influenced at the time). Vignes (yes, it really does translate as 'vines') emigrated in 1826 from the Bordeaux region, arriving in El Dorado, California, in 1831. Vignes was born in Cadillac, a small wine producing town on Bordeaux' Right Bank, that has had, incidentally, a disproportionately large influence on American culture: first with Antoine Laumet de la Mothe, Sieur de Cadillac – who founded Detroit in 1701 and was immortalized with the Cadillac car – and now Vignes, less well known but whose legacy can be felt every time you open a glass of Napa Cab.

Descendants of Vignes still live in California; they look after a family archive that was initially created by Pierre Vignes, brother of Jean-Louis and a man who emigrated to work on his brother's successful vineyard in the 1840s.

Vignes apparently left France, with his wife and four children, in November 1826 intending to establish a sugar plantation in the Sandwich Islands, but instead he ended up near Honolulu, where he raised sugar cane, vines and cattle, before finding a job heading up a distillery. When the distillery closed, Vignes, who was already 51, uprooted his family again, boarding the trading vessel *Louisa* in May 1831 to set sail for Monterey. Two years later he made his way to the pueblo (or small town as it was then) of Los Angeles.

Vignes bought a tract of land adjacent to the Los Angeles River (I'm thinking this would have had a similar layout to the farm one he came from in Cadillac – a wine growing town set on the banks of Bordeaux's Garonne River). Here he laid out El Aliso Vineyard and became the most important winemaker in California, producing as many as 182,000 litres (something like 243,000 bottles) a year. We know that he planted the local Mission grape which was popular at the time, but also that he sent to Bordeaux for cuttings of the varieties that he knew from back home, and that almost certainly included Cabernet Sauvignon and Sauvignon

Blanc. The cuttings were brought in via Boston and Cape Horn and then grafted onto local American rootstock – several decades before other locals popularized European *Vitis vinifera* plants in California.

So much of tracing Cabernet Sauvignon's early journey is guesswork because it would take another century, and Frank Schoonmaker's championing of varietal labelling, to make the concept of recording individual grape varieties a reality. But we have another Frenchman to thank for the first time that we can unequivocally see Cabernet's footprint. Enter our last-but-one dining companion, Antoine Delmas, who arrived in San Francisco aged 31 in 1849. He had been a nurseryman back in France and established a similar nursery in San José in 1851, importing 10,000 cuttings in 1854 alone. It was here that he planted – and kindly wrote down that he did so – both 'Cabrunet' and 'Merleau' (he also imported, apparently, the French snail, with the intention of indulging his culinary passion for them, something that has gone down less well with local gardeners over the years).

By this point, Delmas was far from alone. During the decade from 1852 to 1862, California nurserymen and ambitious winemakers brought in endless vinifera cuttings and rooted vines to plant in California to satisfy a growing thirst. Local records show that in the single year 1855, total sales of still wine came to almost 14,000 barrels and 120,000 cases.

All of which brings us neatly to our final dinner guest, Agoston Haraszthy. This Hungarian nobleman, traveller, writer, distiller, plantation owner and general all-round adventurer gets perhaps the most credit from history for introducing European grape varieties to California. Unquestionably he deserves much credit for importing 100,000 vine cuttings of 300 varieties following his trip around the wine regions of Europe in 1861 (*see* page 19). He was appointed to do this by the Governor of California, John G Downey, and his book *Grape Culture, Wine and Wine-Making*, published in 1862, had a huge impact on local production. He had founded Buena Vista winery in Sonoma back in 1857 and – right up until his death in the jaws of an alligator in Nicaragua in 1869 – was a tireless promoter of quality wine from *Vitis vinifera* grapes. But he was not the first.

Cabernet's fame was cemented over the following decades, when men such as Gustave Neibaum planted the variety at Inglenook in 1883, along with John Drummond in Sonoma and Morris Estee in Napa. In 1885 the most expensive wine in Napa was recorded as a Cabernet Sauvignon from Spring Mountain, called Miravalle, owned by San Francisco financier Tiburcio Parrott, another early proponent of a variety that today dominates the psychological landscape of much of California. But all owe a debt of gratitude to our earlier explorers. Let's raise a glass to them here.

THE NEW NAPA

Harry Waugh was famously the first British wine merchant to champion Napa Valley wines. Here, in his letter from 1971, he finds a region amid great change and discovery, with the 'electric feeling now vibrant in this California air' calling to mind the excitement of the Gold Rush. It is remarkable how quickly some of his predictions for the valley came true.

HARRY WAUGH (1972)

The Napa Valley, which of all the wine districts of California the writer is beginning to know just a little, must surely be the most fascinating, the most exhilarating grape-growing district of the world; remarkable not only for its beauty but for the vitality, the enthusiasm, the expertise and the thirst for knowledge of the winemakers whose willingness to experiment and try out new ideas increases from year to year. This search for perfection, always present in the past, is growing to a crescendo, and is indeed truly exciting.

The concentration on the use of the varietal grape has really only been in being during the past 10 years, but already it has made a vast difference to the quality of the wine and now, although this was certainly not the case in the 1950s, the different vintages are recognized for what they are, and one seldom hears any more that the vintages in California are all the same, for clearly they are not!

The growers, some of the most talented and skilful winemakers of the world, admit freely that all is still new and that there is much to learn. They are not yet certain, for instance, which pieces of ground in the Valley are most suitable, say, for Cabernet Sauvignon, for Chardonnay, or Pinot Noir; this can only be found out by trial and error, that is, by actual experience.

Some growers will tell you it will take 30 years before the real potential of this area can be properly assessed, others say 50 – who knows? But what is certain is that these skilled and dedicated winemakers of the present generation are taking gigantic strides towards perfection.

For proof of this, one merely has to study the Chardonnay to see how this has improved even over the past five years. Many of the wines from this grape seem largely to have lost much of that California taste, though how to describe this taste in words is almost impossible! They seem to resemble more the white burgundy from the Côte d'Or; in fact, before too long a time has elapsed, a number of the Burgundian growers may well have to look to their laurels. Unfortunately, the quantity made of this first-grade California varietal is still all too small. The aim here is not necessarily to make it taste exactly the same as the Burgundian variety, but to produce the best possible quality of which this vine is capable. The recently adopted habit of ageing Chardonnay in French oak seems to have made an important difference: formerly it was possible to distinguish the California Chardonnay from a white burgundy by the bouquet alone; now it is far more difficult and at times (for this writer, at any rate) downright impossible!

The Pinot Noir still appears to be a weak link among the varietals, and the outsider is inclined to wonder why, until the clonal situation has been improved, so much of it is being planted. The answer, most probably, is commercial. All the same, one has only to taste the Heitz 1959 Pinot Noir, admittedly, a *rara avis*, to realize that with the Pinot Noir, too, success is possible.

It is clear that the Cabernet Sauvignon is strongly in the ascendancy. There are not many Everests in this world, but when one comes across summits like the Cabernet Sauvignon of Martha's Vineyard, Heitz and of Bosché, Freemark Abbey (admittedly still of minute production in each case), the future is vastly encouraging. In this land of adventure, this new frontier, as it were, these wines represent but a minute fraction of the as yet undiscovered possibilities.

To touch on Zinfandel for a moment, a foreign visitor finds it something altogether new, and must accustom themselves both to the bouquet and the taste in order to appreciate it properly. Of origin unknown, this vine is grown more widely than any other in California, and the results are most varied. Among the higher echelons of quality, the writer recently tasted the Louis M Martini 1967, Napa Valley, which had a delightful raspberry flavour, and although fairly light, was completely charming, whereas alongside it stood the Parducci 1966 (Mendocino), which has a deeper colour, an attractive bouquet, and was full-bodied and quite different. It must have been either the soil or the vinification, and not so much the vintage, which made the difference – yet each in its own way was admirable.

Even more powerful still is the 1970 Zinfandel from the Occidental Vineyard, which lies in Sonoma County, the grapes of which were transported to Ridge Winery, resulting in a truly astonishing wine, almost black of colour. With a lovely bouquet, it has a great depth of flavour and appears to be of exceptional quality. Unfortunately, only 100 cases are available, so for the rest of the world, quality such as this can only be described perhaps as the glint in the father's eye! It indicates, however, the possibility which still lies dormant in these California vineyards.

In order to counteract the small production of fine quality in the Napa Valley, old wineries are being brought back to life, and thus there are new names

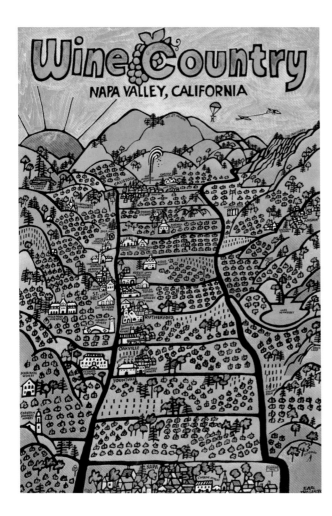

Left: Map illustration by the Napa Valley artist Earl Thollander. This 1971 depiction of the valley portrays a simpler time – the valley's 40 wineries then amount to more than 500 now. And (*above*) Harry Waugh's book published the following year, 1972, sharing his enthusiasm for this 'new' wine region.

with which to contend. A good example of this is Freemark Abbey, where great pro-gress is being made, and there are several completely new wineries where more vineyards have been planted. Prominent among these is that of Robert Mondavi, where under the dynamic control of the managing director a considerable reputation has already been gained.

There are also many new vineyard owners in the valley who will be selling their grapes to the large wineries, and in most cases the old vines, which produced only rather ordinary wine, are being uprooted and replaced by the classic ones such as Chardonnay, Pinot Noir and Cabernet Sauvignon. All of this will help to uplift the general quality. It will, no doubt, take these newly planted vines some 10 years to approach their best, but then, what excitement there will be! How one wishes one could be a young trainee winemaker with all of life ahead, for it will be during this lifetime that the potential of these California vineyards will be recognized throughout the world.

HEARING THE WAKE-UP CALL

Award-winning journalist, author and wine judge,
Elin McCoy, reveals how California embraced organic
viticulture in the 1970s and biodynamism in the 1990s,
and is now looking towards a deeper earth-consciousness
with a future of low intervention, regenerative vine farming.

ELIN McCOY (2021)

At dawn in a Napa Valley guest house about 25 years ago, I woke gasping for breath. Instead of birdsong and breeze wafting from the surrounding vineyard through my open windows, it felt like a toxic cloud of air was invading my space. As I rushed around slamming the casements shut, I glimpsed workers spraying a haze over the vines.

That experience vividly forced me to think about how chemicals might be affecting wines that I loved.

Since then, happily, there's been a sea change in attitudes towards organic and biodynamic grape growing at wineries in California. It's a story of disillusionment with conventional pesticide and herbicide-laden, irrigation-heavy farming; a shift to thinking of wine as an expression of terroir from its own complex vineyard ecosystem – and reflects the increasing awareness of the damage that's been done to the earth.

Essential to this narrative have been passionate people: eco-conscious, radical winemakers and the charismatic, ahead-of-their-time viticulture consultants who advised them; all trailblazing and ready to convert others.

I'd hoped by now that even more of the state's wineries would have embraced these revolutionary vineyard eco-practices, but the story is still evolving as California wine country faces wildfires, new pests and the full effects of climate change. New forms of farming are constantly emerging.

So how did we get here? The earliest organic efforts in California wine in the 1970s and 1980s – well before my own personal wake-up call – happened around the same time as organic farming in general was beginning to capture a wider interest in the US. But the movement's roots go back even further, to 1942 and J I Rodale, who popularized the term 'organic' for growing food without pesticides, and began publishing *Organic Gardening and Farming* magazine. In 1972, Rodale

Left to right: 'Amigo Bob' (Bob Cantisano), Phil Coturri and John Williams, vocal pioneers of organic vine growing in the Napa and Sonoma valleys, who practised what they preached and were responsible for converting many hundreds of vineyard acres to the cause.

Press was one of the five founding members of the International Federation of Organic Agriculture Movement, which met in Versailles. Its ideas were picked up by back-to-the-land hippies and others, who also gleaned advice from counter-culture publications like *The Whole Earth Catalog* (1968–72) and *The Mother Earth News* (1970–).

Before World War II and the availability of chemicals, most grape growing had essentially been 'organic', and some old-timers carried on farming that way, but there were no national standards about what 'organic' actually meant.

THE PIONEERS

Visionary organic consultant Bob Cantisano, known to everyone as 'Amigo Bob', helped define the term. In 1973 he and a few others founded California Certified Organic Farmers (CCOF), which campaigned for the state to pass a legal definition of organic practices, which it did six years later. The rules held that no synthetic pesticides, herbicides, fungicides and fertilizers should be used in vineyards, and, instead, cover crops should be grown and compost applied.

Cantisano and Sonoma-based viticulturalist Phil Coturri made a huge impact on what happened next.

Cantisano, who sadly died at the end of 2020, spent decades traveling the state in his truck, spreading knowledge like a veritable green guru. He sported a ponytail, a seriously bushy mustache, rainbow-coloured tie-dye t-shirts, shorts, sandals and always a floppy hat.

Among the first family wineries to be inspired were Frey and Fetzer, both in Mendocino. (Maybe that's why today nearly 25 percent of the county's vineyards are organic, more than any other California region.) Frey Vineyards bottled the first wines in the US made from certified organic grapes.

For the Fetzer family, the shift came through the wild success of a five-acre organic garden it had enlisted a famous organic farmer, Michael Maltus, to plant at its property in Hopland, on the west bank of the Russian River. Impressed by how tasty the resulting vegetables were, Jim Fetzer contracted Amigo Bob to convert the vineyards too. By the time they sold the winery in 1992, the family was farming 1,200 acres of certified organic grapes. Under company president Paul Dolan, the new corporate owners continued to champion organic growing for the Bonterra label, spreading the idea to grape growers across California. Demand for wines made from organic grapes has grown by double digits annually since the 1990s, which shows just how much the world is changing.

The Fetzer experience drew in John Williams of Frog's Leap, founded in 1981, to become the first Napa Valley winery to go organic, with Amigo Bob's help. Spottswoode, another client, has been farming organically since 1985. Amigo Bob was who you called if you needed to find eco-friendly solutions to pest and disease problems, as Honig did when trying to combat Pierce's disease, spread by sharpshooters (leaf-hopping insects that inject lethal bacteria as they feed from the vine).

At the same time, Phil Coturri, who also sports a ponytail, was following a similar path; he planted an organic Cabernet vineyard on Sonoma's Moon Mountain in 1983 for screenwriter Robert Kamen's Kamen estate. For nearly four decades he has managed hundreds of acres of exclusively organic vineyards, with clients like Laurel Glen, Bedrock, Hamel and Oakville Ranch. His brother Tony's Coturri winery has made wine from organic grapes since 1979.

But the early organic movement was hardly restricted to northern California. In Santa Barbara, Richard Sanford was the first winemaker to get his grapes

California's earliest organic efforts began with the publication of J I Rodale's *Organic Gardening and Farming* magazine (*left*) in 1942, and picked up pace through the 1960s and '70s supported by new journals, *Whole Earth Catalog* and *The Mother Earth News*.

certified, in 1983. He once recounted how he got mealy bugs and ants in the vineyard under control by spreading peanut butter on the bottom of the vine trunks.

What all these early pioneers discovered was that going organic required a different mindset, a way of seeing that everything in the vineyard is interrelated.

Thanks to US government complications, though, most of the wines couldn't be certified 'organic' unless they avoided adding sulphur as a preservative – something that was permitted in European organic definitions. Instead, most winemakers use 'made from organic grapes', for which the USDA provided a uniform definition in 2002.

By 2010, organic grape growing was firmly in people's minds and even those who weren't organic were talking about using fewer chemicals. Cover crops to attract beneficial insects and contribute nutrients to the soil were fast becoming de rigueur. Winemakers who used to show off their temperature-controlled stainless steel tanks now wanted to walk the vineyard, talk about the stones and soil, and how 'wine is made in the vineyard'.

The list of certified organic vineyards is getting longer, and the best wineries, like Rosemary Cakebread's Gallica, for which she buys grapes from several different sources, make clear which are certified organic and which are farmed organically, but not certified. Cakebread's fabulous, layered Grenache from Sonoma's Rossi Ranch is, and it's farmed by Phil Coturri.

We think of organic farming as something prestigious, high-end wineries do, but by 2021, according to Pam Strayer of the wine country geographic blog, the biggest organic grower had become Fred Franzia, who converted 8,000 of his 40,000 vineyard acres in California's Central Valley. The owner of the popular entry-level brand Two Buck Chuck, sold nationwide in Trader Joe's supermarket stores, Franzia now uses this organic fruit for his brand Shaw Organic.

Yet in Monterey and San Luis Obispo counties – both sources of some top wines – the dangerous pesticide paraquat, linked to Parkinson's disease, is still being sprayed on grapes.

ENTER BIODYNAMICS

The biodynamics movement in California proved much more controversial, and for more than a decade it seemed to have a kind of woo-woo, anti-science aura.

Its era started in the 1990s, with Alan York, another charismatic consultant, and the Frey family, both of whom worked with and were inspired by British horticulturalist Alan Chadwick. Frey Vineyard was the first winery in the US to be certified biodynamic.

The principles of biodynamism come from the farming philosophy of the Austrian Rudolf Steiner (1861–1925), which is based on organic principles, but goes further, towards a holistic view of the vineyard (or farm) as a living organism. Adhering to a planting calendar based on phases of the moon and using special preparations to build soil structure – prepared and stirred in a dynamizer – are part of its methodology. But some of the mystical elements and the practice of stuffing a cowhorn with manure and burying it in the vineyard have come in for scepticism and descriptions of vintners' 'voodoo'. (In 2010, outspoken Stu Smith of Smith-Madrone (Napa), briefly, but famously, wrote a blog entitled 'Biodynamics is a hoax'.)

Experiments with biodynamics had been going on at wineries in the 1980s and early 1990s in Europe, especially in the Loire Valley and Burgundy. In 1985, Demeter, an international biodynamic certifier, formed a branch in the US to assist in maintaining recognizable production standards. A handful of California vintners were intrigued and turned to Alan York for help.

His collaborations with the Fetzer family at Bonterra and McNab Ranch and the Benzigers at their estates in Sonoma, which were certified in 2000, became showcases. They brought widespread attention to biodynamic concepts, and drew in others: Quivera, Robert Sinskey, Araujo Estate (now Eisele Vineyard), Spottswoode and more.

By 2007, when I moderated the second Biodynamics in American Wine conference in San Francisco, more than 300 people showed up to listen to a panel of believers that included Alan York, Mike Benziger, Katrina Frey, Paul Dolan and Randall Grahm of Bonny Doon, people weren't laughing. But that doesn't mean they joined the bandwagon.

Some producers didn't go after official Demeter certification, or they ended up dropping it even though they followed the same farming practices. The reasons for this were two-fold: first, because of objections to the fee structure; second, because they considered the rules too rigid, lacking sensitivity to the needs of the individual sites.

GOING FURTHER

The rise of natural wine is an even more recent phenomenon, with an increasing following among young winemakers in California. Their mantra is to adopt low-intervention, minimalist methods: farming that starts with organic and biodynamic grapes (but not always) and extends to the way they work in the cellar, using natural yeast and adding nothing to their wines. Tony Coturri, for example, doesn't add sulphur, a key in defining natural wine in Europe.

In fact, for a surprising number of California winemakers, organics and biodynamics have been stops on the road in their quest to understand the secrets of soil and the best ways to farm grapes for long-term sustainability. In the past

Ted Lemon sees biodynamic regimes as too structured, and prefers a more rehabilitative approach to farming, stressing the regeneration of topsoils.

decade, they've been thinking of grape growing as part of a much bigger agricultural picture and redefining what they do.

Pinot Noir and Chardonnay-maker Ted Lemon of Littorai, on the West Sonoma Coast, travelled the organics and biodynamics route to his own concept of a model farm at the property outside Sebastopol he and his wife Heidi bought in 2003. He adopts a biodiverse, self-sustaining ecosystem that he refers to as generative agriculture, and which he sees as the only path forwards to a healthy planet. It encompasses woods and a stream, open pasture with cows mooing and sheep bleating (both producing manure), chickens scratching, a 30-acre vineyard, a winery built with straw bales, and herbs grown on the farm that are dried for biodynamic preparations to build the soil. Lemon waves off biodynamic certification; he sees its regime as too rigid, not responsive enough to the specific conditions of an individual piece of land.

The soft-spoken Lemon, who started his wine career in Burgundy, has influenced many others, starting with grape growers like David Hirsch, from whom he still purchases grapes. Another new direction is through regenerative organic agriculture, the wine world's latest buzz term, which links organic viticulture with environmental and social justice solutions. Last year, Tablas Creek, a pioneer in Paso Robles and a partnership of the French Rhône Valley Perrin family and the American Haas family, became the US's first Regenerative Organic Certified vineyard. The winery, founded in 1989, has grown grapes organically from the beginning and also added biodynamic techniques. This new step takes them further, committing them to farm worker fairness, animal welfare and a wider view of what healthy soil means. Other wineries are sure to follow.

Perhaps the most radical vision of how to farm vineyards is in the Sierra Foothills at La Clarine Farm, founded by Hank Beckmeyer and his wife Caroline Hoel in 2001. They, too, started out organically and biodynamically, their vineyards certified by Demeter. Then Beckmeyer became fascinated by the writings of Masanobu Fukuoka, the Japanese author of *The One-Straw Revolution* (1975), and his 'no-till' farming philosophy. Beckmeyer began to rethink his own role as a farmer and how both organic and biodynamic methods in the vineyard were a form of control. What would happen, he asked himself, if he became more of a caretaker, stepped back and trusted in natural processes in a route to making delicious wine? As he writes on his website: 'Some surprises may be found. New ways of thinking can emerge.'

So let me come back to the idea of sustainability in the face of climate change and the need to repair much that is wrong with the world. That's something Steve Matthiasson, a viticultural consultant to many top wineries, such as Accendo Cellars, as well as a winemaker at his own eponymous winery in the Napa Valley, founded in 2003, takes very seriously. Yes, all the vineyards he works with, including his own, are certified organic or transitioning to that status. But his view is wider, obsessed with building organic matter in the soil, increasing biodiversity, reducing his wines' carbon footprint, conserving water and paying employees a living wage. In other words, organic viticulture is good, but it takes more than that for winemakers to respect the planet.

Sustainability, Matthiasson likes to say, is a continuum, not a state, an ongoing effort with no end in sight. In California, as elsewhere, that's today's challenge.

2

UP THE COAST... SONOMA AND BEYOND

Without the presence of the mighty Pacific Ocean, there would be no wine in California. Its soothing presence and cool breezes create pockets of possibility – enclaves north and south, chilled enough to succeed with the state's most elegant white grape and its most pernickety red.

CLARE TOOLEY MW (2021)
Without the Pacific, We're Nothing...

GERALD ASHER (1996)
The Mysteries of Edna Valley Explained

REX PICKETT (2004)
Two Guys on Wine

STEPHEN BROOK (2021)
In Pursuit of 'Burgundian' Pinot Noir

WITHOUT THE PACIFIC, WE'RE NOTHING...

Clare Tooley explains why there would be no winemaking in California without the presence of the mighty Pacific Ocean.

CLARE TOOLEY MW (2021)

California's golden Eden owes it all to a vast, deep ocean. The Pacific's perpetual movement brings the weather and life to its shores, creating an existence so inherently attractive, the West Coast is a source of continual inspiration to all who experience it or yearn to. The coastal roads demand a trip, its beaches a holiday. The cities of saints and angels along its ragged edges draw a constant stream, a population of pilgrims, who come in search of gold and fame or to work in the silicon and salad fields. Just offshore, its marine life equally teams with itinerant forms. Breaching to breathe, pods of migrating whales use it as a briny runway to warmer waters and wet-suited surfers, with salty lips and tousled hair, play dice with the sharks to find their flow. They watch its show of colours every evening, straddling their boards, as it bathes the fierce sun and puts it to bed.

But this is no serene, maternal garden paradise. Hewn by great violence, California's coastline is a mass of shattered rocks. The waves rage furiously as if distraught at the beauty they have created. The ocean remains so bitterly cold, it steals breath even on the hottest days. The coastal regions perch on a knife-edge of existence, bracing against the fault lines that trace certain future destruction. No wonder vines are planted here, on the very edge of the world. Wine is needed to stake a human claim, fleetingly, in a place as wild as we are insignificant.

The ocean accommodates this manmade endeavour. Grudgingly perhaps, but without its presence there would be no California wine. Ocean weather is as intemperate and as dramatic as the body of its water is massive. Its storms bring showers to soak vineyard soils enough to germinate, yet rain hard enough to cause catastrophic erosion. Its winds circulate cooler air to mitigate the heat of a sun that has long ago petrified huge tracts further inland. Yet those winds equally drive the state's fires that burn so hard and black as to eclipse the sky. It brings the fog, the most obvious transference of water to earth and of most benefit to viticulture. Every day, the ocean breaks its boundaries to meet with land, tryst-like.

Big Sur, 'not a place but a state of mind' (Lillian Ross): this 114-kilometre (70-mile) stretch of California's dramatic Pacific Coast is skirted not just by great cliffs but by a narrow highway, Route 1, from which the meeting of two great masses of land and sea, can be viewed, felt and savoured.

The surf's cresting, white-tipped waves splinter into a million droplets and turn to milky mist. The fog rolls inland, smothering the beaches in sepia first before funnelling up the tributaries and waterways. It breaches the mountains before its swash flows between vine rows. It has a slightly unnerving habit of disappearing when your attention is drawn elsewhere. Turn back and you have missed its ebb.

The ocean shares its cold and warm fronts with the land, lending texture to the coastal air. It is soft, warm and balm-like in the south. The air changes in the north and, at times in San Francisco, feels like a thousand papercuts of cold. It turns creamier yet cold still in the verdant banana belt of Mendocino. While no marine flavours tincture the crops, it is these textures, keenly felt on human skin, that translate to the fruits and vegetables that grow south to north. No salt lick, but a plush plumpness to the green velvet of avocado flesh and red berry pulp of Pinots in the south. No brine, but a seam of tangy acidity in the blood-orange persimmons and bright green Sauvignons to the elevated north.

More constant still, and once the fog recedes, the Pacific's reflective expanse affects the very nature of California's natural sunlight. To the south, daylight in Santa Barbara is golden with amber edging, but blue in San Francisco Bay, turning verdigris to the north. The vine leaves photosynthesize this shimmering light source to produce synaesthetic coastal fruit of kaleidoscopic flavours. The best wines are both ripe and bright, superbly focused on the palate, their fruit profile as if caught in a cabaret spotlight.

For the wine lover, California's coastline offers a lifetime of entertaining pleasure. The Central Coast covers a vast region of tectonic fertility. Its mountains, valleys and gulleys, chiselled by the movement of the ocean, are a mass of fractured soil rich with possibility. Its beauty and bounty are rightly blessed by its congregation of saints that give their names to the missions and cities along the Camino Real. Travelling northwards from Santa Barbara, through Santa Maria, Arroyo Grande, San Luis Obispo, past the Edna Valley, through Paso Robles to Monterey and Santa Cruz, on to Napa and Sonoma, beyond to Lake and Mendocino, it is possible to taste more wines from more grape varieties than can possibly be good for you.

Unbridled by time and history, defined less by permission and place (as in Europe) than by American immigrant ambition, the coastal pockets of grape production revel in their youth and diversity. Almond and fruit orchards have been uprooted to make way for a panoply of grape varieties, their perfumed blossom, barely perceptible still, evoked faintly in the new berry crops. From Pinot Noir to Cabernet Sauvignon and Albariño to Zinfandel, Chardonnay shares cellars with Grenache Blanc while Syrah sits in barrels next to Malbec and Tempranillo.

The cool air and coastal fogs at the seaward end of the Arroyo Grand Valley preserve the acidity of its fresh-tasting Pinot Noir and Chardonnay wines. By afternoon, the fogs have rolled away to the beaches and the sun shines.

Edna Valley has the longest growing season of all the California AVAs, and this gives its wines greater depth of character and complexity. Its Chardonnays are among the most desirable in the state.

Marsanne meets Riesling, Pinot Grigio and Petit Verdot. Grenache, Dornfelder and Tannat rub shoulders with pungent Mourvèdre and tongue-staining Petite Sirah. Heady Viognier makes room for daisy-fresh Picpoul. Wine blends indulge the wealth of this diversity. Single varieties, hardy enough to resist the drought and mine the volcanic soils, dig deep roots, to become wines that express their determination. Like the pioneering individuals who make them. Energized by the tidal pull, the coastal wines and winemakers are visceral and vital.

Paso's red wine richness – some like fruit cake stuffed with figs and boozy plums, others more earthily baked – evokes the long hot summers that keep winemakers strapped to their surf boards. The Edna Valley, one of the coolest appellations in California, leverages its colder air currents and long growing season to concentrate perfumed aromatics in the shyest of white varieties. The vineyards of Arroyo Grande enjoy million-dollar sea views, but their wines wear this luxury lightly. The best are graceful, as light as soufflés, with fruit tannins like lace. The vineyards, perched at altitude in the Santa Lucia Highlands and Chalone, look down to the ocean and mirror its marine life making wines with backbones of mineral acidity as athletic and flexible as the vertebrae of fish that shoal in the waters below them.

Sonoma and Napa's historic wines are better known and documented than most. Their vines enjoy the cool morning ocean fog, their valleys are equally fissured and soils as significantly patchworked by the shifting plates. Yet the ocean's influence here is geographical in a wider sense. These wines have traversed the oceans to bring the story of the west coast Eden to a wider world. They are served to a larger audience, are influenced by an extended world, and combine a taste of origin with a flavour of their travels.

Heading north into Humboldt and Mendocino, however, the land and wines quieten and become more secretive, muffled by the towering redwoods and damp ferns of emerald forests. The coastline here, more than anywhere else, bears the scars of an enraged ocean. Few vineyards brave its force, and most are set back to avoid the tides that heave rocks onto the shore. There are beaches of bowling boulders complete with long channelled grooves millennia-old and stretches of crushed glass smoothed by the motion of the surf to multicolour pebbles. The crisp dry white wines of northern California match the sweetest fresh crabmeat sucked straight from the claws. Heartier Mendocino red wines wash down the tough sea snail meat of abalone brought to the beach by divers who swim deep with knives drawn. The iridescent shells are scattered through the coast's campsites, their pearl buffed and degraded by the sandpapered salty air.

The Pacific Ocean tempers the sun and keeps time with the moon to create seasons of fruitfulness. It owns California and its wines entirely.

THE MYSTERIES OF
EDNA VALLEY EXPLAINED

Gerald Asher reveals how California's most prestigious Chardonnay appellation came to be born in a small coastal community midway between (and totally unaffected by) Los Angeles and San Francisco…

GERALD ASHER (1996)

The winter rain of 1992 ended six years of drought and left California looking like a child's picture-book image of spring. Between vines, under fruit trees, and across hillsides that had been barren only weeks before, California poppies, flowering mustard and lupins splashed orange, yellow and blue on the bright green of new grass. At the end of a drive south from San Francisco to San Luis Obispo – about 370 kilometres (230 miles), much of it along the Salinas Valley where crews were already bringing in the first spring crops – I was so entranced by the transformation that I overshot my freeway exit and was almost at the ocean before I realized my mistake.

Granted, San Luis Obispo, hidden from the highway that serves it, doesn't announce itself with the visual equivalent of a trumpet blast. But inattention had brought home to me how close to the Pacific the town is – as automobiles run let alone as crows fly. The fishing boats of Morro Bay and the surfing of Avila and Pismo beaches are in the town's backyard. In this special situation, open to the ocean yet a little protected from it, San Luis Obispo has what is probably California's most equable climate. It's also one of California's most agreeable places to live. Almost midway between San Francisco and Los Angeles, San Luis Obispo is compact, friendly and independent of both. It has advantages unexpected for its size – galleries, bookshops, cafés, good movie theatres (the town's Fremont is an Art Deco gem) and lively, unpretentious restaurants – thanks to Cal Poly, with its busy and prestigious schools of engineering, architecture and agriculture.

The town's tie to agriculture in particular is made plain every Thursday, when four blocks of Higuera Street, not far from the sprawling 18th-century mission, are closed to traffic at the end of the business day and allowed to become, for a few evening hours anyway, a giant street market for local farmers. San Luis Obispo County is known for the quality of its fruits and deliciously tender vegetables. Bright days, cool nights and the humidity of sea fog even in the driest summers combine to give local strawberries their intense flavour, and Higuera Street vendors offer them by the crate, along with bell peppers, basil and coriander. In season, there are artichokes and snow peas, onions and zucchini, a multitude of lettuces, bok choy and apples, broccoli and avocados, cucumbers, sweet anise, oranges and walnuts. Beef ribs and local sausages are available from huge barbecue pits set up on the sidewalks; flowers massed on all sides sell for a couple of dollars a bunch; and, at every corner, there is a musician, a juggler or some other street performer trying, usually in vain, to divert attention from fat tomatoes and garden-grown corn sweet enough to eat straight off the cob. In fact, Thursday evenings in San Luis Obispo are as much celebration as commercial endeavour, and except when it rains, the whole town turns out for this weekly paseo.

Jack and Catherine Niven, whose family once shared ownership of California's Purity food chain (service- and quality-driven, it didn't survive the great wave of supermarket expansion in the 1950s and '60s), already knew of San Luis Obispo's reputation for fruits and vegetables when they were looking, in the early '70s, for land suitable for vines. They were not surprised to learn that Edna Valley, abutting southeastern San Luis Obispo, had been recommended for potentially high-quality wine production in the Winkler-Amerine study of California's

The vendors of the 'SLO' (San Luis Obispo) farmers' market gather weekly on Higuera Street, their produce ranging from fresh clams to barbecued corn cobs, served alongside street music as varied as the gastronomic offerings.

The Missíon San Luis Obispo de Tolosa, founded by Junípero Serra in 1772 – one of 21 Spanish Missions that lined the California Coast from San Diego to San Francisco. It still functions as a Catholic church, but what was once the fathers' soup kitchen is now a youth centre.

wine regions, completed back in the 1930s. Jack Foote, San Luis Obispo County Farm Advisor (now retired), had planted an experimental plot of vines in 1968, in fact, and by 1972, when the Department of Viticulture and Oenology at the University of California, Davis, made some wine from those grapes, there was general agreement that viticulture in the area was worth pursuing.

For those who cared to look for it, other evidence pointed in the same direction. The Franciscans who had accompanied Junípero Serra in his trek up the coast of California to establish the early missions had planted vines to meet their domestic and religious needs wherever they set up a community. The wine produced at San Luis Obispo was so good, however, that, as word got out, production was stepped up to a commercial scale. The mission's vineyard was extended, and by the first decades of the 19th century, according to Dan Krieger, history professor at Cal Poly, Father Antonio Martinez of the San Luis Obispo Mission was making over a hundred barrels of wine a year and trading it with whalers and other missions at a good price. Records show that the San Luis Obispo Mission had the highest revenues of any in California.

That vineyard at San Luis Obispo was temporarily abandoned when Mexico secularized all mission property in declaring herself independent of Spain; but then, some 20 years later, in the 1860s, it was acquired and reconstituted by Pierre Hippolyte Dallidet, a French immigrant. His son, also Pierre Hippolyte, predicted in a local board of trade pamphlet of 1887 that San Luis Obispo's vines would eventually bring great wealth to the county. By then, says Krieger, local farmers

– the McCoppins and the Hays, the Andrews and the Taylors, the Atwoods and the Hasbroucks – were already shipping grapes, raisins and wine to San Francisco from a new wharf at what is now Port San Luis, railhead of the narrow-gauge Pacific Coast Railroad built to connect both wharf and port with the town itself in 1881.

Despite skirmishes with phylloxcra and the economic depression of the late 1880s, vineyards continued to flourish in Edna Valley until they disappeared completely with Prohibition. It took the Nivens and Norman and Carolyn Goss to get them started again. The Gosses (Norman was a Los Angeles restaurateur aware of the quality of San Luis Obispo produce) came to the valley independently of the Nivens but at about the same time; both families bought land in 1972 and planted vineyards the following year. In 1975 Andy and Liz McGregor planted 63 acres of vines; and then in 1990 and 1991 several hundred more acres of vines were planted as yet more growers moved in to join those who by then were already well established.

It was never the Nivens' intention to make wine. But in order to grow grapes successfully for others, they had to think of themselves as winemakers. Their Paragon Vineyard Company had had little but theory and the narrowly focused experiments of Jack Foote to guide it in planting five red varieties and three whites in different sites to see how each would react to the range of soils, altitudes and exposures to sun and wind. As Jack Niven tells the story, it was soon evident that the valley was too cool for Cabernet Sauvignon and Zinfandel, and Merlot just wouldn't set fruit. Equally as clear was proof that any Edna Valley Chardonnay could be successful. But, as no one alive could remember having tasted wine made from Edna Valley grapes, the Nivens attempts to sell their fruit were at first disappointing.

Their chance to show how good Edna Valley Chardonnay could be came quite fortuitously. Chalone, a winery on a limestone bench 610 metres up in the Gabilan Mountains and about 160 kilometres (100 miles north) of Edna Valley, had a reputation for Burgundy-style Chardonnay and Pinot Noir unequalled at the time. The limited supply tended to be kept under wine merchants' counters for a favoured few, and the long drive from San Francisco deterred all but the most ardent from attempting to buy directly at the winery. The last part of the three-hour drive leads up a twisting road through miles of parched mountain landscape resembling nothing so much as a Dutch primitive's idea of St John the Baptist's habitat. In the early 1970s, what's more, the winery itself, eerily remote and virtually without either water or electricity, did indeed have an almost religious austerity about it; its domestic-type well and small generator didn't come close to supplying its needs. Since then, the company that owns Chalone has

Given its spectacular isolation (*above*), it seems improbable, but the Chalone winery – famous for its third-place Chardonnay at the Judgement of Paris – gave Edna Valley its first big break.

brought in a power line, and that in turn has allowed the winery to install pumps to bring water up 11 kilometres (seven miles) of pipeline from a well in the valley floor. Chalone extended its vineyard in 1977 and also built a new winery large enough to receive the increased crops.

From the beginning, Richard Graff, Chalone's president, had a policy of using only grapes grown in Chalone's own vineyard for wines sold under the Chalone label. But he hoped to find a use for the winery's spare capacity until the new vines were bearing. At about that time, in the late 1970s, John Walker, an eminent wine shop in San Francisco's Financial District, wanted Chardonnay to sell under its own label and knew that Le Central, a nearby bistro popular with Montgomery Street bankers and stockbrokers, was looking for something similar. Their need, Chalone's space and the Nivens' grapes consequently came together in a private-label programme. Begun in 1977 as an arrangement of convenience for all concerned, the programme became an enormous success, launching the Edna Valley appellation among a knowledgeable and well-heeled clientele.

By 1979, when Chalone was compelled to take fewer of the Nivens' grapes in order to make room for its own, Richard Graff fully recognized Edna Valley's potential and was loath to cut himself off from it. As a result, he and Jack Niven developed the idea of a joint venture between Chalone and the Nivens' Paragon Vineyard Company to make and sell Edna Valley wines. The Nivens had a winery built on their land to Graff's specifications, and this they leased to the new enterprise, Edna Valley Vineyard, in addition to supplying the grapes. Graff's Chalone undertook the responsibility of making the wine and marketing it, and the entire operation was up and ready for the 1980 crush.

If the arrangement with Richard Graff grew out of happenstance, so did Paragon's relationship with Charles Ortman. By the late 1970s, Ortman was Napa Valley's Mr Chardonnay: he had advised, consulted or actually made Chardonnay for an impressive number of important wineries there, including St Clement, Spring Mountain, Far Niente, Fisher and Shafer. Whether inevitably or by chance, Ortman's involvement with Edna Valley, like Graff's, gave the region a great boost in acceptability.

Ortman remembers first working with Edna Valley grapes in 1979. 'The Nivens offered me some that had lost their home,' he told me recently, reminiscing, and alluding perhaps to the changed situation at Chalone. 'So you could say I got the grapes by default. The wine I made from them was bottled under my own label. I was impressed by the fruit and bought again in 1980 and in 1981.

'I didn't have another opportunity to work with Edna Valley grapes until 1987. The wine I made then had still not been released when in 1988 I concluded an agreement with Beringer Vineyards, which bought my brand name, Meridian, and applied it to its new winery near Paso Robles. Beringer's management shared my enthusiasm for Edna Valley, and, as we already had that stock of the Meridian Edna Valley 1987 Chardonnay, the appellation was integrated into the new Meridian programme from the start. We've continued to take grapes from Paragon every year, but we have also bought land there and have now planted a hundred acres of Chardonnay of our own.'

A number of other wineries also began buying Edna Valley fruit after the 1979 vintage. Because the grapes could be relied on for flavour and texture, the grapes sometimes disappeared into a Central Coast or other blend. Over the years several wineries have earned their Chardonnay laurels thanks to a judicious proportion of Edna Valley grapes. Very few wineries have been able to offer a Chardonnay produced from Edna Valley grapes alone, however, because the quantities available have been so limited. The first vineyards planted, in 1973 and 1975, included fewer than 450 acres of Chardonnay – enough to produce a grand total of about 100,000 cases of wine when the vines could be persuaded to produce at the rate of four tons to the acre, which was seldom. A further 300-plus acres of Chardonnay have recently come into bearing. But there are still fewer than 800 acres of Edna Valley Chardonnay compared with nearly 57,000 acres of Chardonnay in the state of California as a whole.

I had driven down to San Luis Obispo to take a look at Edna Valley, to try to understand what made its Chardonnay unique. For in any Edna Valley Chardonnay certain characteristics stand out regardless of the style of the person who made the wine. The Edna Valley Chardonnay by Charles Ortman at Meridian, though not to be confused with other Edna Valley Chardonnays – whether by Steve Dooley at Edna Valley Vineyards, Brooks Painter at Leeward, Michael Martella at the Thomas Fogarty winery, Gary Mosby at Chimère, Clay Thompson at the Gosses' Chamisal or at his own Claiborne & Churchill winery in San Luis Obispo – is closer to all of them than it is to the Santa Maria Valley Chardonnay also made at Meridian by Ortman.

The phenomenon intrigues me not just because I like Edna Valley Chardonnays but also because Edna Valley, declared an approved American Viticultural Area in 1982, is one of the very few to meet what should be consumers' expectations of all such geographically defined wine regions. An Edna Valley Chardonnay is distinctive, it's recognizable and it's consistent. And, because Edna Valley vineyards are overwhelmingly Chardonnay (more than three-quarters of the acreage planted in the valley is devoted to this one variety; the rest is divided among many), to ask for a bottle of Edna Valley wine is almost like asking for a bottle of Meursault: within reasonable limits, the buyer knows exactly what to expect.

Though I hadn't known it at the time, I'd begun to unravel Edna Valley's mystery when I'd overshot San Luis Obispo's freeway exits and found myself on the beach. The maritime influence is pervasive in the valley – to a far greater extent than in any other wine region along the Pacific Coast. The very soil in which the vines grow is made up largely of marine sediment deposited 25 million years ago, when sea levels rose at the end of the Ice Age. The marine sediment is rich, of course, in the tiny shell fossils that give Champagne and Chablis in France their chalky soils. But it is supplemented here by degraded granite and tufa from a chain of 14 ancient, greatly eroded volcanos that stretch in a line parallel with the valley from southeast of San Luis Obispo to the ocean. This spectacular formation, some of the peaks worn down to stumps while others loom to a thousand feet or more, seems to end at El Morro, at the entrance to Morro Bay, but actually continues offshore to finish under 1,100 metres of ocean with Davidson Seamount, the underwater volcano. If soil composition affects the taste of grapes, as is commonly supposed – soil stores the water and nutrients needed for vine growth while its form and texture control rooting patterns – then it must inevitably affect the taste of any wine. Given the unique soil of Edna Valley, this relationship is particularly relevant.

TWO GUYS ON WINE

In an excerpt from Rex Pickett's book, and film, *Sideways*, 'Jack' and 'Miles' explore the Santa Rita Hills – home of California's western-most AVA – and clink glasses over a coastal-cooled 'La Rinconada' Pinot Noir.

REX PICKETT (2004)

I punched the cell off, flung both arms in the air in mock exasperation and commanded: 'Get thee to a winery!'

Jack laughed. 'Amen, brother.'

I leaned back and stared at the highway unfurling in front of us. Jack slipped the new Flaming Lips CD into the dash and raised the volume.

We settled into the rhythm of the road. North of Santa Barbara the terrain grew increasingly rural. The hillside homes gradually disappeared, giving way to gentle slopes covered with swaying grasses. The confluence of broad colours resembled a constantly changing impressionist painting... The ocean coloured into view on our left, a cold expanse of cobalt blue. From the immediate north, the Santa Ynez Mountains approached, looming like leviathans. We flew by slow-moving RVs, piling up the miles between us and LA.

An hour into the drive, we laboured up a curving pass through the mountains, battling an early-afternoon wind that had started to kick up and was buffeting the car. As we crested the pass, a breathtaking view of the Santa Ynez Valley yawned before us and a pure feeling of elation washed over me. Once I was over this hill and down into the valley, where I had vacationed so many times before, I would feel as though I had completely shed the alienating concrete sprawl of LA. I was entering a new pastoral realm of wine and tranquility, where insomnia and Xanax were a thing of the past.

'As far as the eye can see,' I said, fanning my arm across the length of the windshield, 'there are wineries. Some good ones, too.'

'Excellent,' Jack said. 'Excellent. Let's wet our whistles.'

Sales of California Pinot Noir increased by 16 percent after its endorsement in the 2004 film *Sideways*. Seen here Jack and Miles, played by Thomas Haden Church and Paul Giamatti (right and left), are understood to have tasted mostly grape juice while filming.

'You don't want to get a motel first? Shower and clean up?'

'I need a bevie. Take the edge off.'

I fished out my Santa Barbara County winery map from the glove compartment and studied it briefly. 'Hmm... let's take the Santa Rosa turnoff and hit Sanford.'

'What's their specialty?'

'Burgundian. Pinot and Chardonnay. One of the best producers in Santa Barbara County. And, more importantly, they're the closest one.'

'I thought you didn't like Chardonnay?' Jack asked.

'I like Chardonnay. I like all varietals. I just don't like the way they manipulate it, especially in California. Too much time in oak, too much secondary malolactic fermentation.'

'What's that?'

'After the first fermentation, many vintners will introduce lactic bacteria into the wine to stimulate the growth of lactic acid. It converts the tarter malic acid – think green apple – and produces lactic acid: caramel, banana, dairy, not sweet, but a cloying appearance of sucrosity.'

Jack turned very slowly and raised his eyebrows. 'Sucrosity?'

'Sweetness,' I said. 'The French don't use ML – as it's known in the trade – as much in Burgundy, which is why I like Sanford's Chards. They're trying to emulate that Burgundian style and not trying to create some treacly concoction to sell to undemanding palates.'

Jack was staring straight ahead, shaking his head. 'You should get a job in a wine store. Solve your money crisis.'

'Yeah, like that would be smart.'

Jack laughed as we floated down into the Santa Ynez Valley. 'I want you to teach me all about wines on this trip, okay?' he shouted over the wind rushing in through the open windows.

'You're ineducable,' I needled.

'Don't start on me.'

Just south of Buellton, we angled off at the Santa Rosa exit and turned west onto a narrow, one-lane shoulderless road. Vineyards bloomed into view, leafed out and dappled in autumn hues of yellow, ochre and rust. On closer inspection, we could make out grape bunches drooping from the trellised, gnarled vines, the harvest imminent.

I gestured to a tiny sign that indicated the turnoff to Sanford and Jack hung a hard left. We rode slowly on an even narrower gravel road through an arbour of overhanging oaks. More vineyards bounded the road, row after perfect row of Santa Ynez's finest. We forded a mere trickle of a stream and then dead-ended at a small, ramshackle, wood-framed structure with a corrugated aluminum roof set in a clearing.

The sun felt warm as we climbed out of the car and stretched our limbs and drank in the unspoiled view. We were at the foot of the Santa Ynez Mountains, imposing hills carpeted in native grasses and dotted with gnarled oaks. After LA, with its incessant automotive noise, putrid air and constant congestion, the vista was positively invigorating.

'God, it's so gorgeous here,' Jack said.

'Always love coming back,' I said, feeling a smile break out on my face. I turned to Jack, clenched two fists. Shook them in the air, and said: 'Let's get into some wines, shall we?'

'Yeah!'

We marched over to the quaint tasting room. The inside smelled of wood and wine. A gentle breeze wafted through the open windows and acted as a natural air conditioner. A tall, middle-aged hippie with long hair tied in a ponytail was conducting the pouring duties. He wore a white Stetson adorned with a beaded Indian band. His weathered face evidenced equal exposure to sun and wine and was barely disguised by a wispy beard. We were clearly on the early side because the only other people in the room were an elderly couple who had already advanced to the reds.

Jack and I bellied up to the bar where a chorus line of uncorked bottles gleamed at the ready. After we each paid a five-dollar fee, the pourer set down tasting glasses in front of us and reached automatically for the first bottle: 'Would you like to begin with the Sauvignon Blanc?' he asked.

'Absolutely,' Jack said.

The pourer poured tiny amounts into our tasting glasses and recorked the bottle.

'Look at the wine in your glass up against the light,' I instructed Jack as I held up mine and examined it. He did the same. 'Now, set it back down on the counter and introduce some air into it.' We both swirled the wine around. 'Now, stick your nose in it and take a whiff.' Jack imitated me bending over and putting my nose in the glass. Then, I upended the entire tasting amount into my mouth and sloshed it around as if it were mouthwash, then swallowed. Jack followed suit. 'That's what I want to see you do with every one.'

Jack smiled, happy to have such a rigorous tasting regimen imposed on him. 'Okay.'

We went down the line. The Sauvignon was steely: mineral and gunmetal on the palate, but bright and citrussy. The Chards were pleasant enough, not too buttery or flaky, but not thrilling either. I couldn't find any depth in them, only a vestige of what might have been. The Pinots dramatically improved, and I started to get interested.

'Do you have any of the '99 La Rinconada?' I asked, referring to Sanford's maiden bottling of a new single-vineyard Pinot that had been getting glowing reviews.

'Yeah, but we're not tasting it,' the pourer said.

'How much is it a bottle?'

'Fifty-five,' he replied.

I turned to Jack and said: 'It's supposed to be monster.'

'Get it,' Jack said cavalierly. He turned to the pourer. 'Can we drink it here?'

'Sure can,' he said.

While I paid for the La Rinconada, Jack went out to the car to retrieve some chicken sandwiches he had picked up at the gas station in Montecito. The pourer uncorked the wine, stuck the cork halfway back in the bottle, and set it on the bar in front of me. I gathered it up with the two tasting glasses and walked outside, where I found Jack sitting at a weathered picnic bench under a spreading oak that dappled him with oblong splotches of shade. He was munching on a sandwich and looked pretty content sitting there all alone. I wanted to take a picture of him, but I didn't have a camera. Then he saw me and shot his arm into the air. I hurried over with the wine.

I poured two ample glasses of the La Rinconada and handed one to Jack. The wine was a deep, almost opaque purple in the glass. Against the sunlight it turned carmine, but you still couldn't see through it. On the nose it was full-throttle blackberry and leather and spice with hints of raspberry candy. The mouthfeel was explosive of highly extracted, but still young, Pinot Noir grapes draped in tannins. I suspected that another year or two would tame its exuberance, but it was fun to capture it now in its youthful promise.

'What do you think of it?' Jack asked, chewing the wine in his mouth.

'Lovely,' I said, pouring us a little more. 'Big and gamey, almost irreverent for a Pinot. I like it. A perfect beginning to this weeklong adventure.'

We clinked glasses. Jack was relieved to see my spirits lifting. He handed me the other chicken sandwich and we ate them ravenously while continuing to revel in the La Rinconada. Over the vineyard, a turkey vulture wheeled in slow circles. Then, suddenly, as if it had been shot, it dive-bombed out of the sky and disappeared into the vines where it produced a violent struggle. Moments later, it ascended with a great clattering of furiously flapping wings, clutching a partially eviscerated rodent in its talons.

'I hope your marriage works, because that's what divorce is like,' I observed, as the huge, black raptor winged away.

First published in *Sideways* by Rex Pickett, St Martin's Press (New York) 2004. Reproduced with kind permission of the author and publishers.

IN PURSUIT OF 'BURGUNDIAN' PINOT NOIR

From 'True' Sonoma Coast to the cool-climate of Santa Barbara, Stephen Brook seeks out the best producers of the 'heartbreak grape', Pinot Noir, and asks if the California Coast really does have all the answers.

STEPHEN BROOK (2021)

There are parts of the world, just a few, where it is possible to grow Burgundian and Bordeaux grape varieties alongside each other. But it's a stretch, and it has always seemed obvious that Cabernet-dominated California would never be a paradise for Pinot Noir. Some early versions of the latter seemed to bear that out. I recall Firestone Pinots from the Santa Ynez Valley in Santa Barbara. The 1970 was perfumed and impressive if far from Burgundian. But it was a false dawn. Santa Ynez is a warm part of the county, and other vintages of Pinot from here, such as the 1977, 1982 and 1984, were weak.

Joseph Swan in Forestville, Sonoma, planted Pinot in the dark ages of 1969, producing his first vintage in 1973. It was warmly received, and Swan developed a cult reputation for the variety. I tasted the 1978 (vegetal), 1987 (dilute) and 1997 (medicinal), so it's clear I never signed up to the cult.

THE PINOT PIONEERS

Yet there were some good Pinots starting to emerge from Sonoma, notably from the Russian River Valley. Joe Rochioli planted the variety in the late 1960s, selling the fruit to local wineries such as Davis Bynum. Rochioli was primarily a farmer and understood that Pinot was a delicate variety that soon lost quality and typicity if overcropped. He began vinifying some of those grapes from 1982, and certainly the 1987, which I tasted blind, was a lovely wine. The elegant Burgundian 1988 Pinot from Williams Selyem was equally fine. By this time some other Russian River growers were producing grapes of exceptional quality, which they could sell at a high price to Williams Selyem and others.

At the same time growers in Carneros such as Saintsbury and Acacia were achieving good results from Pinot, and many tasters believe the region, cooled by its proximity to San Pablo Bay, would become California's 'hotspot' for the variety.

But it hasn't quite fulfilled its promise, and the wines, while good, do often lack nuance and finesse.

If Rochioli and others such as Tom Dehlinger were clearly demonstrating that Pinot Noir, planted in the right place, could produce convincing and stylish examples of the variety, this was still very much a niche market. Cabernet Sauvignon and Zinfandel had far more commercial importance and popularity. However, there were other outcrops of good Pinot elsewhere in California that were worth turning to. The late Jim Clendenen, who had made wine in Burgundy in 1981 before setting up Au Bon Climat in Santa Barbara, was making good Pinots from low-yielding vineyards, and soon huge grape farms such as Bien Nacido and Sanford & Benedict were winning a high reputation for their Pinot, which was allocated to a handful of wineries with a passion for the variety. I tasted five 1987 Pinots from Clendenen and they were all delicious.

Josh Jensen was another budding winemaker intrigued by burgundy – he worked for a vintage at Domaine Dujac. It's hard to underestimate the influence of Jacques Seysses of Dujac on a generation or two of Californian winemakers. Jacques' Californian wife Roz ensured there was no language barrier, and they were generous in sharing their exceptional cellar with aspiring winemakers from the New World. (I speak from experience, having spent 10 days there as a cellar rat myself, though my practical contribution to the 1987 vintage, all were agreed, was minimal.)

Burgundy spoke terroir, so Jensen sought out the one soil type in short supply in California: limestone. He found it high up in the Gabilan Mountains near Monterey, where he planted single vineyards that he would bottle separately. He made some outstanding Pinots in the early 1980s, but his Calera wines were marred by inconsistency. Ted Lemon was another Dujac graduate. In 1971 Seysses was flat on his back with sciatica. Ted learned how to make Clos St Denis by following Seysses' instructions and bringing tank samples to his bedside for assessment. Later, in 1984, he would be that rare specimen, an American winemaker in Burgundy, overseeing production at Roulot in Meursault. In the 1990s Lemon founded Littorai, seeking out coastal sites in Sonoma and Mendocino and initiating organic and biodynamic practices. By the late 1990s he was releasing wines of rare purity and finesse, as he continues to do to this day.

THINK ABOUT THE DIRT

Even the most 'Burgundian' of California's winemakers, such as Ted Lemon, Eric Sussman of Radio Coteau and Joe Davis of Arcadian, recognized that the West Coast's climate and soil were quite different from the Côte d'Or. Sussman summed it up: 'Burgundy has to worry about rain, dilution and rot. Here, we worry about

The vineyards of the Santa Rita Hills run from from frigid Lompoc to balmy Buellton, producing Pinot Noirs from as-light-as-lace to heavier 'Syrah-like' styles. It's not just the cooling ocean fogs at play here, as the geology at foot – soils from fossil shells to dark alluvium – has its influence too.

excessive sugars and unbalanced wines.' Joe Davis and others who bought grapes from existing vineyards usually contracted to do their own farming of chosen blocks. This allowed them to adapt the viticulture towards earlier ripening and lower sugars. Left unchecked, grape growers would be reluctant to take chances with ripening, and aimed for generous crops with robust flavours. That explains why the same vineyard (Bien Nacido, for example) could be the source of Pinots at 13% and others up at 15% plus.

Few of the most dedicated Pinot producers own their own vineyards. Following the general Californian model, grape farming and winemaking are often separate activities. The drawback of this is that the winemaker is not in full control of viticulture. The advantage is that top growers such as Larry Hyde in Carneros, the Miller family of Bien Nacido (Santa Maria Valley) or the Dutton family in Green Valley (Russian River) have a deep understanding of their terroirs and clones and are experts in what they do. The proliferation of such quality-driven vineyards throughout California has encouraged Pinot enthusiasts, many of whom already mentioned, to buy allocations of fruit each year.

In general, Pinot winemakers do their best to control or influence the farming as much as possible. This can work well or can be a source of conflict if there is a lack of tact on either side. When the relationship is good, the winemaker can determine to a large extent criteria such as irrigation, yields and harvesting dates. The grower makes money by selling tonnage, so winemakers often contract to buy per acre rather than by weight, so that the grower doesn't lose out when asked to reduce yields. It's usually a complicated relationship, but it does allow winemakers without personal fortunes to gain access to some of the best Pinot (or other varieties) in the state. The system is remote from the estate-based Burgundian model, but it can yield fine results, as consumers seem to relish being able to choose from a wide range of single-vineyard wines from among their favourite winemakers.

REINING IN THE RIPENESS

In the 1990s and 2000s winemakers were not always unanimous in their approach to ripeness. Some, such as Ross Cobb, planted Pinot in extremely cool sites. His vineyards were in Occidental (Sonoma), just three miles from the Pacific Coast. His aim, usually achieved, was to have fully ripe grapes at low sugar levels. Indeed, some of his wines were well under 13% alcohol. The risk was that by pushing for aromatic purity and modest alcohols the wines could flirt with greenness. Moreover, the wines' lack of opulence meant they could take a few years in bottle to reveal their complexity and finesse. Occasionally, Cobb's wines could veer in that direction and the same could be true of Clos Pepe in the Santa Rita Hills.

Jamie Kutch has followed a similar path. A Wall Street trader turned winemaker, he persuaded the growers he works with, mostly along the Sonoma Coast, to farm in order to achieve ripeness about 100 days after flowering. 'That would be considered normal in Europe, but most California winemakers consider it as far too early.' Sometimes he has produced Pinots with 12.2% alcohol but no greenness. The drawback, he concedes, is that without the flesh and sweetness conferred by alcohol and glycerol, his wines can be austere when young, a tendency enhanced by his fondness for retaining stems during vinification.

Concurrently, however, there was another school of thought. There were those who thought it self-defeating to fight the California sunshine. Kosta Browne sourced its many single-vineyard Pinots from cooler sites in Sonoma, yet the wines still managed to be high in alcohol. Their sumptuous character may have been atypical of European Pinot Noir, but the fleshiness of the wines appealed to American palates, and to American critics. Purists such as Cobb sometimes lamented that the blowsier styles of Pinot attracted high scores, although they were wines that were unlikely to age well.

Ted Lemon was willing to accept that most American wine drinkers preferred a voluptuous style of Pinot. 'Younger winemakers aren't intent on paying homage to burgundy. Instead they reflect the American palate, which favours bigger, heavier wines. Most younger winemakers as well as consumers don't know anything else, and have never been exposed to great burgundy. It's a style that ignores terroir, but that too doesn't bother most drinkers.'

One of those winemakers, Adam Lee, with his Siduri collection of single-vineyard wines, corroborated Lemon's view: 'My introduction to Pinot wasn't Chambolle-Musigny but Williams Selyem. And California's vineyards are so dispersed that terroir makes less sense than in Burgundy.'

THE HOTTER SIDE OF COOL…

One bizarre phenomenon of the early 21st century was the production of high-alcohol Pinots from sites that were acknowledged to be 'cool'. Santa Rita Hills, with a valley moving inland from frigid Lompoc to balmy Buellton in Santa Barbara County, was a case in point. It had a track record: vineyards such as Sanford & Benedict were acclaimed for the elegance of their Pinots. But other wines were blockbusters.

For years I had a running argument with the winemakers at Sea Smoke in the Santa Rita Hills. A large property, it was planted and farmed conscientiously with the aim of producing outstanding Pinots, yet the wines lacked typicity. They were as dark as Syrah (but were 100 percent Pinot), charred in aroma, rich and plummy in flavour, and very high in alcohol. While conceding that California shouldn't try to ape burgundy, how could such wines be considered exceptional Pinots?

The winemakers explained that the soils gave wines with high tannin levels, so if the grapes were picked too early the wines would be tough. Phenolic ripeness lagged behind sugar ripeness, so high alcohols were inevitable. The last thing they (and their customers) wanted was herbaceousness, so ripe seeds and tannins were essential, even at the risk of high sugars. The most sought-after of the Sea Smoke bottlings was 'Ten', which was also the most atypical. At Melville, down the road, Chad Melville acknowledged the same dilemma: 'The cool summer days mean we have a very long growing season, and our acidities remain high. By the time they drop to palatable levels, we end up with high sugars and alcohols.'

One solution was to add water. Some wines were so extracted and concentrated that dilution wasn't much of a risk, but water would cause acidities to drop drastically, so it then became necessary to acidify. All this manipulation did the balance of the final wine no good. As Joe Davis remarked: 'If you pick overripe fruit, you have to fix the problem in the winery. Far better not to create those problems in the first place!'

Jim Clendenen concurred: 'You eat bananas when they're yellow, not when they're brown. If you end up with grapes with a high pH and ridiculously high sugars, it means you're no good at farming. I add no water. I just go for terroir and low alcohol. It can be done!' But it was Ted Lemon who provided the clinching argument, for me, on wines from overripe fruit: 'When you aim for overripe fruit, you are harvesting a lot of raisins, and one raisin tastes much like any other.'

STICK TO THE COAST?

Pinot Noir, as has often been observed, is an unforgiving variety. You can make some errors in cropping Cabernet or vinifying it, but it will usually survive. Not so with Pinot. Farming is crucial. The 'True' Sonoma Coast, the coastal ranges close to the Pacific, was hailed as a new mecca for Burgundian varieties. Flowers was one of the first growers to arrive, and others soon followed. For me the supreme Pinot grower was usually David Hirsch. In the hands of a gifted winemaker, a Hirsch Pinot can be sublime. I recall being poured a 2004 Hirsch Vineyard made by Steve Kistler, and swooned with the sheer gorgeousness of the aroma.

But the coastal range is not as cool as many believe. Vines are planted at up to 610 metres, and that elevation means they are above the fog line. Grapes lapping up unbroken sunshine are going to develop high sugars whatever their altitude. Further north in Mendocino, the cool sites that make possible California's best sparkling wines at Roederer Estate still allow Goldeneye to produce Pinots at 14.5% and 15%.

Even in Burgundy, of course, consistency can be a problem. This is even more the case in California (or Oregon) with its multiplicity of terroirs, clones, yields and winemaking skills. But the likes of Ted Lemon, Jim Clendenen and others, such as Dan Goldfield of Dutton-Goldfield, Jeff Brinkman at Rhys in Santa Cruz, and Marimar Torres, have shown what can be achieved. If there are still wineries that opt for that lusher, overripe style of Pinot, well, that is their choice, and there is certainly a strong domestic following for such interpretations.

The major change I have witnessed over the decades has been a philosophical approach. The jammy or astringent versions of Pinot from the past resulted from vinifying the variety as though it were Cabernet Sauvignon. Those with some Burgundian experience realized this and opted for the gentler, less interventionist techniques of France. Not all their wines were good, but at least they were operating with acknowledged reference points. The delicate and perfumed wines of Ted Lemon, Ross Cobb, Jamie Kutch and many others show what can be achieved.

No one has taken this trend further than Sashi Moorman of Domaine de la Côte. He began his career two decades ago, making wine at Stolpman in Santa Barbara. A few years later he met Rajat Parr, the wine director for a large restaurant group who was very much influenced by Jim Clendenen. In 2010 the two men set up Sandhi Wines, with enviable financial backing. However, by then Moorman

Ted Lemon's Littorai vineyards on the 'True' north coast of Sonoma – 85 percent of the vines are farmed biodynamically here, but with an emphasis on 'generative' farming that actively benefits the soils and environment. Don't be surprised to find sheep grazing among the vines.

was also involved in an international project called Evening Land Vineyards that developed sites in Oregon as well as California.

Moorman was tasked with that part of the project based in the Santa Rita Hills. He pushed 'cool' to an extreme, choosing sites near the town of Lompoc and thus closer to the Pacific than the great majority of other Santa Rita vineyards. Instead of planting the fashionable Dijon clones of Pinot Noir, he preferred to use the traditional and often overlooked Californian clones that, in his view, had evolved within a Californian context, with better acidity than the French clones. Temperatures here rarely exceeded 27˚C, Arctic conditions for a Californian vineyard, and clusters remained very small, giving intensity of flavour at alcohol levels that rarely exceeded 12.5%. In some spots he daringly planted ungrafted vines at a density of 17,000 vines per 2.5 acres (compared to Burgundy's 10,000).

By 2011 Evening Land was in trouble, and two years later Moorman and Parr took control of the vineyards, which they renamed Domaine de la Côte. There is no irrigation after *veraison* (the ripening stage at which the grapes change colour), which both keeps yields low and allows the stems to lignify so that they can be retained during fermentation. The use of new oak is minimal so the typicity of each site can express itself. He has no interest in producing the 'consistent product' required by large wineries reluctant to disturb their clients with variation. His

Pinots (and Chardonnays for that matter) are individual wines. I am not suggesting that this is necessarily a model for all Californian producers of Burgundian varieties to follow. A gifted and experienced winemaker such as David Ramey (Russian River, Sonoma) regularly produces Chardonnays of greater richness and weight that are equally valid as expressions of the variety. But Moorman's success suggests the notion that California is simply too warm for great Pinot to be feasible is simply incorrect. When I'm tasting with Moorman and commenting on the brilliant intensity of the wines, he echoes Jim Clendenen: 'Yes, and it's not that hard to achieve! Anyone can do this if you farm correctly and retain high acidity in the grapes.'

Gaining mastery over what has often been described as 'the heartbreak grape' is not just a Californian ambition. Pinots from Oregon have achieved far better balance over the past decade, and there are exciting wines from Australia, especially Victoria and Tasmania. Making Pinot appeals to intellectually curious winemakers, as it requires the temperament to walk a tightrope that's not required, say, for Merlot.

This survey has largely ignored the nuances of vinification. Californians with a passion for Pinot have long ago mastered the techniques, such as the use of whole clusters, open-top fermenters and the avoidance of reduction. By and large they know how to adjust the vinification to the nature of the fruit they are dealing with. They have learned not to over-extract (although a few still like to extract enthusiastically because the resulting wines appeal to their clientele) and what kind of barrel-toasting works best with the wines they like to make.

I have focused instead on viticulture because that is where the challenge lies: where to find the right place to plant, and how to farm in such a way as to avoid excessive sugars and thus alcohols. There is far more to be said, especially on clones. Californians couldn't wait to get their hands on the celebrated Dijon clones, but before too long it became apparent that in some places these simply weren't suited to the Californian sunshine. So now there has been a return to heritage clones such as Swan and Pommard, which, if less showy than the Dijon clones, are arguably better adapted to the West Coast climate.

Certain grape varieties seem to invite failure. It's hard to recall the last time I had a fine Viognier from California, although Calera and Chalone made some honourable attempts. Yet Pinot Noir, in just a few decades, has triumphed here. In the US, it used to be considered an exclusivity of Oregon, but no longer, and it's been fascinating to follow the variety's progress from the often clumsy versions of the 1970s to the superbly refined examples routinely produced today.

3

1976: WHAT CHANGED? (THE PRICES, CERTAINLY)

Forty-five years ago, a modest English wine merchant named Steven Spurrier staged an event that was to set about the democratization of the wine world. Here's how the Judgement of Paris changed the game…

GEORGE TABER (2006)
California vs France

STEVEN SPURRIER AND PATRICIA GASTAUD-GALLAGHER (2021)
'1976? Of Course it was a Competition!'

HUGH JOHNSON (1984)
New Classics on the Block

FIONA MORRISON MW (2021)
Wine on the Mountain

DR WILLIAM KELLEY (2017/2021)
In Pursuit of Ripeness

CALIFORNIA vs FRANCE

Tasted blind. Scored out of 20. California Chardonnay and Cabernet vs Burgundy and Bordeaux. George Taber was there to witness the confusion on May 24th 1976 as top critics at a simple blind tasting in Paris made a judgement that was to alter the course of wine forever…

GEORGE TABER (2006)

The nine judges seemed nervous at the beginning. There was lots of laughing and quick side comments. No one, though, was acting rashly. The judges pondered their wines carefully and made their judgements slowly. As I stood only a few feet from them, I could listen to their commentary and I copied into the brown reporter's notebook that I always carry with me such phrases as: 'This soars out of the ordinary', 'A good nose, but not too much on the mouth' and 'This is nervous and agreeable'.

From their comments, though, I soon realized that the judges were becoming totally confused as they tasted the white wines. The panel couldn't tell the difference between the French ones and those from California and they began talking to each other, which is very rare in a tasting. They speculated about a wine's nationality, often disagreeing.

At one point Raymond Oliver was certain he had sipped a French wine, when it was a California one from Freemark Abbey. Shortly after, Claude Dubois-Millot said he thought a wine was obviously from California because it had no nose, when it was France's famed Bâtard-Montrachet.

The judges were brutal when they found a wine wanting. They completely dismissed the David Bruce Chardonnay, Pierre Bréjoux giving it 0 and Odette Kahn just 1 point out of 20. The David Bruce was rated last by all of the judges. Robert Finigan had warned Spurrier that he'd found David Bruce wines at that time could be erratic.

After the white wines had been tasted, Spurrier called a break and collected the scorecards. Using normal procedure for wine tastings, he added up the individual scores, divided this by the number of tasters (his and Patricia Gallagher's marks not being noted) and ranked them from highest to lowest. The judges spoke quietly to each other and I talked briefly with Dubois-Millot. Even though he did not yet know the results, he told me a bit sheepishly that: 'We thought we were recognizing French wines when they were Californian and vice versa. At times we'd say that a wine would be thin and therefore California, when it wasn't. Our confusion showed how good California wines have become.'

Spurrier's original plan had been to announce all the results at the end of the day, but the waiters were slow clearing the tables and getting the red wines together and the programme was getting badly behind schedule, so he decided to announce the results of the white wine tasting. He had been personally stunned and began reading them slowly to the group:

1 Chateau Montelena 1973 – 14.67
2 Meursault-Charmes 1973 – 14.05
3 Chalone Vineyard 1974 – 13.44
4 Spring Mountain 1973 – 11.55
5 Beaune Clos des Mouches 1973 – 11.22
6 Freemark Abbey 1972 – 11.11
7 Bâtard-Montrachet 1973 – 10.44
8 Puligny-Montrachet les Pucelles 1972 – 9.89
9 Veedercrest 1972 – 9.78
10 David Bruce 1973 – 4.67

When he finished, Spurrier looked at the judges, whose reaction ranged from shock to horror. No one had expected this and soon the whole room was abuzz.

After hearing the results I walked up to Patricia Gallagher. The French word in the winning wine's name had momentarily thrown me. 'Chateau Montelena is Californian, isn't it?' I asked a bit dumfoundedly.

'Yes, it is,' she replied calmly.

The scores of the individual judges made the results even more astounding. California Chardonnays had overwhelmed their French counterparts. Every single judge rated a California wine first, Chateau Montelena was given top rating by six judges, Chalone being rated first by the other three. Three of the top four wines were Californian. Claude Dubois-Millot gave Chateau Montelena 18.5 points out of 20, while Aubert de Villaine gave it 18. Chateau Montelena scored a total of 132 points, comfortably ahead of second-place Meursault-Charmes which got 126.5.

As I watched the reaction of the others to the results, I felt a sense of both awe and pride. Who would have thought it? Chauvinism is a word invented by the French, but I felt some chauvinism that a California white wine had won.

Gary Myatt's *The Judgement of Paris* – painted in 2012 and measuring 6 x 3 metres – depicts the amazement of the eleven-strong panel. At the table, *from left*: the restaurateur Raymond Olivier, Patricia Gallagher, Pierre Tari of Château Giscours, Michel Dovaz of the Académie du Vin, Pierre Brejoux of the INAO (Institut National de l'Origine et de la Qualité), Odette Kahn, editor of the *Revue du Vin de France*, sommelier Christian Vanneque of Tour d'Argent, Aubert de Villaine of Domaine de la Romanée-Conti, Claude Dubois-Millot, Jean-Claude Vrinat of the restaurant Taillevant and, seated at the front, Steven Spurrier. The on-lookers wear hats: Sir Peter Michael, who commissioned the work, stands on the left, and George Taber of *Time* magazine watches from the right.

But how could this be happening? I was tempted to ask for a taste of the winning California Chardonnay, but decided against it. I still had a reporting job to finish and I needed to have a clear head.

As the waiters poured the reds, Spurrier was certain that the judges would be more careful and would not allow a California wine to come out on top again. One California wine winning was bad enough; two would be treason. The French judges, he felt, would be very careful to identify the French wines and score them high, while rating those that seemed American low. The French reds, with their classic, distinctive and familiar tastes, would certainly stand out against the California reds.

There was less chatter during the second wave of wines. The judges seemed both more intense and more circumspect. Their comments about the nationality of the wine in the glass were now usually correct. 'That's a California, or I don't know what I am doing here,' said Christian Vannequé of La Tour d'Argent. I looked at my card and he was right; it was the Ridge Monte Bello.

Raymond Oliver took one sip of a red and proclaimed: 'That's a Mouton, without a doubt.' He too was right.

Because of delays in the earlier part of the tasting, the hour was getting late and the group had to be out by 6pm, so Spurrier pushed on quickly after the ballots were collected. He followed the same procedure as he had for the Chardonnay tasting, adding up the individual scores of the judges and dividing the total by nine. The room was hushed as he read out the results.

1 Stag's Leap Wine Cellars 1973 – 14.17
2 Château Mouton Rothschild 1970 – 14.00
3 Château Montrose 1970 – 13.94
4 Château Haut-Brion 1970 – 13.55
5 Ridge Monte Bello 1971 – 11.50
6 Château Léoville-Las Cases 1971 – 10.78
7 Mayacamas 1971 – 9.94
8 Clos du Val 1972 – 9.72
9 Heitz Martha's Vineyard 1970 – 9.39
10 Freemark Abbey 1969 – 8.67

This time the stir in the room was even more pronounced than before. A California wine had won again! Who would have believed it? The judges sat in disbelief. To confirm that I had heard Spurrier correctly, I walked up to Gallagher again and asked: 'A California wine also won the red?'

'Yes,' she replied.

Excerpt from *Judgment of Paris – California vs France and the Historic 1976 Paris Tasting that Revolutionized Wine* by George M Taber, Scribner (New York) 2005.

'1976? OF COURSE IT WAS A COMPETITION!'

As an Englishman and an American in Paris, many thought Steven Spurrier and Patricia Gastaud-Gallagher bold, foolish even, for setting up a wine school there. But the success of their Judgement of Paris event, comparing the best wines of France and California, meant the influence of their Académie du Vin was eventually felt far and wide. Steven and Patricia share some of their memories of that breakthrough day…

STEVEN SPURRIER AND
PATRICIA GASTAUD-GALLAGHER (2021)

1 Were you really so naïve? Deep down, did you both know you could be stirring up something big?

SS At the Académie du Vin we gave tastings of all kinds and although our Paris event was much bigger than many, we weren't aiming to create a stir. What we wanted to do was to draw attention to the quality of wines from California, principally those of Napa, and in this we succeeded. It was Patricia's idea – we wanted to show the wines of her country at their best.

PGG Commercially speaking, there was absolutely nothing to gain by promoting California wines. Steven did not sell California wines at Caves de la Madeleine and Académie du Vin students were only interested in French wines. Our objective was to share the pleasure of wines that we

had only recently discovered ourselves. No one could have anticipated that our guests would confuse California and French wines – we couldn't possibly have contrived that. But we were naïve in reporting the results. John Movius, editor and publisher of *The Wine Scene*, wrote to us saying that a 'simple "t-test" analysis would have shown a four-way tie among the Chardonnay wines of Chateau Montelena, Meursault-Charmes, Chalone and Spring Mountain, and a four-way tie for a "true rank" of first among the Cabernet-based wines of Stag's Leap Wine Cellars 1973, Mouton Rothschild 1970, Château Montrose 1970 and Haut Brion 1970.' Did the American wines defeat the French? Statistical analysis, according to Mr Movius, said 'No'. Steven and I admitted to statistical illiteracy, but adopted t-tests at our

The lineup of blind-tasters at the 1976 Judgement of Paris. Patricia Gastaud-Gallagher and Steven Spurrier are seated at the centre. Organizing the event had been 'good fun'.

subsequent tastings, which went on to have the exact same result.

2 You aimed high! Did you consider showing the California wines against the Médoc's Third or Fourth growths?

SS No. The decision to make it a blind tasting was mine only a week before the tasting. The burgundies and Bordeaux tasted were the benchmarks from their regions and matched the California wines in varietals and vintages.

3 Neither of you had ever been to Napa, but you knew there were great wines out there. How tough was it to make your final selection?

SS The inspiration came from wines brought to us at l'Académie by producers and journalists, particularly Robert Finigan and Alexis Bespaloff. Once the idea was in play, Patricia went to Napa in September 1975 and made a basic selection from 'boutique wineries'. I followed in late April 1976 to make the final choice.

PGG I had read favourable commentary by Robert Finigan in his *Private Guide to Wines* (1972) and the previous year Robert had introduced me to wineries whose wines he thought would please French palates. Steven then made the final decision based on the ones I suggested.

4 What was your budget to create an event like this?

SS Whatever the expenses were, they were financed by the Académie du Vin. We paid for the wines (which were not expensive); they were shipped free, thanks to Joanne Dickenson of TWA. The space at the Intercontinental Hotel was offered free, too, kindly allowed by its Food & Drinks manager Ernst van Damn.

PGG My trip to Napa was at my expense (I was already in California to visit my sister and brother-in-law at Palos Verdes). I was hosted at the home of Robert Cudaback, the father of friends of mine at the *Herald*

Tribune who encouraged this trip, and he also lent me a car to drive. There was no budget for this tasting, nor did we need one. Steven always said that he gave the sommeliers at the Hotel Intercontinental 200 francs.

5   How did you feel when you realized the judges, tasting blind, were genuinely confused as to which wines were French and which Californian?

SS Personally, I was more concerned with the functioning of the day. The results of the white tasting showed their confusion and it was evident that there was confusion with the reds too. But I could not pay attention to this as I was tasting seriously myself!

PGG I had no idea as I was intent on tasting the wines. If I had known, I am sure I would have underreacted: 'Really? How interesting.' Publicizing the results of the tasting was not on our minds.

6   Warren Winiarski famously called the Judgement of Paris (JOP) 'a Copernican moment' – it changed our wine-thinking as dramatically (and controversially) as Nicolaus Copernicus' revelation that the earth revolved around the sun and not vice versa. What was your favourite reaction from the winners?

SS When Warren first heard the news that his wine, Stag's Leap Wine Cellars 1973, had been placed first among the reds, he didn't realize the full impact of the result. He simply said: 'That's nice.' That is my favourite comment.

I think his 'a Copernican moment' probably overstates it!

PGG Jim Barrett summed it up perfectly with: 'Not bad for kids from the sticks!' Modesty is always becoming. His wine, Chateau Montelena, had come first among the Chardonnays...

7   Whose feathers were the most seriously ruffled?

SS Of the producers, the Bordelais reacted strongly – one winemaker said: 'You've spat in our soup!' and I was *persona non grata* in the region for a while. But in 1986, when we held a 10th anniversary re-run of the tasting, we proved that their wines had not been tasted too young – which had been their major complaint. A great wine will show its greatness whatever its age.

Of the judges, plainly Odette Kahn, the editor of the *Revue du Vin de France*, who said: 'Monsieur Spurrier, I demand to have my scorecards back!' (I refused, pointing out that they were not hers, but mine.) Then she accused us of running 'a false test, because California wines are trying to become too much like French wines'.

PGG Which of our guests had the most to lose when the tasting was reported in *Time* magazine as a 'A defeat for all Gaul'? Definitely Odette Kahn, who was widely admired as a wine taster but who confused French wines and California wines – as did others – and who had to answer to the owners of the magazines for which she was editor-in-chief. Pierre Tari, owner of Château Giscours and secrétaire général of the Syndicat des Grands Crus Classés, and Aubert de Villaine, manager of the Domaine de la Romanée-Conti, each faced criticism for participating in the tasting but did not blame their friend Steven.

8 Without the Judgement of Paris, how long do you think it would have taken for California wines to get noticed?

SS It was a slow burn. Even the East Coast US had no interest in Napa before 1976.

PGG I think it would have taken decades for California wines to gain the recognition brought by this single tasting once it was reported by George Tabor and published by *Time* magazine. I would be curious to know what percentage of wines from the wineries we presented at our tastings is now sold abroad. My guess is, it's tiny. Our tasting put California wines on the map – in America!

9 The Paris tasting has become a template for comparative wine tastings. Is this its greatest legacy?

SS Yes, certainly. This is its legacy and what has made it so important in the world of wine. It championed real quality over the preconceived idea of quality and became a model for further comparisons – not least with Chilean wines at the Berlin Tasting of 2004. It paved the way for unknown wines to have a 'voice'.

PGG We broke a glass ceiling, that's for sure. Did we actually provide a template? I don't think so. With our low budget and the lack of commercial interest in its results, our tasting to celebrate the US bicentennial was unique!

10 It was a tasting whose time had come and the stars were aligned. What were those stars?

SS The stars did seem to be aligned: Patricia's original idea and her commitment to it right from the start; the fact that the Académie du Vin was well respected and the top judges all agreed to attend; the 200th anniversary of American independence was a key (it was a great reason to show the progress this country's wines were making), as was all the help we received. Never, at any moment, did I feel we were doing anything but good in holding this event and the stars shone through.

PGG It's hard to imagine now – we are talking about almost 50 years ago – and no one, but no one, beyond state lines, with the exception of a small number of wine lovers and collectors, had any focus on California as a source of world-class wines... But the stars were indeed aligned for the event Steven and I decided to organize in celebration of the Bicentennial one spring morning in our picturesque Académie du Vin offices near the Place de la Concorde.

NEW CLASSICS ON THE BLOCK

In his seminal essay of 1984, Hugh Johnson registers the effect on the rest of the world – on both consumers and producers of wine – of the new front-runner suddenly arriving in their midst, California.

HUGH JOHNSON (1984)

The wine world is conservative. It bases its notions of quality and even correctness on concepts that have taken centuries to shape. It uses the word 'classic' without self-consciousness, giving it a widely understood meaning.

What is that meaning? Does it apply to California wines? Is it begrudged them? What have they done, are they doing, or must they do to win 'classic' status? A little history is essential to understand how the 'classics' arose and, most puzzlingly, why they arose where they did. In every case, five elements were essential in conjunction: a tolerable soil, a tolerable climate, a suitable vine, an active local market (or easy transport to one) and the right cellar conditions. Good growing conditions are important, but in the long run, if quality is the aim, not so important as the conditions, natural or artificial, under which the wine is made and then matured.

This is the basic reason why northern European wines are historically superior to southern – and, by extension, to those of regions like California with a Mediterranean climate. The weather at harvest time was cooler, the *chais* or 'cellars' cooler, the fermentation cooler, and the storage at a lower and steadier temperature. Cooler vintage weather and slower ripening started the wine with better acid balance; natural atmospheric conditions were ideal for its development.

It is scarcely necessary to list the classics that came about in this way – almost all in the time of the Roman Empire: Bordeaux, an entrepôt with a maritime climate; Saint-Emilion, with its limestone cellars; Burgundy, with one of Europe's main highways as its shop-window, already chilly by harvest-time; the Rhine and Mosel, water-highways with long, misty autumns and dank barrel-cellars; Champagne, equally chilly and equipped with huge chalk pits for storage; Piedmont, cold in the autumn; the Loire with its caves . . . there are even exceptional cases of excellent cellars in southern countries producing 'classic' wines: Rioja and Frascati are two, even if Frascati chose grapes with no inherent balance and stability, so that its wine could not leave its deep cellars without starting to disintegrate. For each of these areas the growers selected grapes whose natural timing of flowering and ripening suited the local conditions – mostly, in fact, fruitful local strains of the woodland vine. Having no means of controlling nature, in other words, they carefully observed it and made the best of what it offered. The results, refined through centuries, have such fully evolved identities that they are now benchmarks no explorer can ignore. They are the classics. They even remain the classics when they are far from being good wine.

The concept of wine quality can also be considered quite separately from membership of the classical elite. A truly vigorous, well-balanced, satisfying and long-lived wine is often made right outside the classical traditions – and vice versa. Wines we call 'great', and unanimously agree in appreciating, are usually those that combine intrinsic quality with a classical idiom.

California is still asking itself whether these two recurrent themes are necessarily complementary, or even necessarily compatible. The question being asked is whether, let us say, California Pinot Noir should be judged by how far it resembles a Côte d'Or wine, or Riesling by how clearly it evokes the Rhine (or the Mosel). The answer is no: it should be judged for its qualities in isolation. But the real-life answer is that comparisons will be made. The problem is that having adopted a 'classic' model, it is extraordinarily difficult to set it aside in making judgements.

What happens when established classic and California aspirants are brought face to face in competition? The answer was given dramatically at a famous blind tasting in Paris in 1976 (*see* pages 66–73). French and Anglo-Saxon tasters alike were taken by surprise. Their training had led them to look for certain 'classic' attributes, and to judge a wine, broadly speaking, by how much of the desirable taste and smell in question it offered.

In the Old World it is only in the most successful vintages that these characteristics are found in full concentration. The 'claret' we are accustomed to drinking year in year out, for example, is a fairly light, distinctly astringent wine, extremely variable from vintage to vintage. The French tend to drink it brisk and young, appreciating its tannic and acidic 'cut'. Anglo-Saxons usually prefer to wait until vigour has been replaced by smoothness and bouquet – admittedly running a risk of missing the point where the flavour is at its juiciest.

Faced with very ripe California wines, many of them with higher alcohol levels than their French equivalents, the judges' first thought was that they had French wines of exceptional vintages before them. On the superficial examination of a blind tasting, they matched up closely to their ideal prototypes. I am not saying that they will not do the same in the long run; simply that a single blind tasting cannot provide this information.

I have discussed the matter at length with a number of European friends whose own work in wine is, to say the least, progressive. Piero Antinori, whose influence is changing the face of Chianti, pointed out to me another reason for the striking performance of California wines in such comparisons: 'There is an obligatory phase in a market where the consumer is quite new and needs to easily recognize a product. Varietal character is therefore maximized as the distinguishing feature for the public to remember. The more aggressive it is, the greater its initial impact.'

Even to experienced French and British palates, it seems, this learning phase is necessary in discovering the real identity and merit of California wines. The trouble, as we all rapidly learn, is that high-impact wines can all too soon pall. Piero Antinori makes another point that I have found worth pondering. 'In a short time,' he says, 'California's winemakers have been able to make some of the best wines in the world and have created a prestigious image, first in California... now even in Europe. All of this is the result of great love and enthusiasm united with solid know-how, plenty of money and a favourable environment – but above all due to the fertile imaginations of some avant-garde producers who have positively influenced the whole field. Their great skill has been in spreading and publicizing some particular technical aspects, definitely important but maybe not determining quality factors, and in making them into the real banner of California oenology. The outstanding examples are the temperature-controlled fermentation of white wine, and the ageing of red and some white wines in small barrels of high-quality oak of various origins. These and other aspects so well publicized have, in my opinion, contributed perhaps more to the prestige and image of their products than to their intrinsic quality.'

Modifications in present practice suggest that Antinori's point has already been taken by some winemakers. The day of the 'show wine', the big statement in the clearest terms (with or without accompanying maps of sub-divisions of the forests of France) is probably coming to an end. The drinker can add an important reason why it should. It concerns the sheer drinkability of show-stopping, high-alcohol, high-extract, usually low-acid wines. I was astonished when I first met what I now call a 'one-glass' wine. To one who is accustomed to finish the bottle, each glass leading teasingly to the next, promising more interest and refreshment, I was affronted and disappointed to find that by the end of the first glass, however splendid, I had no desire for another.

Edmond Maudière of Moët & Chandon, who has the privilege of making wine in both Champagne and the Napa Valley, is precise about the 'pre-conceived and false notions' that have led to such disappointments in white wines – above all, the idea that high degrees of alcohol are either desirable or unavoidable. It is,

The thin sea-bed soils of Mount Veeder are difficult – sometimes treacherous – to farm, their steeply angled slopes unsuited for most vineyard machinery. But great wines are made from vines that 'struggle' to survive, and the Chardonnay and Cabernet produced here prove this.

he says, easy to control by picking at the right '*equilibre physiologique*'. Twelve to 12.5% alcohol is as much as Chardonnay needs for balance and delicacy. To make white wines like red, macerating the skins in the juice and fermenting in oak, is to lose control of their balance and their eventual harmony. Instead, Maudière advocates fermenting in stainless steel or any neutral container, then ageing whatever seems the proper proportion of the wine in oak – leaving the final assembling of the wine until tasting has determined precisely how much oak influence gives the best result. (This is, of course, the philosophy behind the *cuvée* of champagne.)

Maudière's enthusiasm for California's potential is strongly felt, but very specific. He finds the general standard of red wine far above the whites. Like all Frenchmen he attributes at least as much to soil as to climate. The Carneros region can grow extremely fine Pinot Noir of great delicacy, perfect for his *cuvées*, more on account of its poor, hungry soil than its Bay-influenced coolness. He finds excellence in the Chardonnay grown on Mount Veeder and in the thin soils of other Napa hillsides. Monterey and Mendocino, he considers, are both at present underrated for the delicate wines he is looking for.

It is interesting to hear a contrary view to both Antinori and Maudière. Miguel Torres, whose family's work has put Penedès in Catalonia firmly on the fine-wine map, likes heavy, strong Chardonnays because they are different, with a distinct image of their own. Rather than wanting to reproduce the harmonies of classic wines, he sees the virtues of inventing new ones. He is not afraid of alcohol, in the right place. Zinfandel he likes best at 14%. On the other hand, he cites the advent of 'light' wines as proof of the vitality of the industry. As a Spaniard, he would, not surprisingly, like California's winemakers to try Spain's best varieties as an alternative to what risks becoming a narrow range of accepted varieties. The Parellada, which serves him so well for white wine in Penedès, should grow excellently in the North Coast counties. Torres is particularly concerned with costs and prices, reserving his strongest admiration for Gallo, which has shown the way to very drinkable white wines at a lower price than any advanced country can match. It is no coincidence that the Torres company has started production in Chile, which has an ideal environment for the vine. Perhaps it is surprising that California's winemakers have not.

The international consensus seems to be that California has proved herself more conclusively so far with red wines than with white. Fritz Nerath, whose work with the great German Seitz filter company brings him to California at least twice a year, is very specific. Napa Cabernets, he says, have always been outstanding. 'There are always people who overdo things,' but there is no questioning the stature of the finest California reds…

It is widely agreed that one towering advantage California has over Europe is its open mind. Rapid adaptability is simply not possible in the classic European regions. Law and custom slow change down to a crawl. To see the speedy, unhampered development of new ideas, you must look to such areas as Sicily or the Midi, which have minimal controls.

I do not doubt that the soil – not just the 'dirt', but what the French call *terroir*, the land in all its aspects – is next on the agenda for serious study in California. The 100th Anniversary (July 1980) issue of *California Agriculture*, the journal of the University of California Division of Agricultural Sciences, an issue devoted to viticulture and oenology, contains no chapter on the land itself and only a single mention of the word soil (in relation to pH). If French concern with soil can sometimes seem blinkered, this is surely sand-blind, if not (as Launcelot says of Old Gobbo in *The Merchant of Venice*) high-gravel blind.

Indeed, where academics have failed to lead, experienced farmers are now finding their own way. Wines from named vineyards were rare exceptions three years ago. Today they are becoming commonplace. It will, of course, take many years to plot the significance of their terroir as against the variety and age of their vines and other factors, but this is certainly the next priority in California's search for its own classics.

Excerpt from California Wine: An International View, Hugh Johnson's introductory essay to *The University of California/Sotheby Book of California Wine*, editors Doris Muscatine, Maynard A Amerine and Bob Thompson (California) 1984. Reproduced here with permission of the author and publishers.

WINE ON THE MOUNTAIN

Fiona Morrison talks to Paul Draper of Ridge Vineyards, whose Monte Bello 1971 was ranked fifth in the Judgement of Paris, and explains this is one wine that has *not* changed as a result of that famous moment.

FIONA MORRISON MW (2021)

Let me take you back in time to a California that was re-awakening. The missions and the gold panners had left the Golden State long ago and the native wine business was just beginning to stand up and shake itself off after the miseries of financial crisis, Prohibition and a punishing Vietnam War.

There were signs of hope: one of them was to be found just off the highway at Cupertino, at a time when Apple's presence there was just a small research and development campus and its 'Infinite Loop' headquarters was yet to be built. The name Cupertino then signified a small town at the base of San Francisco Bay, not far from Palo Alto and the hallowed corridors of Berkeley. I first travelled there in the 1980s but mine was a loftier destination. After we turned off the highway, we climbed 800 metres up into the Santa Cruz Mountains, to a ridge high up in the Monte Bello Reserve. Once the deep fog had swirled away towards the end of the morning, the views stretched to the Pacific Ocean to the west and the nascent sprawl of cranes and scaffolding in Silicon Valley to the east. It seemed an unusual place to find one of the key figures of the Californian wine scene.

My first winery visits that trip had, naturally, been to the Napa Valley where new cellars were opening monthly. Shiny counters in each tasting room offered an incredible array of different varietal wines, all grown in the same valley vineyards and presented for trial by perky hostesses. The sun beat down. The wines tasted sweet. And this was only the beginning of the wine theme park that Napa was to become.

But here on the San Andreas Fault was another world: a rediscovered territory, a remote outpost, a hippy-sounding collaborative that seemed worlds apart from the manicured marketing of Napa. The memory of this first excursion remains brilliantly clear: as we twisted and turned up the Monte Bello Road, I remember imagining back to a century earlier when the first settler up here, an Italian doctor, planted vines on these barren slopes. This place served as a reminder that California wine was about more than just Napa and that in the decades ahead, new valleys, new districts and new mountain sites were about to be discovered at a pace not seen since the Mission times.

Making his way towards us that spring morning was a rather diffident, intellectual, somewhat pixyish man with wire rectangular glasses (I don't think he has ever changed the shape), a lush moustache and goatee beard. He reminded me of my philosophy tutor at university. As he recognized my companion, Gerald Asher, he did a little hop of excitement and his face came alive, parting the fog and any residue of doubt. This was Paul Draper.

More than 30 years on, I, like so many others, think of Paul with great warmth. I love that rolling accent of his, the rather deep, stony voice that drops and pauses as he speaks: he talks in a very conversational style, using his hands to express his points. He always says 'we', never 'I', to emphasize that Ridge has always been a synergetic effort. He never puts himself forward. I look through the notes that I have taken over the years, spreading tasting books all over the floor as I pick up Paul Draper quotes. His clear, simple sentences leap from the pages, talking about how it is the balance in wines that he loves most and how his goal has always been to show the character of the vineyard. Very early on, long before we thought of the ageability of California wines, it was Paul who explained to me that it was the soil and climate that give us wines worth ageing.

Paul would protest at the thought, but he has probably inspired and taught just as many winemakers and wine lovers as did the ebullient, media-savvy Robert Mondavi, doyen of the Napa Valley. The number of winemakers, researchers, scientists and dreamers that have spent time here up on this high ridge is impressive, and many have become passionate devotees of Monte Bello as a result. Of course, Paul will be the first to say that success of this wine was not only due to him, so to understand his wine's perennity, we must go back to the beginning of the Ridge story.

STARTING OUT AT RIDGE

The circumstances that led to Paul arriving at Ridge were as serendipitous as much of his history. It all started with a 1960s 'Grand Tour' of the vineyards of France and Italy, which in a roundabout way led him to Chile. Down in the south, he found a dry-farmed site of old Cabernet Sauvignon vines that caught his attention and put a stop to his travels – he stayed and made wine for three years, until California called him home…

Winemaking in the 1960s was intuitive and empirical, not academic. When four Stanford University scientists – fellow virtual reality researchers – decided

Left: Paul and Maureen Draper at their wedding celebration and (*below*) the crush station at Ridge Vineyards, circa 1898; the first Monte Bello was crushed here in 1892. Ridge's original stone winery was built in 1895 by Dr Osea Perrone of San Francisco.

to revive the old Monte Bello winery at Cupertino, it was the reality of nature that drew them to this site: it seemed to balance the virtual world they worked in. These brilliant hi-tech developers had a basic need to keep their feet on the ground. Paul Draper became their winemaker in 1969. The tale of their first wine is a wonderful story, best told in Paul's own words: 'In offering me the job of winemaker they had me taste the '62 and '64 Monte Bellos made from Cabernet replanted in the 1940s. They had never made wine before and had simply picked the grapes on a Saturday, crushed them into a small fermenter (adding no yeast) and gone back to their jobs. They had placed a grid in the vat to keep the crushed grapes submerged within the vessel and came back the next weekend to find them fermenting nicely. A week later the wine was dry and they pressed-out the grapes, adding back the press wine and a minimum of sulphur dioxide.

'The wine went through a full, natural secondary fermentation and what I tasted with them six years later was the finest, most complex California wine I had ever had – and I include in that the best-known wines of the 1940s and '50s. The guys had simply not gotten in the way. It was clear they had an exceptional site and I knew if I joined them I would have the chance to make some very fine wine.'

Paul did not set out to make Bordeaux in America, but he knew this vineyard was blessed with a similar magical ingredient: limestone. Prized in Bordeaux and rarely found in California, the soil here was offering up a challenge to him: the chance to make really fine, fresh wines on this high mountaintop.

He and his team made wine using the pre-industrial methods of the 19th century; practices that remain in place at Ridge to this day: natural yeasts are used, very gentle pump-overs, simple racking into barrels, and that is about it: no additives, no chemistry. Paul talks with awed reverence of the old Bordeaux that straddled the 19th and 20th centuries, the historic California wines, such as Inglenook, dating back to the 1930s: they were all made this way. You can hear the nostalgia in his voice. But then it all went wrong. Europe had two world wars to interrupt its history of great wines and California had Prohibition. After a 13-year total ban on alcohol, from 1920 to 1933, many of California's early 20th-century winemakers had retired. Viticulture was pretty much on its knees, with poor, abandoned soils and no one around to do the myriad of small tasks that are necessary to take a vine naturally through from pruning to harvest. By the 1940s, to get things kick-started, the chemical companies and technicians found a quick solution: synthetic products – fertilizers, herbicides, pesticides, fungicides – were liberally applied to the vineyards, forcing them back to life and transforming the natural fauna into a wine park.

Today, it is once again fashionable to talk about non-interventionist winemaking and California growers are steadily turning their backs on such invasive technology. But at Ridge, the wines hadn't needed that post-Prohibition shove; they had steadily carried on making themselves.

KEEPING IT LOW-KEY

So perhaps, after all, Paul's isn't the best example of 20th-century California winemaking. What is remarkable, however, is that he has kept his head when all about him were losing theirs. He has resolutely continued to make wines in the same way he made his first vintage in 1969. Perhaps these days he has the luxury of more precise technology for measuring data. To examine grape components and phenols Ridge boasts one of the most sophisticated labs of any of California's fine wine producers, but this has only served to help him to become less and less interventionist in his winemaking.

I believe that there is another advantage to Ridge's remote location. Far away from the hype and the fashion of Napa, there have been no neighbours to compete with, no obligatory tourist trap to maintain and, above all, no bling surrounding the winery. While Napa has run the gamut of wine trends from high-toast new oak barrels to dark, inky, extracted, high-alcohol wines, Ridge has been able to potter along doing its own thing, while wine trends whizzed by. As Paul says, he and his team were just left alone to make their own way.

So, how is the recipe kept so simple? Well, simplicity here belies the precision and attention to detail that's required to make these wines. Using cover crops in the vineyards to provide organic matter, soil stability on the hills and the nitrogen vines need; nurturing the yeasts and malolactic bacteria that naturally occur in the vineyard and complete the process of primary and secondary fermentation; nudging the wine gently through barrel ageing by racking every three to four months. Everything feels so natural, so timeless, yet behind the scenes there is a strict discipline and pragmatic science. Paul was probably the first to insist on ingredient labelling on his bottles to prove that all his winemaking was natural and transparent.

Influenced greatly by Europe and his international winemaker friends, Paul Draper was one of the first to see the value of separating vineyard parcels, making the batches of wine one by one and assembling them based on blind tasting; there can be as many as 70 individual parcels from the Monte Bello vineyard.

There is so much about each site that is unique, and this uniqueness is probably what spurred Paul on to seek out other distinctive sites across California: he now has over 10 – there's Lytton Springs in Dry Creek Valley, where old vine

The combination of Monte Bello's high elevation (at 400–800 metres), cool climate and green stone, clay and decomposed limestone soils gives its wines a profile that's unique in California.

Zinfandel is grown, and the Geyserville estate in Alexander Valley with field blends of vines over 120 years old, to name just two.

At Monte Bello, it is the ancient limestone sub-soils, the high altitude and the influence of the Pacific Ocean that imprint the wines with a freshness that, as California winemaking entered the 21st century, was to prove vital with the reality of global warming. Natural acidity – a far cry from powder added at the start of fermentation – was to prove as important a backbone to fine wine here as tannin. It is one of the secrets of Monte Bello. Call it luck, call it serendipity or call it intuition but it was in recognizing this acidity that Paul knew he had all the ingredients to make California wines that shine. No wonder Monte Bello has been a beacon for so many others.

Most top wineries are resolutely wedded to maturing their wines in French oak, but I love the fact that Ridge has always used American oak. When I mention this to Paul he warms to a lovely story about when he was making wine in Chile, having travelled around Europe learning about vines and oak trees. He had been fascinated by trials done in Bordeaux in the 1870s where winemakers aged wines in oak from several different regions. His friend, Philippe Dourthe (then owner of Château Maucaillou in the Médoc), who Paul met when they were both working in Chile, had backed-up these theories with his doctoral thesis on oak ageing that made use of a 10-year study by the University of Bordeaux of ageing in several different oaks at each of the First Growth châteaux in the great vintage of 1900. After tasting the wines blind at each château for 10 years, the results were identical to those from the trials in the 1870s. The Baltic oaks came in first, American white oak second, Bosnian oak third and oak from the centre of France fourth. In the late 19th and early 20th centuries the top classified growths used Baltic oak.

Then for Paul, the real revelation came when, thanks to Michael Broadbent at Christie's, he had the chance to buy the greatest wine he has ever experienced: the 1864 Lafite from the cellars of Glamis Castle. At just over a century old, the Lafite 1864 had been matured in Baltic-oak casks and was in superb condition. Its beauty convinced Paul that he would attempt to make wines that would age. Using French oak would imply, wrongly, that he wanted to make his California wines more like Bordeaux, so instead he celebrated the native white oak that had shown so well beside the Baltic oak a hundred years ago.

CLIMBING EVEN HIGHER...

Let's come back to the 21st century and pan out for a moment to view Ridge Vineyards from above. Today, the top of the mountain is stratified with rows of vines – they follow the bends and folds of the slopes like the contours of a map or the lines of a giant's thumbprint. One hundred years ago they were even more extensive, reaching to the top of the mountain at 1,000 metres. However, 50 years ago Prohibition had caused much of this area to revert to bush, oak and madrone; small patches of vines clung on between the homesteads that dotted the landscape. Ridge Vineyards still feels like a homestead: above sits the winery, below it the elegant but low-key visitors' centre and tasting rooms with their sail-like voiles and parasols offering welcome shade. A little further off is the home that Paul and Maureen Draper have made here.

Planted originally from the mid-1880s at 700 metres, the site was replanted to Cabernet in the late 1940s – it was these Cabernet vines that inspired the friends from Stanford to purchase the 79-acre ranch in 1959. It would be thrown into the spotlight just over a decade later when the 1971 vintage, Paul Draper's third vintage at Monte Bello, won fifth place at Steven Spurrier's Judgement of Paris tasting in 1976. Paul worried at first that this victory would create a backlash for Californian wines in Europe but he soon saw that the French wine tasters had paid him the ultimate compliment of accepting his wine in a league with their own.

When we talk about our mutual friend and his famous Paris tasting, Paul remembers that Steven had originally told him that he had planned to show just the California wines, but realized the French tasters might dismiss them too easily. So he decided to include top white burgundies in the Chardonnay flight and top classified growth Bordeaux in the Cabernet flight for comparison. Given his love of Bordeaux, Paul had been tasting his 1970 and 1971 Monte Bello alongside several 1970 First Growths. He was delighted when Steven told him that he was going to do the same. 'I remember wondering why he didn't take the 1970 vintage which I felt would go on forever,' Paul reminisces. 'Perhaps it was because 1971 was a cool, elegant vintage at 12.2% that Steven chose it.' When I ask him why his 1971 did so well, he explains: 'Because I have never believed in the overripe style of California. We are 24 kilometres (15 miles) from the ocean, sited at 400 to 800 metres altitude; winter can arrive before we have full ripeness in flavour.' In 40 years, the alcohol levels at Ridge have only risen by one percent to around 13.5%. Meanwhile, wineries in the warmer Napa Valley have decided to leave the grapes on the vine until they reach overripe flavours at 15%, or even 16%, then cut them back by adding water until they reach 14%.

Funnily enough, I have never thought of Paul as the winemaker at Ridge, and nor, in many ways, does he. He seems more like the guardian, the gatekeeper, the curator of a vinous treasure, and over the years our wine conversations have always been more sensual than technical. Fortunately, the partners recognized Paul's value to Ridge early on and offered him an equal share of the ownership. Paul has remained at Ridge for his entire career. That consistency and longevity is unusual. I last talked to him a few days before his 85th birthday, over 50 years since he first arrived. He remains as a very active chairman of the board and in mid-May 2021 completed the second and final assemblage of a superb 2020 Monte Bello vintage with the Ridge vineyard and winery team.

Wine has been made at Ridge since the early 1890s when all the wines carried the name Monte Bello. For many of us, Ridge will always be timeless, the perfect legacy of a great man and his site at the service of a wonderful wine. When I first tasted Ridge Monte Bello in the 1980s, I don't know if I fully understood it. It was almost too easy to like. I was wary of its sheer drinkability; its smoothness; the fresh, abiding exuberance that seemed so natural; its fine tannins which seemed in balance with all the other components – fruit, soil, oak, acidity, age; its presence in my mouth which seemed to come with a built-in memory. Quite simply, it was, and still is, the most delicious Californian wine I have ever drunk, and I really can't imagine not having a few bottles always in my cellar. It makes me happy. It makes me smile and when I tell Paul this, he smiles too.

IN PURSUIT OF RIPENESS

William Kelley charts the dramatic transformation of Napa Valley Cabernet Sauvignon over four decades – since its wines first found acclaim at the Judgement of Paris – and finds this grape moving towards an era of extreme ripeness.

DR WILLIAM KELLEY (2017 / 2021)

What is ripeness? It's a complex question. As grapes mature on the vine, sugar accumulates and acidity levels drop, while tannins and pigments develop – not necessarily in synchrony. So ripeness is not a moment but a continuum: herbaceous spiciness gives way to bright fruit, which in turn segues into compote, dried fruit and, finally, roasted aromas of coffee and grilled meats; tart acids mellow; thin, green tannins gain in amplitude and grip before becoming lush and supple. Deciding when to interrupt these processes determines a great deal about a wine's style and character. In fact, it's the most decisive choice a winemaker makes each year.

Nowhere has the definition of ripeness been explored more thoroughly, or pushed to greater extremes, than in California's Napa Valley; and Cabernet Sauvignon, its calling card, tells the story eloquently. The United States Department of Agriculture's annual California grape crush reports reveal that the average sugar content of Napa Cabernet has never fallen below 24 degrees Brix – a measure of sugar equivalent to around 14.3% potential alcohol – since 1997. In 2013, the figure hit a record 26.3 Brix – that's 15.6% alcohol. And while data on individual wines is a closely guarded secret, anecdotal evidence suggests that many of Napa's most expensive and sought-after wines run considerably higher than those averages.

Whichever way you look at the numbers, they chart a dramatic evolution: contemporary Napa Cabernet Sauvignon has never been so rich, ripe or high in alcohol. There's no doubting its popularity – the Napa wine trade contributed nearly $34 billion to the US economy, even in 2020 in the midst of a paralyzing pandemic – but it's nonetheless a polarizing style.

Veteran winemaker David Ramey, by no means one of Napa's latest harvesters, speaks for many when he argues that Californians 'should embrace the ripe fruit that is our birthright'. For others, however, the facility with which grapes ripen here makes imbalance an ever-present danger. 'Excessive temperatures in Napa Valley make it a challenge for the wines to belong on a world-class level,' admitted Christian Moueix, proprietor of Dominus Estate, in a candid interview.

For long-time observers of Napa Valley trends, the debates of the present day evoke a sense of déjà vu. In their day, after all, the powerful Cabernet Sauvignons of the early 1970s drew similar criticism. Those 'massive, often charmless wines' appealed only to those who valued scale above 'balance, subtlety, and just plain drinkability', complained Gerald Asher in 1984. 'It was a time,' agreed Warren Winiarski of Stag's Leap Wine Cellars, 'when California winemakers were asking what Cabernet Sauvignon grapes *could* give, as opposed to what they *should* give.'

The extremes of the present, however, in fact bear only a superficial resemblance to the extremes of the past: Asher's 'massive, often charmless wines' are mere striplings compared with the cult Cabernets of the new millennium. Today's winemakers are prepared to accept unprecedented levels of sugar – and concomitant alcohol – in pursuit of fruitier flavours and riper tannins. What were the forces that drove this radical transformation, which was accomplished in a mere three decades?

AN INCONVENIENT TRUTH

Let's pause to consider how Napa Cabernet Sauvignon compares with that of Bordeaux, this grape's home. Back in the 1960s, A J Winkler's groundbreaking *General Viticulture* (1962) classified California's grape-growing climates by counting the number of hours during which temperatures exceeded 50 degrees Fahrenheit (10°C) over the course of the growing season – a rudimentary but effective metric of a region's capacity to ripen grapes. Winkler's research indicated that the Napa Valley was comparable to Bordeaux, and thus ideally suited to growing Cabernet Sauvignon.

More recent research, however, reveals that the valley is actually considerably warmer than Winkler realized. *General Viticulture,* for example, stated that Oakville enjoys 2,300 hours above 50 degrees Fahrenheit (10°C), a dead ringer for Pauillac; but the true figure is more than 3,200. Saint Helena, assessed by Winkler at 2,900 hours, in fact racks up over 3,700. These numbers have more in common with Provence than the Médoc: palm trees and aloes may not be indigenous to the Napa Valley, but it's no wonder they thrive here.

The differences, moreover, run deeper than temperature alone. Oakville's latitude, translated into European terms, places it somewhere to the south of Lisbon, so the sunlight that bathes Napa's grapes is notably more intense than that which shines in Bordeaux. A similarly stark contrast can be drawn between

Bordeaux's humid maritime climate and the dry air of Napa Valley afternoons: since humidity impedes photosynthesis, grapes in drier climates accumulate sugar faster while the maturation of their tannins and flavours lags behind.

All this means that Napa Valley Cabernet Sauvignon is inevitably going to pack more of an alcoholic punch than classical claret. But it doesn't explain why contemporary Napa Cabernet is picked at such dramatically higher sugars than it was in the 1960s and '70s. Certainly, many of that era's wines were tannic and herbaceous; but plenty of bottles from producers such as Heitz, Stag's Leap, Chappellet and Joseph Phelps survive to prove that great Cabernet below 13.5% alcohol was a real possibility in Napa Valley not so long ago. What changed?

A VITICULTURAL REVOLUTION

One answer lies in the vineyards. A landscape littered with different pruning systems reflects decades of experimentation. Gnarled head-trained vines, dry-farmed and planted two metres apart, are relics of the 19th century. Then Prohibition wiped California's viticultural slate clean, and in its aftermath new vineyards were planted with wider spacing, designed to accommodate cumbersome tractors and pickup trucks. By the 1970s, a rudimentary 'T-trellis' had been introduced, with wires to lift the canopy above the fruiting zone, the shoots flopping down between the rows in what became known as California Sprawl.

There were problems with California Sprawl, especially in fertile sites on Napa's valley floor. Planted at low density and often generously irrigated, vines grew extravagantly: 'It rapidly became a jungle, with more leaves than anything else,' says Chris Howell of Cain Vineyards. 'Yields were bigger and green flavours lingered longer,' recalls Cathy Corison.

The notion of varietal wines – made from one grape only – was crusaded before World War II; but until 1976 no one knew that Cabernet Sauvignon (*left*) would be crowned their 'king'.

By the 1980s, winemakers were exploring alternatives, and many looked to Bordeaux for inspiration. A decade earlier, a young Ric Forman had already travelled to the Médoc and returned to plant experimental vineyards at Sterling, emulating the careful trellising and close spacing he observed there. On a later visit, in 1980, Forman was joined by David Abreu, an up-and-coming vineyard manager, whom he inducted into the mysteries of French viticulture. 'David was just enthralled by the whole thing,' Foreman remembers, and Abreu returned to Napa eager to implement the best of French practice, soon emerging as the valley's premiere viticulturalist.

Around the same time, Tim Mondavi also began experimenting with closely spaced, trellised vines – imitating the techniques he had observed at Château Mouton Rothschild, the Mondavi family's partner in their new joint-enterprise, Opus One. Pruned close to the ground and spaced just over a metre apart, Mondavi's vineyards could have been transplanted directly from the Médoc.

Many followed suit, and others pursued similar experiments independently, drawing on similar inspiration. And their intuitions were compounded by advice from viticultural scientists, led by the Australian consultant Dr Richard Smart, who conducted workshops and advised wineries, including Mondavi. Smart preached opening up canopies to light and air; and to winemakers wrestling with unruly California Sprawl the message seemed timely.

Change, in short, was in the air; and it was dramatically accelerated by the second coming of phylloxera at the end of the 1980s. Vast swathes of Napa's vineyard acreage were ripped out and replanted; and many took the opportunity to put new viticultural theories into practice on a grand scale.

Closer spacing and more sophisticated trellising were paired with new rootstocks and virus-free Cabernet Sauvignon clones – many adapted to Bordeaux's comparatively cool and humid maritime climate – which favoured earlier ripening. The higher vine densities meant that drip irrigation, already commonplace, became the norm – and, conveniently, fertilizers and treatments could be applied through the water supply simultaneously. 'It's a growing system not dissimilar to hydroponics – growing plants without soil,' says John Williams of Frog's Leap, one of the valley's most ardent advocates of farming without irrigation, 'and it created all sorts of problems.'

The new vineyards were beautiful. But there were unintended consequences: the wines didn't taste the same. 'It took me 10 years to figure out I was wrong,' admits Howell, who had studied in France and began experimenting with Bordelais pruning systems shortly after he arrived in Napa in 1984. 'I began to notice that the tannins were different,' he recalls, 'but I was such a committed Francophile that for a while I questioned my own perceptions.'

In retrospect, it's hardly surprising that viticultural practices designed to maximize ripeness in Bordeaux's marginal climate should have proven poorly adapted to the Napa Valley's considerably warmer conditions. Not only were the wines' tannins more aggressive, but their flavours were also intensely green and herbaceous.

New techniques in the cellar couldn't solve the problem, and gradually it became clear that the only solution was to pick later, harvesting riper fruit with higher sugars. 'To make the wines softer, we had to make them bigger,' explains Chappellet winemaker Philip Corallo-Titus, who typically picks his grapes at around 28 Brix today.

Since the early 1990s, of course, viticulture has progressed considerably: Napa grape growers are more careful to avoid excessive sun exposure; a small but growing number are pursuing dry-farming too. Trellising has evolved, and several growers are even rejecting it altogether, reverting to the head-trained pruning of the 19th century: 'It's better adapted to our climate and helps the vine self-regulate,' argues Graeme MacDonald, who stewards some of the oldest head-trained Cabernet vines in the valley and has first-hand experience of the system's advantages.

So while the legacy of vineyards which only ripen grapes at high sugar levels is very much with us, it's increasingly the subject of critical thinking. 'We're still learning,' concludes Chris Howell, 'and that's good.'

A MATTER OF TASTE

If Napa Valley viticulture has changed radically since the 1970s, then so too has the valley's collective palate. Even the old guard has relented a touch. 'I don't like the gaudy character Cabernet Sauvignon can get, but I am picking a bit later,' admits Ric Forman: 'I think everyone's taste has changed that way.'

'I've come to think that wines don't need to be mean in their youth to age well,' concurs Philip Togni, who trained in Bordeaux in the 1950s and whose Spring Mountain Cabernets are a watchword for longevity.

Forman, Togni and other classically-minded producers such as Heitz and Diamond Creek have evolved subtly. Others have made a more dramatic break with the wines of the past, pursuing a plush, opulent style of Cabernet that proudly broadcasts the valley's sunshine and warmth. 'In the 1980s, my dad was usually one of the last to harvest; now we're among the earliest – we haven't changed, but everyone else has,' says second-generation winemaker Alex Kongsgaard.

It can be difficult to buck the trend. In Bordeaux or Burgundy, those who wait to harvest are living dangerously, but in Napa's balmy climate, with warm and dry days frequently persisting until Thanksgiving, it takes courage to be the first to pick. 'There's maybe an element of group-think at play,' suggests Cathy Corison. 'You have to have the guts to say, "It's not green, it's fresh!"' observes Mike Dunn.

In retrospect, the 1997 vintage seems to have been the tipping point. 'Yields were so generous that we ran out of tanks to ferment all the fruit,' remembers John Williams. 'We had to leave grapes hanging on the vine, harvesting them several weeks later.' Like many, Williams believed that the ensuing wines were fatally overripe, but they received rave reviews from wine writers awed by their richness and impact.

By the beginning of the new millennium the moral of the story was clear, and more and more winemakers began picking later: some were relieved to be unshackled from convention, free to explore riper tannins and flavours; others simply followed the market. An accident had unleashed a revolution.

Revisiting the 1997 Napa Cabernet Sauvignons two decades later suggests that while ripeness may be a continuum, exploring its extremes is a high-wire act; deft winemaking and above all a great site are critical to attaining balance. Today, the best remain dazzling wines, full of vitality; others are already tired and oxidative; and some are simply rather dull.

So is the era that began in 1997 finally coming to an end? After three decades of experimentation, plenty of lessons have been learned. There's certainly a lot more talk about elegance, freshness and restraint in contemporary Napa Valley. But it would be rash to prophesy a revolution. Instead, expect incremental change and refinement. It's an exciting moment in the history of a region that has achieved so much in so short a time.

First published in *Decanter* magazine in 2017 and reproduced here with kind permission of the author and publishers.

FIRE, DROUGHT, PESTILENCE AND DESPAIR...

From the twin devastations of phylloxera and Prohibition to the perils and pluses of being a seismic hotzone, California wine has its fair share of troubles – but few will be surprised at the energy with which it turns adversity into good fortune...

HUGH JOHNSON (2020)
Stopped in its Tracks

JON BONNÉ (2013)
The Eye of the Hurricane

NORM ROBY (2021)
Phylloxera Returns

ELAINE CHUKAN BROWN (2021)
Drought, Fire and the Future

CLARE TOOLEY MW (2021)
A Greater Threat than Flames?

STOPPED IN ITS TRACKS

Just as it was getting going, California's young wine industry was dealt the crushing blow of Prohibition. From 1920 to 1933 alcoholic drinks were banned from production, transportation, importation and sale. Hugh Johnson explains how it all panned out…

HUGH JOHNSON (2020)

It was as World War I ended, and the prospect of normality was rekindling spirits everywhere, that America produced the black joke of Prohibition. No one, at least in America, could say they had not been warned. The temperance movement, despite its complicated internal power-struggles, had been gradually gathering strength all the while America itself had been growing and learning to use its power. It was like a cancer in the body of the country built on freedom; a coalition of quite disparate interests, of sincere reformers and power-brokers on the make, that joined in exploiting what they chose to see as a weakness: the freedom of men and women to refresh and restore themselves as their ancestors had done since history began.

This is not the place either to retail the machinations, or even to deplore the obvious consequences of the catastrophe. It is hard to imagine a greater spur to law-breaking even by agents seeking to destroy the nation. Its moral repercussions were horrifying. The systematic hypocrisy it introduced into public life was as bad as the simple slaughter of individuals who were caught in the wrong gang of bootleggers at the wrong time. The best excuse of those who promoted Prohibition is that they had no idea what its consequences would be. Nowhere is this more true than in the world of wine. Its net effect was to add more than half as much again to America's wine consumption. Production averaged over 284 million litres a year over the 13 years the law was in force, compared with 190 million litres in the record pre-Prohibition year. Nobody knows how much wine was smuggled in from abroad (although the figure offered by the champagne industry is over 265 million litres during the years in question).

The wine industry did not even have to go underground. Although it was strictly policed (at least 1,000 enforcement officers were found guilty of extortion, conspiracy, perjury and other offences), it was still permitted to make wine

The pledge of abstinence, introduced as early as 1800 in the eastern US, culminated in the 18th Amendment, banning the sale of alcohol, in 1920. Much wine had to be tipped away.

for medicinal and sacramental use. Anyone could call himself a rabbi or indeed found a 'church'. Every drugstore sold medicinal wine, and every doctor would prescribe Paul Masson's excellent 'Medicinal Champagne' for any patient suffering from an otherwise incurable thirst.

These legitimate exceptions, though, made up only perhaps five percent of the wine that Americans drank during Prohibition. By far the greatest portion was also made more or less legally, and was made possible by a gaping loophole in the so-called Volstead Act, the 10,000-word document that put flesh on the bones of the 18th Amendment.

The loophole was a sentence in Section 29. It read, in part: 'The penalties provided in this Act against the manufacture of liquor without a permit shall not apply to a person for manufacturing nonintoxicating cider and fruit juices exclusively for use in his home...' – up to a limit of 909 litres a year. 'Nonintoxicating' apparently was too long a word for the millions of Americans who suddenly became home winemakers. A demand grew almost overnight for grapes in quantities never transported before. It was bad news for the wineries, but a bonanza for grape growers, and for railroad companies. Within two years the price of grapes in California rose to three times its average before Prohibition as dealers filled every waggon they could find to rush them to the cities of the east. Wine grapes, table grapes and raisin grapes were all just grapes to them – with the proviso that the thicker the skin and the darker the juice, the better.

The ideal, and the grape that was planted massively at the expense of better varieties, was the Alicante Bouschet – the red-juiced '*teinturier*' that M Bouschet had bred to lend colour to the pallid production of the Languedoc. So dark was its pulp and skin that after it had been pressed, a second and even a third batch of 'wine' could easily be made by fermenting sugar and water on the remaining 'marc'. Its thick skin also survived the railway journey better than any other. The New York yards of the Pennsylvania Railroad became the auction room for the grapes as they arrived. 'What Wall Street is to the investment business, the Penn yard is to the grape business', as *Business Week* explained. In 1928 one buyer bought 225 carloads of Alicante Bouschet as a single auction lot: enough to make over nine million litres of 'wine'. This, of course, was very much the wholesale side of things – the bootlegging business that principally supplied restaurants and speakeasies. On the retail side, although many turned up at the Pennsylvania yard with everything from wheelbarrows to baby buggies, most citizens, having experimented with one sticky bathful of grapes, were prepared to pay extra for convenience.

'Grape bricks' of concentrated juice were one solution, each one bearing a warning: 'Do not add yeast or contents will ferment.' A far more imaginative procedure was dreamed up by Paul Garrett, the creator of Virginia Dare: to use federal funds to 'save the bankrupt grape industry' by making and marketing juice concentrate. What industry was more in need of President Hoover's farm relief programme? Fruit Industries Inc was the name of Garrett's enterprise, uniting his interests in California and grape growing New York.

In 1930 'Vine-glo' was advertised – in terms which suggest a certain over-confidence, to say the least. Eight varieties were offered to the public: Port, Muscatel, Tokay, Sauterne, Virginia Dare, Riesling, Claret and Burgundy. Not only was the concentrate delivered to your home, but a service man came with it to start the fermentation, and came back again 60 days later to bottle and label the (presumably 'nonintoxicating') wine – and more than likely bring another keg.

So audacious a scheme attracted compliments from the highest quarters. Al Capone is reported to have banned Vine-glo from Chicago on pain of death. More seriously, a Kansas City court saw straight through the whole charade. But by this time the end of Prohibition was in sight. The next year, with Roosevelt's election as President, California became the first state to repeal its Prohibition laws, and from December 1933, in the depths of the Depression, the 'noble experiment' petered out ingloriously across the nation.

If there was rejoicing in the vineyards, it was to be short-lived. By vintage time Repeal had been imminent enough for wineries (most of which had not made wine for years) to wind up for action. They were to discover that the realities of restarting were less attractive than the idea. Most of the vineyards had been replanted with 'shipping' grapes. Much of their equipment and cooperage was unusable. Many were inexperienced or rusty in even the principles of their craft.

Wines made in a hurry, some still fermenting, were rushed to the Christmas market. Bottles that had not turned to vinegar exploded in shop windows. Nothing could have persuaded the public more effectively that it was better off with the home-brew it was used to – on which, besides, there were no taxes to pay.

America had lost not only its wine industry: it had lost its taste for wine – orthodox wine, that is, for drinking with meals at home as part of daily life. Dry wines depend on good grapes and on reasonable skill in winemaking. Tastes vitiated by a dozen years of home-brew were looking for something sweet and strong. This was the way the industry had to go. The historian Leon Adams worked as a journalist in San Francisco through the whole unhappy period. 'Most of the people in the industry thought of wine as a skid-row beverage,' he recalls. 'The bankers regarded wine as one by-product of the grape industry... Some growers, such as John Daniel of Inglenook, tried to secure larger loans to plant premium wine varieties – but grapes were grapes as far as banks were concerned.'

In 1934, in the giddy aftermath of Prohibition, 800 wineries had licences, three-quarters of them new, in California. A few years later barely more than 200 were still in business. It was a desperately slow climb back, led by a handful of men whose faith was not to be shaken; true heirs of Jefferson who understood that natural wine stands apart from all other beverages. Among them were the aristocracy who had survived: the firms of Krug, of Inglenook, Beaulieu and Wente, Martini and Paul Masson. Most active in the politics of the business were the Rossi twins, Edmund and Robert, whose Tipo wines from their Italian Swiss Colony winery in Sonoma County never made claims to greatness, but who passionately took up the cause of wine against hard liquor and laid the foundation of today's Wine Institute of California. Quietly getting on with their business of making low-price wine in ever-increasing quantities in the Central Valley were three Italian firms, the future giants of the industry: the Franzias, Louis Petri and the brothers Gallo.

Excerpt from *The Story of Wine, From Noah to Now*, Chapter 41 'Fifty Years of Crisis', by Hugh Johnson, Académie du Vin Library (London) 2020.

THE EYE OF THE HURRICANE

There were bumps in the road, of course, as California wine climbed steadily out of Prohibition towards new heights. But did it climb too far? Jon Bonné tells the story of the mavericks who paved the way to glory and the storm they created when they got there.

JON BONNÉ (2013)

'We were a big, young country,' Robert Mondavi wrote in 1998, 'oriented towards mass production and scientific research, and in our winemaking we emphasized crop yields, sugar levels and profit margins. The great European wineries, with centuries of tradition and craft behind them, put their emphasis on less tangible qualities such as style, character and bouquet. To my mind, the contrast was stark: we were treating wine as a business, the great European châteaux were treating wine as high art.'

That was his conclusion after his first trip to Europe in 1962. Mondavi returned to his family's winery, Charles Krug, determined to elevate California. He spent years trying to redirect Krug towards fine wine, but he always lost the argument, his family convinced he was becoming ever more the snob. Things exploded after he punched his brother Peter in a scuffle over a mink coat for Robert's wife, Marge, and he was essentially barred from the family's winery. By 1966 Robert was courting investors to pursue his own dream for California.

Even in the 1960s Mondavi was targeting the chasm between the art of wine and the technocratic winemaking that had flourished in the postwar era, the treatment of wine as just another industrial product. To this day, it is California wine's great shortfall. What the state lacks in historical legacy it has typically tried to make up for with a combination of brashness and rigid science. Indeed, the tension between the two – winemaking as cultural expression and winemaking as commercial endeavour – has defined California's struggle.

SIGNS OF REVIVAL

After Prohibition there was a desire in California to make great wine again. In the mid-century period following World War II, the industry's true believers insisted that rebirth had to come not by pursuing simple wines but by attempting to make

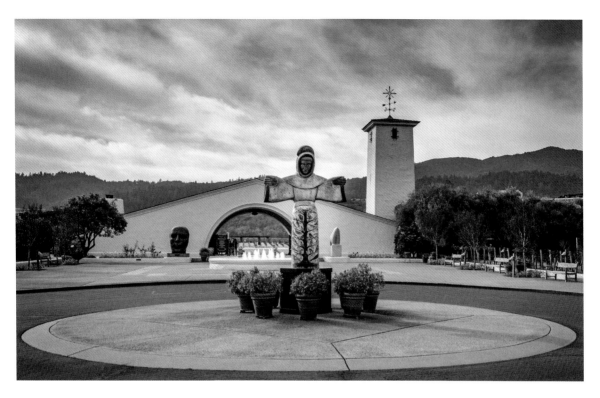

Flanked by the mighty Mayacamas Mountains and the prestigious To Kalon vineyard, the entrance to the Mondavi winery in Napa's Oakville district is one of the most iconic in the world.

great ones, a belief they shared with Robert Mondavi. This group included John Daniel Jr of Inglenook and André Tchelistcheff of Beaulieu Vineyard, who crafted the era's greatest Cabernets, and renegades like Martin Ray in the hills above Saratoga, who strived to rival Burgundy with his Pinot Noir and Chardonnay.

Consider this the beginning of California wine's modern era: when the Mission-style arch of the Robert Mondavi Winery appeared along Napa's Highway 29 in 1966. Designed by architect Cliff May, whose work on ranch houses and *Sunset* magazine's headquarters reflected the essence of California postwar design, it was a revelation, evoking the best of both California's Spanish history and mid-century present, a stark contrast to the rustic barns and chunky industrial buildings that dotted the valley, or even the occasional Victorian remnant of 19th-century greatness, like Beringer's Rhine House in St Helena.

The creation of the Mondavi winery, of May's timeless arch framing the Oakville benchland, was meant to serve as a visual cue for Mondavi's evangelism. Very quickly, the early Robert Mondavi wines became benchmarks for a more refined chapter in California, wines like the inaugural 1966 Cabernet Sauvignon, or the 1968 Fumé Blanc, a Sauvignon Blanc that Mondavi renamed with a French moniker, which hinted at both its oak ageing and the grandeur of Pouilly-Fumé, one of the world's great Sauvignon Blanc-based wines.

Mondavi's wasn't the only big dream. The Chappellet family had established itself on Pritchard Hill, building a pyramid of a winery overlooking the valley. In 1972 a Frenchman named Bernard Portet co-founded a new winery in Napa's Stags Leap District, Clos du Val, with businessman John Goelet. That year brought a raft of new wineries, including Caymus and Warren Winiarski's Stag's Leap Wine Cellars. Around the same time, a lawyer named Jim Barrett partnered on the old Chateau Montelena property in Calistoga. Further south, young Paul Draper had taken the helm of tiny Ridge Vineyards in the mountains above the town of Cupertino. In the Central Coast's remote Gabilan Mountains, a Burgundy lover named Richard Graff tapped into calcium-rich soils, hoping to make Pinot Noir and Chardonnay to rival those of the Old World.

BRAND CALIFORNIA

By the late 1970s, the state was flush with the success of the Judgement of Paris. Wine lists across the country added California fare, just as California cuisine was redefining modern American cooking. Ambitious young winemakers like Ric Forman were pioneering advances like barrel fermentation for Chardonnay. A passel of winemakers trained at University of California, Davis, were quietly taking over cellars, people like John Kongsgaard, whose family had been in Napa for several generations, and Cathy Corison, who along with Zelma Long was among the first female winemakers in modern California.

Most of the attention was on wines with the pedigree of the California coast, but in fact the state's great grape engine had long been found in hotter inland vineyards – perhaps from the Lodi area, east of San Francisco Bay, and more often from the Central Valley, the stronghold of California's mid-century industry, in cities like Stockton, Fresno and, of course, Modesto, whence came E&J Gallo, the state's largest wine company.

These were the seeds of Brand California: a somewhat hazy belief in the quality of the California appellation, one that didn't make geographic judgements. Even as the best of California wine was becoming more refined in the 1970s, Brand California was largely being built on the cheap wine that had ruled the market since Prohibition's end, although the packaging was getting fancier.

As Brand California grew, the chemistry-based curriculum at UC Davis, intended as a teaching tool to help students understand the basics of winemaking, was quickly coming to dominate cellar practices. The programme emphasized sanitary practices over creativity; it insisted on commercial cultured yeasts to ensure uniform fermentation, even though for centuries wine had been fermented using indigenous yeasts found in vineyards and cellars; it advocated routine acidification, in which acid is added to wine to balance its chemistry. On the vineyard side, for many years the Davis curriculum taught that, aside from variations in water retention, the different composition of various types of soil didn't particularly matter.

All these ideas were based on sound academic principles, resulting in a curriculum that would suit everyday industrial work. But the programme also spread the belief that winemaking could be done according to a formula. While the Europeans had their own issues – particularly when it came to microbiological problems that left some wines tasting unclean – Californians increasingly believed that wine could be engineered to be delicious. As Ridge's Paul Draper put it: 'Basically Davis rejected traditional winemaking as old wives' tales that made bad wine.'

Even on the matter of California's most famous wines, let's not romanticize the past. The era's winemaking had its shortfalls; Joe Heitz and many other top vintners would frequently make acid adjustments – often on moderately ripe wines that didn't need the chemistry tweak – in order to approximate the chemistry of European wines.

Research conducted during and after World War II tried to sort out where specific types of grapes should be grown, in essence dividing hot California from cool California. But according to that model, climate was everything. 'The whole idea of soil versus climate in California was decided in favour of climate many years ago by professors Amerine and Winkler,' Richard Graff, one of the early hunters of limestone soils, said in 1977, 'for the simple reason that the factor of climate produces differences in grapes which are measurable in the laboratory. The differences in grapes which are the result of soil are not measurable in the laboratory.'

Nor was 1970s farming necessarily a point of pride. The era's less efficient practices in the field – high yields, wide spaces between rows, sprawling trellises, inefficient irrigation – might have held California's ripeness in check. But with it came an obsession with high yields, which meant that farming practices were dictated less by biological balance than by balance sheets.

Most wineries in the 1970s were utterly focused on growth. So-called small operations, for example Mondavi and Beringer, had an expansion boom, producing hundreds of thousands of cases. By the time wine scientist Richard Peterson showed up at an ambitious new project, the Monterey Vineyard, it already had 10,000 acres of vineyards sprawled across the Salinas Valley, the heart of Steinbeck country.

Soon the Davis graduates of the 1970s would be the new rock stars. A handful, like Kongsgaard and Corison, put their chemistry-heavy learning at a distance, eager to mirror the practices of old European hands who had resettled in Napa, like André Tchelistcheff and Philip Togni, a student of famed Bordeaux oenologist Emile Peynaud. But more often, the Old World equation – in which the vintner toiled in both field and cellar – was replaced by winemaking as a self-contained job. Here was California's other great chasm. Winemakers were winemakers; growers were growers. Unless you were a maverick like Winiarski, farming was just a field hand's job.

FIGHTING VARIETALS

By the time the 1980s arrived, California wine was booming – and feeling more than a bit self-satisfied. A grape glut in the late 1970s plus ambitious growth projections (in 1970, the Bank of America predicted Americans would drink nearly two billion litres of wine annually by 1980) had given rise to an ever-increasing raft of inexpensive wine. While the table wines of the past were typically blends from low-grade grapes – like Gallo's Hearty Burgundy and Almaden's Mountain Chablis – the turn of the decade brought a novel concept: selling cheap wine by varietal name.

The notion of varietal wines had been championed since writer and merchant Frank Schoonmaker crusaded for it before World War II, hoping to emulate Europe's finer practices, but the boom in plantings had given rise to a belief that Americans would, in fact, drink more wine if they could better understand it, especially if it was packaged in a proper 750-ml bottle with a cork rather than a jug or box. The so-called fighting varietals entered the scene in the early 1980s. Brands like Glen Ellen and Mondavi's Woodbridge soon soared.

No one was entirely sure which varietal wines would stick, and the spirit of exploration was still strong; Johannisberg Riesling, Chenin Blanc and Napa Gamay, for example, all fought in the varietal wars. But the Paris tasting had crowned a king and queen. Nothing could match the dominance of Cabernet and Chardonnay. The latter, a one-time asterisk in the book of California winemaking, was of particular interest after a San Francisco lawyer named Jess Jackson produced one in 1982 under his Kendall-Jackson label. Its slight touch of remaining sugar found favour with drinkers, especially women. Soon Chardonnay was virtually synonymous with white wine. America had found its beloved beverage.

There were speed bumps in California's progress, of course. As the Reagan era unfolded, a backlash – fueled, in part, by the French – arose, as some considered California wines too big, too robust. In response, some vintners became occupied with the prospect of creating 'food wines'. Picked earlier and often doctored with acid, they were, by turns, either vibrant or screechingly tart. To believers in the 1970s boom, these moves seemed foolishly reactionary. The wines were soon savaged by a new breed of wine critic, including an upstart publication, the *Wine Spectator*, and an ambitious young reviewer from Maryland, Robert Parker, who was shifting his focus from Bordeaux to the West Coast.

THE LONG BOOM

Right on schedule, the predictions of the early 1970s were coming true: America was finally becoming a nation of wine drinkers, and California wanted to capture every last dollar.

But there was one other fly in the ointment. Throughout the 1980s, evidence kept mounting that the AxR-1 rootstock on which many of California's vineyards were planted had a fatal flaw: susceptibility to a new biotype of the vine louse phylloxera. Only in 1989 did Davis finally issue a decree to stop using AxR-1, but by that point the damage was done. As phylloxera devastated vineyards, growers were forced to tear out their relatively young plantings and start again. Thousands of acres would have to be replanted, at an eventual estimated cost of more than a billion dollars. The runaway success of the California wine industry finally faced a hurdle it couldn't muscle past.

As the 1990s began, California launched another planting boom, though not a wholly voluntary one, given phylloxera's toll. This new wave of vineyards corresponded with a massive influx of money, particularly into Napa Valley. Previously, the model for success had been at large scale, but a few wineries had deliberately stayed small, charging top dollar and selling scarce wines in small amounts, often via mailing lists, to justify those high prices. Hints of this cult-like status had emerged in the late 1970s, notably with Al Brounstein's Diamond Creek, which became the first Cabernet to top $100 with its 1978 vintage.

But the first winery created with the sole purpose of becoming a cult hit was arguably Harlan Estate. Bill Harlan, who had founded the real estate firm Pacific Union, bought property west of Oakville in 1985. Having spent years in Napa Valley, as co-founder of St Helena's posh Meadowood resort and part owner of the Merryvale winery, he had a sense for the financial workings of wine. So he decided to create a project with a remarkable focus; he produced fewer than 2,000 cases each year, sold either through restaurants or a nearly impregnable mailing list.

Harlan wasn't alone. New money was surging into California. Napa had long hosted its share of escapees from elsewhere; early modern pioneers, like the Chappellets and the Davies family, which bought Schramsberg, had come from Los Angeles and even further. But the Napa they settled into was pastoral and quiet. Now serious cash was flooding the valley. By the time Harlan's first commercial vintage was released in 1996, he had a raft of competition – names like

Colgin, Bryant Family, Dalla Valle, Araujo and, most notably, Screaming Eagle. Some had arrived earlier than others (Dalla Valle in 1982), and a few acquired long-standing properties, as when Bart and Daphne Araujo purchased the legendary Eisele Vineyard in 1990, a site responsible for some of the great 1970s Cabernets.

The cults, born out of the industry struggles and the vineyard devastation of the 1980s, quickly came to represent the pinnacle of California winemaking, an industry built around big money and meticulously tended, usually young, vineyards. Grow big? No, the new game was to blossom small. This new goal was encapsulated by Jean Phillips of Screaming Eagle, who in 1986 acquired a 57-acre vineyard. It was mostly planted in white grapes, but she soon decided to replant it and make her own wine. The 1992 debut vintage of Screaming Eagle hit the wine industry like a neutron bomb. At less than 200 cases, and with a 99-point rave from the increasingly influential Robert Parker ('one of the greatest young Cabernets I have ever tasted'), Screaming Eagle set the standard for unattainability.

Napa was becoming addicted to prestige and was quickly turning into the Hamptons West. The annual Napa wine auction, which had once been a relatively quiet community affair, spiked from collecting $447,000 for charity in 1988 to a dazzling $9.5 million in 1999. (This figure would be eclipsed again in 2005, on the far side of the dot-com boom.) Public Napa kept churning along, with its winery tours and bustling traffic along Highway 29. But the real action now was in private Napa. Wineries were built far from the public eye, shrouded in mystery; for many years Screaming Eagle, hoping to discourage looky-loos, managed to keep its address a secret. Here was a way for California, or at least an elite set of newcomers, to redefine the terms of engagement with the Old World.

'EYE OF THE HURRICANE'

And what of the wines? They were getting flashier, with deep extraction of flavours and lots more new French oak, the typical signals of attempted self-importance. Restrained, traditional winemaking began to seem quaint, its practitioners stuck in the previous decade.

A handful of talents for hire emerged, each with a knack for crafting wines that made the desired impact. While Harlan relied on his longtime winemaker Bob Levy, Dalla Valle and Screaming Eagle turned to Heidi Peterson Barrett, daughter of wine scientist Richard Peterson and wife of Chateau Montelena's Bo Barrett, and she soon became synonymous with a stylish and successful style of wine. But one person more than any other set California on a path towards the style that would define it for the next 15 years. 'Certainly,' James Laube, the senior editor for California at the *Wine Spectator*, told me one day over lunch, 'Helen Turley is in the eye of the hurricane.'

A Georgia native raised by teetotalling Baptist parents, Turley made her name as winemaker for two Sonoma wineries, B R Cohn and Peter Michael, but by the early 1990s she had become a winemaking gun for hire, acquiring a roster of top clients, including Bryant Family and Colgin, plus others like Martinelli in Russian River Valley.

She also worked with her brother, Larry Turley, making the wine for his Zinfandel-focused Turley Wine Cellars when he launched it in 1993. Entranced by the possibility of producing Pinot Noir out on the Sonoma Coast, Helen Turley and her husband, John Wetlaufer, in 1985 hatched their own tiny label, Marcassin, which would extend the cult model to both Pinot Noir and Chardonnay. If California had been seeking a style of wine that would set it apart, Turley was the master of the pursuit of maximum impact.

But the formula for stratospheric success was becoming more broadly evident. Vineyards needed to be fastidiously planted, densely spaced on the vertical trellises that had been northern Europe's great viticultural innovation. These young vines were farmed for dramatically low yields – often two tons per acre or less, perhaps half the standard in European vineyards – with underdeveloped grape bunches cut away weeks before harvest. All this propelled the remaining grapes to dramatic ripeness levels.

Helen Turley's first job was working in the lab at the Mondavi winery; her winemaking then went on to take the world by storm. James Laube of the *Wine Spectator* called her 'the eye of the hurricane' but the revolution she started was more than just a one-woman show.

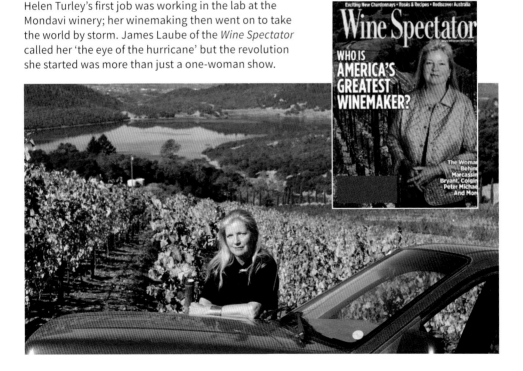

With this meticulous work came a huge spike in farming costs, although prices for the top wines enjoyed a far bigger spike. The master of the form was viticulturist David Abreu, a longtime Napan who had learned farming at Caymus and Inglenook before building his own consultancy, where he employed many techniques popular in Bordeaux. Clients like Colgin, Bryant and Grace Family gravitated to Abreu's precise, manicured and expensive farming methods. Globe-trotting consultant Michel Rolland soon arrived from Bordeaux to offer his own talents. His early work for Harlan caught the attention of others hoping to advance on the cult battlefield. Rolland's long friendship with Robert Parker was, at least tangentially, also a draw; his projects had an uncanny ability to find favour with Parker's publication, *The Wine Advocate*.

Indeed, a symbiotic relationship was emerging between top critics and the top wines. A decade earlier, California wine had been benchmarked mostly by wine competitions like the California State Fair and a handful of regional writers. But as production exploded, after barely budging the previous decade, the state's grape crush figures ballooned nearly 60 percent between 1990 and 2000 – critics, especially Parker, saw an opportunity to become kingmakers, to create a new hierarchy. *The Wine Spectator* shifted from tasting wines as a panel and gave individual critics – in California's case, Laube – full responsibility for evaluating wines.

Critics increasingly swore by blind tastings during which they sampled large flights of wines sent for evaluation. This setup absolved them, theoretically, from making judgements about the source of the wines, but there were still opportunities to game the system. Some of the new elite leveraged the power of their early high scores. Properties such as Harlan and Screaming Eagle soon earned enough clout that they could give writers an ultimatum: either visit the winery and taste in a setting advantageous to the vintner or don't taste at all. Parker actually seemed to prefer tasting this way; it soon became a standard practice.

Lessons about the success of these new practices reverberated through the California wine industry. The Screaming Eagles of the world defined a pinnacle of style. Long growing seasons producing ripe grapes, like 1994, found particular favour, as did wines with softer tannins that were ready to drink upon release. 'The thing is that people used to make their wine and hold it for five years,' Laube says. 'They couldn't do that anymore. The economics dictated that they needed to get their wines out, sold, drunk and reordered.'

LESSONS OF '97

The year 1997 was one that grape farmers dream of: a warm spring and early bud-break, then a warm and constant summer. Harvest began remarkably early, with Napa's sparkling-wine grapes delivered in July. The years of post-AxR-1 replanting were past, the new vines had begun to mature, and the perfect weather delivered a highly productive bumper crop unthreatened by fall rains. Not only could the brave leave their grapes on the vine, further bumping up ripeness, but in some cases they had no other choice, as cellars ran out of room to process all the fruit.

Praise came big, too. Parker doled out four perfect 100-point scores – to Harlan Estate, Screaming Eagle, Bryant Family and Abreu's Madrona Ranch – while Laube didn't mince words, ultimately proclaiming that it was 'the vintage of the century for California Cabernet Sauvignon'.

Finally, here was a signal that affirmed the past decade's work to erase the struggles of the 1980s – proof that crafting wines in the bigger, more dramatic style was not just possible but essential. It was after 1997 that many of California's most successful wines crept north of 14% alcohol – and stayed there. Exuberance was everything. Extreme ripeness was soon seen as the essence of California sunshine.

This exuberance would last precisely one year. The weather in 1998 was everything '97 wasn't: cold, wet and dismal. It could not offer the ripe and almost raisiny flavours, unctuous textures or high alcohols of the previous year. The pure id of the '97s was gone. The 1998 wines were mostly panned.

The following year, 1999, was a more classically styled vintage: the wines were more taut, tannic and fresh than those of 1997, but they were certainly riper than the grim '98s. They got a cautiously upbeat reception, but by that point the standard was clear. Bigger was going to be better. Believe otherwise and you would be punished.

The Screaming Eagle (*left*) and Harlan wine labels – representing two of Napa's most prestigious and sought-after wines. Both recipients of maximum Parker points.

Few were punished worse than Tim Mondavi. By then in charge of wine-making for the Robert Mondavi Winery, which had grown into a powerhouse of a public company, Mondavi was still faithful to the style of wine he had learned not only through the 1970s, but also through his travel to Bordeaux to work on Opus One, Mondavi's partnership with Philippe de Rothschild. Though the winery was at a corporate scale, Mondavi's wines – in particular the 1994 Reserve Cabernet, which, Parker said in 1996, 'may turn out to be the greatest Mondavi has yet made' – were still standard-bearers.

Four years later Parker released his annual California report. He heaped praise on the usual suspects, including Helen Turley's Marcassin, Martinelli, Bryant Family and Harlan (although even he was wary of it becoming 'increasingly expensive'). But when it came to Mondavi, Parker's tone was one of dismay. He chastised Tim Mondavi for 'an almost obsessive mission' to make lighter-styled efforts that, to Parker's taste, were 'indifferent, innocuous wines that err on the side of intellectual vapidness over the pursuit of wines of heart, soul and pleasure'. ('I was a poster child for staid old ways,' Tim recalls, 'and tacked on a board.')

Parker continued: 'I believe he is going against what Mother Nature has given California, the ability to produce wines of exceptional ripeness and gorgeously pure, intense flavours.' Parker found his nearly four-hour tasting at Mondavi to be 'almost agonizing', as he sampled wines with 'intricate aromas that were too subtle and restrained', and that were 'collectively superficial, with tart, almost stripped-out personalities'.

This would be your fate for loyalty to a classic style. California's new mandate was Big Flavour: opulent fruit and the resultant high alcohol. You could hope to be rewarded for compliance. You diverged at your own peril...

Excerpt from *The New California Wine – A Guide to the Producers and Wines Behind a Revolution in Taste*, 'The Rise and Fall', by Jon Bonné, Ten Speed Press (Berkeley) 2013. Reproduced here with kind permission of the author and publishers.

PHYLLOXERA RETURNS

Just over a century after the devastating phylloxera attacks in Europe and similar decimation in California, vine growers once again found traces of the aphid in the Golden State. Norm Roby charts events in the vineyards as they unfolded – and the revolution that followed.

NORM ROBY (2021)

In 1998, at the Premiere Napa Valley mid-winter barrel auction, the tone was upbeat as attention was focused on 'the many new post-phylloxera trends currently seen in the Valley'. Among the trends showcased by the barrel lots were new clones, rootstocks, close vine spacing, trellising methods and vineyard sites.

Winemakers introduced 1997 as the first 'post-phylloxera' vintage. Yes, another post-phylloxera era was brought about by the unexpected return of phylloxera in the 1980s and '90s. But this time it was labelled a 'wake-up call' that resulted in a 'viticultural revolution' – a revolution that led to a 'large-scale change in a compressed space of time', and which was 'a boon to wine quality'.

Make no mistake, 'Phylloxera Redux' was a major event, but over a compressed space of time? Not so much. By 2000 well over 50,000 acres of vines had been infested and removed in Napa, Sonoma and Mendocino, then replanted at a cost in excess of $1 billion. The bug continued to spread here and there, and even in 2021 it has cropped up in the Central Coast and in remote own-rooted vineyards or on vines propagated by massal selection.

CALIFORNIA IN THE 1980s

After the 1976 Judgment of Paris and its multiple re-enactments, California winemakers were on a roll and enjoying the ride. One veiled reference to a Napa vineyard with an unspecified vine disease goes on record in 1981, but the first time the 'P' word is used in public involves a vineyard north of Oakville. That was in 1983.

That the initial response within the Napa Valley was denial is understandable. After all, much like France, California was devastated by phylloxera in the late 19th century. And, of course, most vines established since then had been grafted onto 'phylloxera-resistant' rootstock. Somehow, an old proverb comes to mind: 'Fool me once, shame on you. Fool me twice, shame on me.' Those of us visiting Napa Valley in the early 1980s were aware of burn piles smouldering in the far corner of vineyards but the assumption was that these were old vines being pulled out routinely.

But how could something known to be so devastating return? By 1980 the Napa Valley had changed and was no longer a rural, mixed-agricultural region with prunes, almonds and grapes. From Carneros right the way up past Calistoga, orchards were being replaced by vineyards and the valley was rapidly becoming a monoculture. We now know that vine diseases normally transported by farm equipment and visiting shoes can spread with far more ease when there's just one crop to negotiate, and phylloxera did just that.

During the 1980s, vineyards were using the popular rootstock, AxR-1, which was thought to be resistant. By 1989, growers and winemakers in northern California finally acknowledged that it wasn't, accepting that because this widely used rootstock had been developed from a vinifera parent it was indeed vulnerable.

This phylloxera was labelled 'Biotype B'. New name, but same result. Gradual destruction of the vine's root system and, eventually, the vine itself.

The disease did not play favourites, attacking vineyards of all ages and pedigrees. Cakebread, Staglin, Chimney Rock, Shafer and many other newcomers were hit hard. Peju Province lost all 30 acres of its high-end HB Vineyard, which was pulled in 1995. By the end of the 1990s, the replanting programme eventually included all of Opus One, most of Robert Mondavi's To Kalon Vineyards, and parts of Beaulieu's famous old Cabernet vineyard, Vineyard #2 in Rutherford.

Though the attack was slow, the disease marched on. Sonoma's Alexander Valley was affected first in the south but also wherever vineyards were on AxR-1. As Hank Wetzel of Alexander Valley Vineyards confirms: 'Most vineyards in the Alexander Valley were done in by phylloxera; first in the southern reaches where we are, and eventually all the way to the Mendocino County line. Along with Robert Young Vineyards, we were some of the first landholders to begin removing infected vineyards.' Though relatively young, Jordan's 275-acre estate vineyard a few miles away was not spared.

Parts of the Anderson Valley in Mendocino eventually noted phylloxera damage in both old and new vineyards. Deborah Cahn of Navarro Vineyards recalls: 'It first appeared at Roederer, Navarro and Husch in the late '80s. It showed up in the Anderson Valley a little later than Napa and Sonoma, but it arrived. All the vines that were on AxR at Navarro had to be replanted.'

The costly removal process began in earnest in 1989 with about 1,000 acres in Napa. The pace quickened throughout the valley and removals continued until about 24,000 acres or two-thirds of the Napa total had been pulled and replaced by 2000. The Robert Mondavi Winery estimated that as of 2000 it had spent $50-million in redeveloping 700 phylloxera-stricken acres.

Elsewhere in Mendocino County, as Glenn McGourty, the region's viticultural advisor, recalls: 'By the late 1960s and early 1970s, Mendocino County vineyard acreage expanded to around 11,000 acres. During this rapid expansion, some people planted vines on their own roots and once again, those vines were lost to phylloxera – grafted planting material was hard to come by, and people thought that their isolation might protect them. We had our first confirmed case in 1994. Mendocino County did not experience the sudden rapid decline of many acres as our neighbours to the south did. Our organic farming techniques probably slowed the decline, but since 2000, over 4,000 acres have been replaced with new vines on new rootstocks.'

In other regions such as Lodi and the Central Valley the soils were predominantly sandy and thus, the rootstock proved resistant. In the Sierra Foothills, many older vineyards were own-rooted and fared well. As Bill Easton of Terre Rouge explains: 'Because phylloxera is slow to propagate in areas with cold

There was no alternative. Vineyards succumbing to the deadly phylloxera louse had to be bulldozed and burned in order to eradicate the bug. It took up to 10 years to replace them.

winters and sandier soils, we in the Sierra Foothills experienced only minor phylloxera damage in the 1990s, but it became more advanced in the 2000–18 period. The three-year drought accentuated the damage.

Wherever and whenever the disease showed up, it left growers with one lesson learned. Understanding the soils makes the biggest difference.'

Rootstock selection is now determined by soil composition and vigour. Now popular for shallow, rocky soils are the once-snubbed rootstocks 110R and 1103. Those favoured on average soils are 3309, 5C and 5BB.

And as this rootstock summary suggests, the return of phylloxera was not headline news because a revolution based upon close vine spacing, canopy management, row orientation, sunlight on the fruiting zone, trellising systems and rootstocks is simply far too geeky for public concern – it's just not very sexy.

A WAKE-UP CALL WAS NEEDED

Initially, much of the blame was placed with University of California, Davis, for recommending the failed rootstock and encouraging nurseries to use it when grafting. But it had never been presented as totally foolproof. It was deemed 'resistant' to various diseases based on extensive field experiments on warm sites with sandy soils. Eventually the finger-pointing and blame-casting calmed down and the quest for a solution took precedence. It turned out that rootstock wasn't the only problem – old ways and antiquated techniques had a lot to answer for too.

'Viticultural practices such as head-pruning [leaving the vines freestanding, like small trees] had been around since the age of the telegraph, and were being blindly followed in the 1980s,' notes Doug Shafer. To allow tractors and other equipment easy access, farmers left three metres between each row and two metres between each vine. The number of vines planted on this grid is roughly 500 vines per acre. Typically with this traditional spacing, vines would develop a huge trunk, rich foliage and become loaded with clusters. With its massive foliage, this vine look was coined the 'California Sprawl'.

From the 1960s until the bug reappeared, the viticultural focal point before developing a vineyard was the climate. UC Davis studies of weather during the growing season defined five distinct zones for wine grapes, with 'Zone 1' being the coolest and 'Zone 5' being the warmest (*see* page 50). With the simple goal of matching variety to climate or microclimate, every would-be grower memorized the five zones and their range of degree-days the way school children master their ABCs.

During the North Coast's modern-day planting boom of the 1970s and '80s the primary consideration when planting a vineyard was drainage, with well-drained soils being preferred. So by following rather crude measuring devices concerning climatic zones and drainage, growers often ended up planting one popular variety over numerous soil types and within an area containing subtle but significant microclimate differences.

These basic, rudimentary concepts were widely followed when the vineyard expansion era arrived. Napa's total acreage went from 14,000 in 1970 to 35,000 in 1990. Cabernet Sauvignon increased from 2,600 acres to over 10,000. And then there was Chardonnay expanding from under 1,000 to over 8,000 acres. Sonoma County saw its total acreage double between 1970 and 1990, led by Cabernet and Chardonnay. The latter increased from roughly 1,000 acres to 10,000 in 1990.

In California, the number of wineries increased from 240 in 1970 to 470 by 1980; the boom was on. (If you like comparisons, in the entire decade of the 1960s, nine new wineries were established in the Napa Valley.) With so many newcomers and career-changers entering the wine world, it is not surprising that enrollment in oenology classes, both full-time and short courses, were much more popular than viticulture classes at UC Davis.

So it makes perfect sense that when it came to making vineyard decisions, the newcomers went with the current wisdom and opted to go with the most popular rootstock, AxR-1. Also, the 1980s gave rise to the market-driven 'fighting varietals', inexpensive, drink-now, rocket-aged Cabernet, Chardonnay and Merlot. What also made AxR-1 so widely appealing was that it could support a large crop.

There were alternatives such as the St George rootstock, which were used by many old vineyards, especially those that were dry-farmed. It was a reasonable option at the time. All of Chateau Montelena's 70-acre estate vineyard used St George rootstock. Rodney Strong once quipped that he was forced to use St George because he couldn't afford AxR-1.

ANSWERING THE ALARM

Once phylloxera was acknowledged, research kicked in with a definite sense of urgency. 'We were forced to rethink everything,' said Tom Selfridge, president and chief executive of the Chalone Group of wineries, in 1990. 'If there had been no phylloxera, we would have replanted gradually and made changes as we went along, but this was war. We were forced to make a lot of major decisions quickly, and we knew we had better make the right ones.'

Most of the experimentation in this era had been focused on the science of winemaking and barrel ageing. Several grape-growing research projects were underway, but they were not top priority. The Robert Mondavi Winery began its own experiments with various new rootstocks in 1983. Louis Martini, Wente, Beaulieu and other mainstays had been exploring clones before the crisis arrived. And I remember the Carneros Creek Winery had been exploring Pinot Noir clones, so on several fronts there was interest in changing the old way of growing grapes.

For the state, wildfires have always been an expected phenomenon. The region's climate brings rain only in winter months. So, by late summer the forests and hillsides are covered in a bevy of dried plants that serve as perfect kindling for forest burns. Historically, residents have understood the typical heat spells of late summer or early autumn bring with them the risk of wildfire.

But as climate change has increased the frequency of hot weather events, it has also made the California landscape, and quite literally the humidity of the air, drier far sooner. The result is that the number of days with that perfect combination of low vapour pressure and high temperatures has increased at the same time forests and hillsides are gaining fire kindling.

According to climate change researchers, in the US West Coast between the years 2000 and 2015, there was a 75 percent increase in the proportion of forested area experiencing the optimum conditions for forest fires. In the same time period, the West Coast has also gained nine additional days per year of wildfire potential.[1] Thanks to climate change, wildfire season in California has literally been getting longer at the same time as potential wildfire areas get larger.

VINEYARD IMPACT

For wine growers and winemakers, the challenge of California's elongated wildfire season is its exact overlap with the growing season and harvest period for wine. Few vineyards have burned in California wildfires, and generally only those planted alongside forests in the hottest part of a wildfire. Even so, wildfires during the growing season can cause deep financial ruin for a winery through the cost of smoke taint in a wine.

In 2017, Napa and Sonoma were hit by an unusually intense windstorm a week into October; wildfire erupted across the north coast of California. At the time, what became known as the Wine Country Fires were the costliest fires in the history of the state, leading to more than $9.4 billion in property damage[2], as well as the loss of 44 lives. (Damage from fires in 2018 surpassed the 2017 record.) But even though the Wine Country Fires surrounded the vineyards and wineries, surprisingly little wine was lost from the vintage. When the storm hit in October, Napa and Sonoma growers had already harvested around 90 percent of that year's grapes so smoke taint was not an issue.[3] But in 2020, the situation was different.

---

[1] 'Impact of anthropogenic climate change on wildfire across western US forests', John T Abatzoglou and A Park Williams (October 18th 2016) PNAS vol 113, no 42, 11770–11775.

[2] 'Wine country wildfire costs now top $9 billion, costliest in California history', Dale Kaslerm (December 8th 2017) The Sacramento Bee.

[3] California Wine 2017 Harvest Report (November 8th 2017) California Wine Institute.

On the evening of August 16th 2020, a tropical storm off the Pacific Ocean travelled unusually far north. Overnight, 'Storm Fausto' sparked dry lightning across Northern California, igniting 650 wildfires. At the time, only the earliest of varieties had already been harvested. Vintners scrambled to schedule picks on ripened Chardonnay and Pinot Noir while also facing the likelihood of evacuation. By September 10th smoke had settled on much of the length of the California coast and was being pushed inland over the eastern parts of the state by wind currents. By the end of harvest, only Santa Barbara County vineyards remained mostly untouched by fires or smoke.

SMOKE TAINT AND WINEMAKING

Studies have shown wine grapes are generally most vulnerable to smoke impact in the growing period that begins immediately following *veraison* and lasts until harvest. Grape skins slowly soften when the berries begin to change colour,

Wildfires burning in the hills and vineyards of Sonoma County, October 12th 2017. *Inset*: Fatally damaged? The charred stem of a young vine; grafted plants are less likely to survive.

making them more vulnerable to smoke taint. Volatile phenols found in smoke, then, are more readily absorbed into the skin of the berries where they bond with natural sugars in the fruit. (While berries earlier in the growing season can be affected by smoke damage, it seems to demand extraordinary conditions.)

Part of the difficulty is that smoke taint is not always apparent in fresh juice from impacted berries. Through fermentation and even more so in the ageing process, volatile compounds absorbed from smoke before harvest are released into the wine. Over time, the wine's own acidity cleaves the chemical bonds the smoke's volatile phenols had formed in the fruit. As a result, a wine's smoke taint character can increase over time, producing wines that seem to begin without any apparent impact but revealing it with age.

Studies have found that smoke compounds form primarily in grape skins, and only impact the juice inside the berry in extreme conditions. Testing has also shown that smoke character is fully extracted from grape skins in only two to three days, and usually before the full extraction of either anthocyanins or tannins. What that means is that shortening maceration time for red wine is unlikely to reduce smoke taint in the final wine and making rosé by soaking the juice in skins is likely to extract some smoke compounds as well. Current knowledge does suggest it is possible to avoid smoke impact by seeking a sort of still wine *blanc de noirs*, making white wine from red wine grapes without any skin contact.[4] White wines made without skin contact can also be made without smoke taint character.

Some winemakers have turned instead to making red wines and then using filtering technologies to remove smoke taint. So far, there seems to be little long-term success. Reverse osmosis can remove smoke impact from a wine but also removes other flavour complexity. And, even so, over time, smoke taint character often re-emerges in the wine as acid hydrolysis naturally releases volatile compounds through the ageing process.[5] Some success has been had by fining with carefully selected activated carbon. However, as the activated carbon removes smoke taint character it also removes other desirable aromatic compounds, thus impacting the complexity of the final wine as well.[6] With either method, the recommendations are to sell the wine for quick release or blend it as a small portion of a high-volume wine, thus diluting its presence.

[4] 'Smoke Markers in Red Wines and Maceration Times' (2019) Eric Hervé, Steve Price and Gordon Burns, ETS Laboratories.

[5] 'Smoke taint: practical management options for grape growers and winemakers' (December 2018), Australian Wine Research Institute.

[6] 'Treating smoke-affected juice or wine with activated carbon' (June 2020). Australian Wine Research Institute.

Even so, how smoke impacts grape vines, their fruit or the resulting wine, is less obvious than it might seem. Vintners across California have been collaborating with researchers these last several years. The tragedy of increasing wildfires has at the same time almost exponentially increased our knowledge of how fires form, how their smoke challenges vineyards and how smoke taint evolves in wine. It has pointed us in new directions for research as well.

RETUNING SMOKE STUDIES

The California fires of 2017 through 2020 have shifted how we study smoke impact. Experience from recent fires suggest that the way smoke is absorbed into grape skins is profoundly varied not only within a region but also across any particular vineyard.

It appears that air currents and surrounding weather conditions – including temperature and vapour pressure – have a key role in how smoke settles into and is absorbed by fruit in different areas of a vineyard. Testing has shown significant differences in smoke compound markers found even in neighbouring vine rows.

We do know that the age of the smoke itself changes the impact on an exposed vineyard. The host of volatile phenols[7] responsible for creating smoke taint character in wine seems to dissipate quickly. The fresher the smoke, the more likely it is to impact the wine. Smoke that was made weeks prior seems to have less if any impact on wine quality even if not dissipated. The length of exposure and the overall concentration of the smoke also alter the severity of the absorption. Additionally, different forest types produce different smoke compounds, which are absorbed differently by grape skins.

Studies have also shown that different grape cultivars have differing levels of susceptibility to smoke taint even with the same level of smoke exposure.[8] Further research is being developed in both California and Australia to expand the grape varieties studied and our understanding of how they both absorb and respond to smoke presence. Over time, planting grape types less susceptible to smoke absorption might be one key to evolving wine in response to increasing wildfires.

---

[7] The volatile phenols guaiacol and 4-methylguaiacol have the greatest impact on wine character; 4-ethylguaiacol, 4-ethylphenol, eugeneol, o-cresol, p-cresol, furfural and syringol are secondary markers that can be tested in an expanded panel and are now believed to have an important though less prominent impact on wine character. More research is needed to determine which compounds cause which sensory characteristics.

[8] 'Impact of grape vine exposure to smoke on vine physiology and the composition and sensory properties of wine' (February 2016) R Ristic et al, *Theoretical and Experimental Plant Physiology* 28 (1).

WORKING WITH FIRE

Adjusting how we plant vineyards could eventually alleviate smoke impact in wine but adjusting how we manage vineyard surroundings can also improve the situation. More frequent wildfires have forced regions already prone to them to rethink forest management. While climate change has increased wildfire conditions, fire scientists have also shown that attempts at fire suppression for the last hundred years have actually increased our susceptibility to them.

As the population of California has expanded, more people have built homes in more remote parts of the state and pushed into areas traditionally prone to fire. At the same time, the state has reduced prescribed burns and forest clearing efforts. The result is, quite simply, more fire fuel throughout the region even as climate change has intensified wildfire conditions.

While wildfire conditions due to climate impact will likely continue to intensify, some fire management practices can be improved. Fire scientists recommend prescribed burns in key forest and grassland areas. As counterintuitive as it can first sound, the goal is to use fire to lessen the potential impact of naturally occurring wildfires. Prescribed burns help to alleviate the build-up of pine needles and fallen branches on the forest floor. They can also remove small trees or dried brush, which not only act as fire fuel but are considered to be a kind of fire ladder. The risk is that these younger trees and bushes tend to ignite more readily and help wildfires achieve height above the forest floor, up to a level where they may ignite older and larger trees, which burn for longer. Low-intensity, controlled fires carried out in winter months when temperatures are cooler and conditions naturally wetter can reduce these risks. Forest and land clearing by hand, or with grazing animals, can help property owners reduce excess plant growth as well.

Such practices won't stop wildfires, but they can help reduce fire fuel, and in some cases also create breaks in a fire-prone landscape, thus reducing how serious any particular wildfire can become. For fire scientists, the goal is to shift away from seeking complete fire prevention, to establishing instead institutional and government support for thorough-going fire management. In some cases, such fire management will have to include rethinking where we build homes, or in the case of wine, where we plant vineyards and establish wineries.

RETHINKING THE VINEYARD

As dire as wildfires feel to the wine world, their increase alongside climate change will not result in a complete loss of wine. Nor will it lead to a total loss of any particular region's wine-growing ability, nor a widespread loss of grape varieties. But it will demand a rethinking of how we grow grapes and what we plant where.

As the wildfire season becomes longer, it inevitably arrives earlier. Shifting vineyards to earlier ripening varieties will help ensure they are more likely to be harvested before possible threats of smoke or evacuation. This depends, too, on wineries, regions and their marketing strategies being willing to change. For already-established vineyards, some farming decisions can shift vine development to encourage slightly earlier ripening. But too much change will also change a wine's character.

Fine wine is intimately connected to ideas of terroir and site expression. As regions get warmer, more intervention is required in vineyards to grow the same varieties farmed there before climate change. After a point, such interventions also begin to change flavour and structure characteristics, altering the overall expression of a wine. The effect would seem to be one of expressing farming choices more than innate site character. And here is where bigger changes have to be made.

It is unlikely that a region like the Napa Valley, for example, will have to stop growing Cabernet Sauvignon *in toto*. But it could become more difficult to cultivate vineyards close to forests for fear of wildfire, or to grow Cabernet in the warmest parts of the region without significant intervention as they continue to become warmer.

In the meantime, researchers are evolving the ways they study climate, collaborating with wine regions and wineries to utilize already established weather and vineyard data to evolve both our understanding of wine growing and our changing planet. Remote-sensing technologies, and vine-sensing equipment are making that easier. Most of all, wine's ongoing success will depend on the wine community's willingness to evolve.

A GREATER THREAT THAN FLAMES?

Clare Tooley charts the ingression of marijuana into California's agricultural consciousness since its US legalization in 2016. As a major competitor for vineyard space – the best terroir is the best 'buzzoir' – will it threaten wine livelihoods or create a 'wine and weed' love story?

CLARE TOOLEY MW (2021)

Californian gold has taken on many different hues over the centuries. From gold to white to green, the state is no stranger to the rush it inspires on its land and natural resources. Generations of pioneers, wielding pickaxes, sieves, shovels and trimmers, have tried their hand at emptying the state's natural coffers to make their own fortune. It is a brutal love story of sorts, between man and land. It is the story of California. The relationship falters as greed takes over or fatigue sets in. But there is always another pioneer willing to take up the challenge, who sees gold in the hills. And so it continues, making the history of Californian agriculture one of transformation, driven by market demand.

Vines began to take precedence when the state's 19th-century ranching and grain-growing transitioned to intensive fruit cultivation which included grapes and citrus. California's 'white gold', cotton, peaked in the 1980s when rising water costs and pest problems made its production less lucrative, and almonds, grapes and tomatoes were planted instead. It stands to reason that just as fruits took over from grain and cotton, so other forms of agriculture, under the right circumstances, will eventually displace current crops. In an ideal world, those circumstances would consider the changing climate and its effect on natural resources. The propagation and promotion of less thirsty crops together with a regenerative approach to farming is certainly called for in California where drought and a nation's demand for produce persist in equal measure.

But California is less an 'ideal' world than an 'idea' driven one. It is a creative state, as amply illustrated by its technology hubs, its tourism and its Hollywood film industry. Recreation is key in the Golden State and all that promotes entertainment is eagerly embraced. Climate aside, it is no coincidence that California is both the US's largest wine region and its largest 'weed' producer. The new gold is green, legally green, following the passing of California Proposition 215 for

Cannabis under irrigation in the early morning light. If cannabis cultivation requires 10 times more water than irrigated vineyards, can it sustainably compete with the wine crop?

medical cannabis in 1996 and 64 for recreational use in 2016. While there were millions to be made during the 19th-century Gold Rush, there are now billions of dollars at stake in this century's green rush. Cannabis, therefore, has the potential to transform the state's farming again.

ENJOYING THE GREAT OUTDOORS

The cultivation of outdoor cannabis shares a timeline with grape vines, both dating back to 4000BC. They have coexisted on the same land for thousands of years. Stonework on the Roman temple at Baalbek in Lebanon's Beka'a Valley shows a vine and cannabis plant side by side, and Chateau Musar shared the valley with cannabis for many years before it was suppressed. As old, therefore, as viticulture and related in its power to harness plant life to offer the consumer a natural recreational high, the parallels are obvious and their coexistence inevitable.

In California, cannabis plants have been planted for as long as anyone can remember, some between the rows of vines, with winemakers and locals enjoying cannabis-infused wine on their time off.

Like grape vines, cannabis grows well on flat land but gradient and altitude with specific exposure to the sun gives higher quality flowers with a higher terpene and higher cannabinoid content – these being the chemical compounds responsible for aroma and pharmaceutical effect or 'high', respectively. The Mediterranean climate of California is particularly favourable to the cultivation of cannabis and that, coupled with the state's history of agriculture and vast tracts of land, is what has made California a natural home to cannabis, regardless of its legal status.

The US is the first country to have legalized the possession and cultivation of recreational cannabis alongside its highest value wine grapes, specifically in California and Oregon. The legalization of both medical and recreational cannabis is well underway across the US, making it mainstream; 83 percent of the US population supports legalization, 64 percent believe cannabis to have medical benefits, and over a third of the population are consumers of cannabis products. This would suggest a relatively easy transition for illegal cannabis growers from their hideaways on mountaintops and secret valleys to open spaces, their day in the full sun finally a reality.

The situation is much more complicated, however. There is an appetite for licensing, which is under the direct control and at the discretion of individual counties, but illegal cultivation is still widespread, fuelled in part by the established illegal market. Mirroring its wine business, California has supplied 70 percent of the country's cannabis requirements for years, long before legalization. It will take years to unpick the threads of a cultural fabric so comfortably worn. This, coupled with the high cost of licensing and the stringencies of an imposed cultivation regime, permissions and labour laws, are high barriers to overcome.

Nevertheless, along California's coastline, where grapes and cannabis have long basked together, thriving in the Mediterranean climate, legitimate businesses are beginning to grow. Significantly, outdoor cannabis does not just thrive, it excels in California's wine regions to the north in Mendocino, Humboldt and Lake Counties. This is home to the Emerald Triangle, the country's largest cannabis-producing region, and birthplace of contemporary high-quality cannabis culture.

There is a belief that such world-beating cannabis can contribute positively to any region seeking to lay claim to quality products. Sonoma and Santa Barbara counties, therefore, have embraced legislation, issuing cannabis cultivator licenses and supporting the expansion of legal grows. Napa County stands alone among its premium wine-growing peers in continuing to prohibit cultivation. It is at odds with its neighbours and meets divided opinion within its own communities. Its moratorium suggests a conservative approach that may mirror the political persuasions of its wealthiest landowners. Politics aside, the perceived anti-agricultural stance of such a prohibitive approach is at odds with Napa's Edenic, diverse and inclusive agricultural message, and hence is challenged.

KEEPING THE HARMONY

The return to Eden, peace and pot, a place where everyone sits harmoniously under their own dappled vine trellis, fig tree or weed parasols, is an image promoted by many who embrace both crops. It is not entirely far-fetched. Working in harmony with the land is already embraced by many California cannabis and grape growers who practise sustainability and farm organically and biodynamically. The production of legal cannabis may even be setting a new standard within agriculture in general with its strict residue testing and move towards organic certification. Draft regulations for an organic certification for California-grown cannabis, the OCal Program, comparable to the National Organic Program, have been released by the California Department of Food and Agriculture (CDFA). Regenerative farming is an area of overlap between high-quality growers. The use of companion plants such as yarrow and chamomile by cannabis growers to increase the oil production in the surrounding plants and legumes, and mustard by grape growers in their vineyards to nourish the soil, is part of much common ground between them.

Nevertheless, as an agricultural crop, cannabis competes with others for resources and challenges their financial viability. Land may still be in plentiful supply but is expensive, and California is not as bountiful in other resources as it once was. What was once a land of plenty, is now beset with the natural and manmade disasters of drought, fires, economic instability, labour shortage and an ever-widening eye on profit. It is perhaps the greatest irony that a social and political softening towards cannabis, heralding an unprecedented increase in demand and therefore production, should coincide with a time in California's history when it is at its most challenged to deliver efficiently and least likely to reap the benefits.

Solutions will need to be found to avoid having to make hard choices. Cultivation techniques of grapes and cannabis are not only similar but also highlight the challenge of coexistence. Most cannabis harvests produce a single crop and occur in October, thus coinciding with the grape harvest. Not only are cannabis flowers at their most pungent at harvest time, increasing the risk of potential odour drift to neighbouring properties, but labour requirements for harvesting overlap. The labour involved in the trimming and processing of the cannabis harvest is intensely manual, and cash-incentivized due to federal banking restrictions, begging the question how will a region retain and increase a labour force already straitened by immigration laws.

Combined indoor and outdoor cannabis cultivation requires 10 times more water than irrigated vineyards, prompting one to ask how an agricultural region, already rationed, will choose to distribute its water. These choices will inevitably be guided by the practical, with an eye to the financials. Cannabis potentially trumps grape vines in both cases, firstly by producing within its first year, ensuring a faster return on investment compared to vineyards that take years to reach maturity, and secondly by securing a vastly superior return per acre.

THE BEST IN THE WORLD...

Perhaps the greatest challenge cannabis poses to California's wine industry, however, is less physical and more perceptual. If, indeed, the 'world's best cannabis' is grown in California, it stands to reason there will be connoisseurs seeking California's best cannabis – terroir-driven cannabis. This has considerable potential to disrupt the value of premium grapes for if cannabis culture ever really develops a sense of terroir, or 'buzzoir' as one eminent winemaker puts it, then the wine business could be in real trouble.

The market value of California's viticulture has been defined by its American Viticultural Areas which have allowed regions to differentiate themselves from other regions. They have enabled certain regional producers to charge more for their grapes by conceptualizing and marketing a quality hierarchy as well as by nurturing a reputation for being unique. Competition arises when another product markets itself in the same way, in the same place, to a similar audience. The question then becomes whether both products can retain their exclusivity as a premium product.

The concept of 'terroir' is widely discussed by cannabis experts who talk of the importance of the effects of the terpenes and the differences arising from unique practice and place. It has already been taken up by one Sonoma-based wine company marketing their cannabis product, 'The Grower's Series', as 'an ancient and bounteous gift of mother nature, linked by great care, terroir and temperateness'.

There are now cannabis tour operators established specifically to promote the singularity of the plant grown in their region. An appellation project for cannabis, modelled on the wine industry appellations system, has been commissioned by the CDFA, suggesting location will govern future cultivation sites. The notion that cannabis could claim similar rights to terroir as viticulture may seem implausible by those who believe the chemical and its effects are its attraction, not the 'sense of place'. One could argue, however, that many believe the same to be true of wine.

Cannabis has the potential to be a potent disruptor of California's wine industry. Yet for all the uncertainty, there is an undeniable acceptance that it is here to stay. Global beverage businesses are investing in cannabis distribution, signifying their belief in its potential as a partner or possible alternative to wine. Time will tell whether the opportunity legal cannabis offers California leads to cooperation among the agricultural community or commercial cannibalism. In the meantime, however, the state's long history of pioneering and love for all that its dirt produces, claims the victory as California enters yet another golden era.

5

ANYTHING BUT CABERNET!

With all the publicity and most of the prizes, Cabernet Sauvignon reigns supreme. But Zinfandel is California's prince of versatility, Chardonnay its pretender to the burgundy throne, and its sparkling wine and Sauvignon beat majestic paths all their own.

LISA PERROTTI-BROWN MW (2021)
Survival of the Greatest

LIZ THACH MW (2021)
The Only Way is Fizz

BOB THOMPSON AND HUGH JOHNSON (1976)
Not to be Sniffed At

PAUL DRAPER (2021)
All Hail Zinfandel, Prince of California!

SURVIVAL OF THE GREATEST

Lisa Perrotti-Brown tracks Chardonnay's upward trajectory in California, finding that it now not only gives white burgundy a run for its money but also brings unique new qualities to the fray with its range of heritage clones.

LISA PERROTTI-BROWN MW (2021)

The most ubiquitous of the noble grapes, Chardonnay is also among the most polarizing. There are those that flat-out refuse to drink it, while others will have nothing else.

Chardonnay has become a widely recognized grape variety brand. And yet, at its pinnacle, California Chardonnay stands apart from the herd with its enviably unwavering popularity. David Ramey, one of the state's best-known producers, once quipped that Chardonnay is the red wine of white grapes, an observation that makes perfect sense to hardcore fans of the finest, most singularly expressive Californian examples. This has as much to do with the vineyard landscape as it does with how its unique Chardonnay clonal material has adapted to the land over the course of more than a century since it arrived in California.

After an explosion of global Chardonnay plantings in the 1990s to meet the growing worldwide demand for largely New World-forged, big, oaky, oily, high-octane, butterball styles, into recent times, Chardonnay has, in some circles, become a victim of its own former success. The backlash in the early 2000s was the ABC contingent, who demanded Anything but Chardonnay. As demand for Chardonnay in Europe and the Antipodes dried up, a lot of producers around the world sought to reinvent themselves with leaner, fresher, less oaky or unoaked styles, hoping to ride the next trend wave. Some big-brand, large-volume producers turned their backs on Chardonnay altogether, heading for greener grape variety pastures by replanting to Sauvignon Blanc, Pinot Gris or red varieties.

Californian Chardonnay, on the other hand, didn't miss a beat. Today, as the California Wine Institute attests, Chardonnay remains California's most widely planted wine grape and is the most popular wine in the US, having been so for the last decade. According to the University of California Giannini Foundation of Agricultural Economics in a report on recent trends in the California wine grape industry: 'Throughout most of the last 30 years, Chardonnay yielded the highest average prices among the major white varieties by a wide margin.'

The success of California Chardonnay is largely due to a staunchly loyal domestic following, which has much to do with consistency of quality. Chardonnay shines here, in all its many guises. Granted, there are a lot of ordinary, straight-forward, generic Chardonnays sold at the lower end of the market, accounting for most of the volume. But the success of Chardonnay in the US extends from volume-led brands all the way up to 'icon' status. At the upper end, the successes of 'cult' Californian Chardonnays such as Kongsgaard, Marcassin, Kistler, Aubert, Morlet and Peter Michael have as much to do with sky's-the-limit greatness as with the expression of singular, signature styles, distinctive from white burgundy, which simply cannot be replicated in other regions around the world. This is partly down to that somewhat mystical term 'terroir', a sense of place, admittedly difficult to link with specific characters in a wine. In the case of California Chardonnay, more relevant and easier to demonstrate is the impact that California's heritage clones have on the singular styles, manifesting unique terroir expressions and the extraordinary quality levels of the most highly sought-after labels.

WHAT IS A HERITAGE CLONE?

There's more and more talk nowadays about heritage (also known as 'heirloom') vegetable and fruit varieties. Recently they have gone from specialty products found mainly in farmers' markets and upmarket shops, to dedicated sections in major grocery stores. Heritage varieties are those that have resisted and survived in a location over many years. They have been selected, propagated and passed down by local farming communities, and valued through generations for their unique qualities and ability to adapt to local growing conditions. When methods of industrialized agriculture swept through our modern times, laboratory- and nursery-created hybrids and crossings offered disease and pest-resistant varieties with higher yields at lower costs of production. Sadly, it was then that many of these heirloom varieties of vegetables, fruits and even wine grapes were replaced and ultimately forgotten or lost. But, when it came to California Chardonnay, happily there was a better outcome…

CALIFORNIA'S MAJOR HERITAGE CLONES

The traceable history of Chardonnay in California goes back to the late 1800s – it arrived just after the Gold Rush, when the wine industry was finding its stride, and before it hit the Prohibition wall from 1920 to 1933. But perhaps the most important milestone in California's Chardonnay history came with Carl Heinrich Wente's purchase of a vineyard to the east of San Francisco in Livermore, in

1883. The Wente winery was established in 1912, and soon afterwards Carl's son, Ernest Wente, encouraged him to import Chardonnay planting material from the University of Montpellier in France. Two sources were propagated in the Wente's Livermore vineyards and selected for desirable traits over the next four decades. It is estimated that the overwhelming majority – more than 80 percent – of all California Chardonnay vines today can be traced back to this Wente clone heritage.

Today, Foundation Plant Services (FPS) at University of California, Davis, in California maintains a large collection of Chardonnay clonal selections, most of which are available to the public. The Wente clone selections can be broken down into two major types, the first being what is considered the 'traditional' Wente clone selection, featuring smaller clusters of thin-skinned berries that typically result in 'hen and chicks' or 'shot berries'. That is to say, the bunches contain a mix of larger, riper berries and smaller, greener / less-ripe berries. Technically, this effect is known as *millerandage*, which is generally considered a virus-related affliction, but can also produce astonishingly intense and complex wines. The second, less common type of Wente clone variant is generally referred to as the 'Musqué' clone, nowadays sometimes known by the names of the source, such as See clone or Rued clone. This category of clonal material tends to give more aromatic styles of wine with perfumed floral and spice characters similar to Muscat.

MASSAL SELECTION

Through more than a century since the establishment of modern-day Chardonnay heritage clones in California, selection has shaped (and still shapes) the planting material that is most sought-after today.

'Exposed to many *sélections massales*[1] and clones of Chardonnay in California, I came to favour the Old Wente (OW) for its more classic array of apple, pear, spices and minerals versus the more common exotic and tropical fruit expressed by other clones,' commented Luc Morlet, former winemaker at Peter Michael Winery in Sonoma and now proprietor of his own highly revered label. 'It has been my favourite *sélection massale* to work with by far. First of all, there are many different OW selections, often named after the vineyard or vineyard owner from which the cuttings came, and I would rather call them 'OW selections' than 'OW clones' since each of these selections comes from a multitude of selected vines which differ in their DNA. Over time, I have had the opportunity to work with numerous Old Wente selections, such as Hyde, Hudson, Haynes, Kistler and others.'

---

[1] *Sélections massales* (massal selections) is the French wine-growing term for the practice of replanting new vineyards with cuttings of top-quality vine material that performs well on older sites nearby.

[2] 'Shatter' is when a grape cluster fails to develop to maturity.

Wente vineyards in the Livermore Valley. Home to more than 80 percent of California Chardonnay's clonal heritage – vines that give Chardonnay wines of complexity and character.

As to the allure of Old Wente selection above others, Morlet commented: 'The main reason I love OW is the aptitude of the fruit to express where it is coming from, its terroir. If conducted properly, the winemaking enhances the sense of place of the fruit. Primary aromatics are then subdued; varietal characters seem to quickly fade away to let more mineral-driven aromatics take the lead and express the vineyard site. Why and how do OW selections accomplish that more than other selections or clones? There are still numerous mysteries in winemaking, and I particularly love the charm they bring to the industry!'

Fortunately for the future of fine Chardonnay in California, heritage clone selections have remained more a case for quality, rather than quantity.

'For sure, a reason to favour the Old Wente selections is the smaller yields off the vineyards,' continues Morlet. 'We refer to it as the "clone of the winemaker", as opposed to the "clone of the grower". As OW has typically small clusters and a fair amount of *millerandage*, often no thinning is needed at all. OW is definitely more about quality than quantity.'

And yields are not the only deterrent that would put volume-seeking growers off working with Old Wente clone selections. 'Other challenges linked to OW include shatter[2], due to particular weather conditions (wet and/or cold flowering, excessive winds) or vigour (soils too fertile, excess of water or overly vigorous rootstocks can induce shattering at berry set),' says Morlet. 'Economically speaking, there are obvious drawbacks to smaller yields from the vineyards and off the press; with many small berries, the GPT (gallon per ton) drops from 160 to about 135. Finally, if overly extracted, the juice can quickly become bitter. Yet, all of these challenges are well worth overcoming in order to produce world-class wines, with personality and a strong expression of terroir.'

THE HYDE CLONE(S)

It is nearly impossible nowadays to discuss high-quality California Chardonnay and not give credit to its Wente clone heritage. And there are few living winemakers who know more about the Wente clone than Larry Hyde of Hyde Vineyards in Carneros, who has established his own highly regarded selection known as the Hyde clone. 'In 1981 I called Wente and asked for wood from the small-cluster Chardonnay that had "shot" berries in most clusters,' Larry Hyde commented.

'Hyde clone, in most cases, refers to the plant material that my father received directly from the Wente Vineyards in Livermore,' explained Larry's son, Christopher Hyde, now general manager at the estate. 'This became a field selection carefully propagated by my father and selected for small clusters, and what is now known as FPS 112. There are two other Wente selections we have that originated from Linda Vista nursery, but the Livermore is by far the most well-known and widely propagated.'

When asked what makes this selection unique, Christopher replied: 'We propagated a more mineral selection that produces a fresh, citrus and limestone character, and is prone to shatter. The vines are fertile, allowing for many small clusters. These characteristics, however, do have a lot to do with the site, climate, soil and row orientation at Hyde Vineyards too.'

BEYOND THE 'TRADITIONAL' WENTE CLONES

Apart from Wente clone, the Hydes also highly value another heritage clone widely known as the 'Calera' clone. This is something of a mystery clone, having come from an unknown source in France, and is named after the Calera winery in California's Central Coast. 'The Calera clone has substantially larger clusters and slightly thicker skins,' explains Christopher. 'The resulting wines have a richness and opulence, a fruitier, stone-fruit profile that contrasts with the more austere and bright notes of the Wente clones.'

'Calera fruit has a thick skin which preserves acidity and overall freshness; it gives wines with great mineral undertones and notes of Williams pear,' added

[3] See's Candies is a Bay Area manufacturer of chocolates and sweets founded by Charles See in 1921.

[4] Leafroll, a virus that causes discolouration and curling of the vine leaves, hence reducing their photosynthetic capacity and lowering yields by 30–50 percent due to the uneven ripening of fruit.

Luc Morlet. 'Its main challenge is in the vineyards where it requires serious thinning almost every year.'

The Hydes also grow some Musqué clone. 'Last but not least for us was the Musqué clone,' offers Christopher. 'It's a selection from Long Vineyards that came from the old Martini Vineyard on Las Amigas road (in Carneros), selected for its tropical fruit flavours. This makes up about a third of our Chardonnay acreage at Hyde Vineyards, and comprises wines such as Kongsgaard, Auteur and Massican.'

Morlet also works with Musqué clones, including the so-called See and Rued clones. 'See fruit has a superb aromatic profile, very much on the candied (no pun intended[3]) citrus side; intense and refined,' he said. 'The main challenge is to find very clean cuttings, as leafroll[4] is an issue. Finally, I appreciate Rued in some particular soils (white and very well drained) for its very intense and typical bouquet of flowers (rose, lychee-like) and for its density, as a blending component. Its genetic heritage is obvious, looking at its yellow-skinned berries, it is a relative of Muscat.'

As for other Chardonnay clones such as more recent imports from France (the so-called Dijon clones, etc), Morlet commented: 'I found the other ones (within the conditions I worked with) either too simple and boring, or too varietal driven, not expressing enough the terroir they are from.'

Chardonnay is among the most hardy and malleable of the noble vinifera varieties. Having existed in California for more than a century, it has adapted to the broad variations in climate and soil types, and not only has it survived, it has excelled. Time and *sélections massales* performed by quality-driven producers, most notably the Wente family and those who subsequently obtained bud wood from this source – as the Hydes have done – has, over the years, resulted in an invaluable collection of heritage clones. This collection of superior planting material specifically nurtured within and moulded to the California landscape not only helps to bring out that elusive sense of place within the Chardonnays they produce, but comes to embody the resilient, pioneering, no-compromises spirit of California wine.

References

Nancy L Sweet, *Chardonnay History and Selections at FPS* (Foundation Plant Services, UC Davis) 2007.

Richard Volpe, Richard Green, Dale Heien and Richard Howitt, *Recent Trends in the California Wine Grape Industry* (ARE Update 11(4)(2008): 7–10. University of California Giannini Foundation of Agricultural Economics).

Wente Bros, *The Story of Wente Wines* (A winery commissioned brochure) 1954.

THE ONLY WAY IS FIZZ

From frothy pink Catawba to specialist wines that baffle the Champenoise in blind tastings, Liz Thach charts the rise of the California sparkler from humble beginnings to the dining tables of the White House.

LIZ THACH MW (2021)

American sparkling wine began by happy accident, when Ohio-born lawyer Nicholas Longworth allowed his pink Catawba wine to go through a second fermentation in the spring of 1842. This accidental sweet sparkler turned out to be Longworth's best wine yet, going on to receive compliments from experts in Europe and praise from the poet Henry Wadsworth Longfellow. California did not catch on until 1855, 13 years later, and sadly its first sparkling wine, made at the San Gabriel Winery in Los Angeles, was discontinued after just a few vintages, its winemaker dismissed as 'a humbug'.

Despite this less than spectacular start, California's sparkling wine is today widely extolled at home and abroad, with many of its wines mistaken for champagne by the experts at blind tastings. Other wines, revelling in the state's freedom from exacting winemaking regulations, are made with unabashed pride at their reflection of the sunshine and exuberance of the Golden State.

From just a handful of sparkling wine producers in the 1800s, the number of California proponents has grown dramatically. As of 2020, there were an estimated 150 sparkling wine producers in California, according to CaliforniaChampagne.com. Market research firm Gomberg-Frederickson estimates that from 2016 to 2020 these wineries produced an average of 11.8 million cases of wine per year.

THE FREEDOM TO EXPERIMENT

Being free to experiment with a wide range of grape varieties definitely helped California fizz along its way, as its early history reflects. In 1857, the El Aviso Winery in Los Angeles made over 150,000 bottles based on the honeyed, low-acid Mission grape (called Listán Prieto in Spain, it was brought to California by missionaries who used it to make 'sickly sweet' sacramental wines). In 1859, General Vallejo in Sonoma followed suit, but his son-in-law, Arpad Haraszthy, had more luck with Zinfandel. After studying in Champagne for two years, in 1861 Arpad returned to his family's winery, Buena Vista, in Sonoma, and following a few aborted attempts, eventually produced the first commercially successful sparkling wine in California. It was called 'Eclipse Extra Dry' – a semi-dry wine made from pink Zinfandel grapes that had undergone a second fermentation in bottle. The wine was so successful that it went on to win awards not only in California, but in New York, England and France too.

Another successful early sparkling wine house was Korbel Champagne Cellars, established by the brothers Francis, Anton and Joseph Korbel (who had emigrated from Bohemia, today's Czech Republic, in the 1850s) in 1882. Though they made most of their fortune from timber harvesting, the brothers decided to plant vineyards in the Russian River Valley. Their grapes of choice included Riesling, French Colombard, Chenin Blanc and other popular varieties of the time, and right from the beginning they focused on sparkling wine. Today, their very popular Korbel Brut wine – a blend of Chardonnay, Chenin Blanc, French Colombard and Pinot Noir – still shows the same varietal freedom, while there's also, more conventionally, a Korbel 100 percent sparkling Chardonnay, as well as Korbel Natural, an off-dry (with sugar at seven grams per litre) sparkler made with 65 percent Pinot Noir and 35 percent Chardonnay from the Russian River AVA.

'Our goal,' explains president and owner, Gary Heck, 'is to produce high-quality fruit-forward California bubbly at an affordable price using the champagne method of secondary fermentation in the bottle.' Gary and winemaker Paul Ahvenainen stress that they are not trying to emulate champagne, but instead want their wines to be celebrations of California's sunny climate. 'We harvest most of our grapes at around 19 Brix and conduct secondary fermentation in bottle for 12 to 18 months, but our style is distinctly Californian and we are proud of it,' says Paul: 'We are not trying to copy the Spanish or the French.'

It is partially for this reason that every bottle of Korbel's 1.5 million-case production for the US each year proudly states 'California Champagne' on the label. Though the Champenoise fought fiercely to stop their place-name being used in the US, a 2006 French-American trade agreement permitted any American sparkling producer who had used the term 'Champagne' on their bottle prior to 2006, to continue to do so, as long as they included a US geographical region to differentiate it. 'We've talked to thousands of consumers in America,' reports Paul, 'and no one has ever expressed confusion over where our wine is made. They know it is from California, not France.' The fact that Korbel was established in 1882, nine years before the 1891 Madrid Agreement which laid the groundwork for European trademark recognition, is another factor that is important to Gary. 'We started in 1882. The French government did not certify Champagne as a region until 1956.'

This independent spirit is also reflected in other historic California sparkling wine producers. One of the best known is from the Italian Swiss Colony in Sonoma County, which produced an acclaimed sparkling Muscat, and Hanns Kornell in the Napa Valley, who was well known for his sparkling Riesling wines.

A NOD TO CHAMPAGNE

Despite the fact that many California sparkling producers continue to experiment with a wide range of grape varieties, a few decided to embrace the classic champagne trio: Chardonnay, Pinot Noir and Pinot Meunier. One of the first was the pioneer Paul Masson who emigrated from Burgundy in 1878, and started making sparkling wine from Pinot Noir and Chardonnay. His success enabled him to purchase the famous La Cresta estate in the mountains above Saratoga, and to achieve a win at the Paris Exposition of 1900 – following which, he became known as the 'Champagne King of California'. After his death in 1940, his protégé, Martin Ray, purchased the winery and kept up the tradition of fine bubbles and Champenoise grapes, eventually attracting the attention of LA businessman Jack Davies and his wife Jamie, who became enthusiastic investors. The Davies were so intrigued with the delicacy and vibrancy of the wines that in 1965 they purchased the old Schramsberg winery in Calistoga, which had been lying empty, with the dream of launching the first traditional-method sparkling wine house in Napa.

'My parents were trailblazers,' explains Hugh Davies, their son and current CEO/President of Schramsberg. 'They started with one tank of Napa Chardonnay to make 200 cases of Blanc de Blancs, and today we produce around 90,000 cases annually.' The Schramsberg philosophy is to emulate the delicacy of Champagne, but also to reflect the terroir of California. 'We want to produce wines with finesse,' says Hugh, 'but with flavours that present the brightness of our California fruit. Our style is to only include 10–15 percent malolactic wine in the blend, which allows us to balance that ripeness with a tart vibrancy.'

Indeed, Schramsberg wines have received much acclaim and recognition over the years. The Blanc de Blancs was used for the 1972 'Toast to Peace' between President Nixon and Chinese Premier Zhou Enlai. It has also been served countless times at White House dinners. The Champagne and Cava houses of France and Spain did not fail to notice the prestigious 'newcomer', and in the 1970s and '80s began to search for locations to emulate the Schramsberg success. Thus began the influx to Northern California of more than 10 major international producers.

THE CALIFORNIA 'CHAMPAGNE RUSH'

The first champagne house to arrive in Napa Valley was Moët & Chandon in 1973. It was part of the 'sparkling wine "gold rush"', according to Hugh Davies, with

Left: Schramsberg's Napa Valley sparkling wine was so successful that France's champagne houses began to take note. *Right:* In 1982, Champagne Roederer opted to place its new facility in cooler Mendocino County: its vineyards (Chardonnay vines seen here) are all farmed sustainably.

Chandon's success inspiring others. In 1980, Piper-Heidsieck arrived in Sonoma County to develop Piper-Sonoma, with Freixenet establishing Gloria Ferrer there two years later; then in 1985 Mumm Napa was created. Taittinger arrived in 1987 to create Domaine Carneros, and Codorníu launched Artesa in Napa in 1991.

Further north in the Anderson Valley – land was more affordable and the climate cooler in Mendocino County – Champagne Louis Roederer arrived to create Roederer Estate in 1982. It was preceded by one year by John Scharffenberger, the San Francisco chocolate millionaire, who created Scharffenberger Cellars. Scharffenberger then linked up with Champagne Pommery in 1989, which eventually sold to LVMH in 1998. Today Scharffenberger is part of Roederer Estate, which purchased the winery in 2004.

'We hired scouts to help us identify the best place for us to plant vineyards and build a winery in California,' explains Arnaud Weyrich, the current Roederer winemaker who trained in Champagne. 'The Anderson Valley's proximity to the ocean, and the well-drained soils combined with warm days and cool, foggy nights, are perfect for Chardonnay and Pinot Noir.' Today, the Roederer estate boasts 620 vineyard acres, and hires and houses a full-time vineyard crew to assist with sustainable farming practices. They are one of the few large sparkling houses in California (turning over 105,000 cases of wine a year) to produce 100-percent estate wines. Most others continue to buy a large proportion of their grapes from other properties, maintaining just a few vineyards of their own.

Roederer is also proud to make one of the rare California wines to consistently stump experts in blind-tasting tests. Many believe it is real champagne, and Arnaud explains why: 'We are part of Champagne Louis Roederer, so we have the family DNA in our winemaking. We make a quality promise to consumers: if the name Roederer is on the label, then the wine will reflect our reputation. We do try to keep the house style, but we don't want to be a total copycat. This is still California sparkling wine.'

Arnaud explains that every bottle of Roederer Estate has seen oak twice. Reserve wine, which is stored in wooden casks, is used first to make the initial blend, and second as part of the dosage. 'We take a special selection from our oak casks and add sugar and sulphur. In order to achieve a fresh, lively style, we also use only a minimal amount of malolactic wine – Scharffenberger, on the other hand, uses more malolactic wine as part of its house style.' Every bottle of Roederer Estate is a *cuvée* blended from 100–200 different wines that age for an average of four years. The vintage *cuvée*, L'Ermitage, is produced only in exceptional years.

THE RISE OF THE BOUTIQUE SPARKLER

The influx of European sparkling houses coincided with the arrival of a tranche of new boutique ventures. The Central Coast (not far from Edna Valley) has boasted Laetitia Vineyard & Winery from 1982, and Carneros the Schug winery since 1983. J Winery, created by Judy Jordan in 1986, uses the classic grape trio sourced from the Russian River Valley; the brand was sold to E&J Gallo in 2015 and has now increased in production size. A more recent entrant is Breathless Winery, established in 2012 by three sisters – Sharon Cohn and Rebecca and Cynthia Faust – in Sonoma County. They have won multiple awards for their sparkling wine, produced by Penny Gadd-Coster.

Probably one of the most illustrious boutique wineries is Iron Horse, launched in 1976 by Audry and Barry Sterling in one of the smallest and coolest appellations of California, the Green Valley AVA. The Sterlings, who had lived in France for a number of years, had a vision to create a 'Château model', focused on producing estate wine. When they first saw the Green Valley with its fog-enrobed hills, they fell in love with the site and bought it within two weeks. Today, the 300-plus-acre winery produces award-winning bubbles that have been served at the White House for six consecutive presidential administrations.

'Our goal,' says Joy Sterling, current CEO and daughter of Audry and Barry, 'is to create sparkling wines that set off the memory bells for champagne quality and finesse, but show fruit that is unmistakably Californian – Sonoma County,

Russian River and most specifically Iron Horse – in style.' The wines are exclusively produced at the estate and have a minimum of three years ageing *en tirage* (on the yeast lees). Joy believes that people can taste the difference between France and California just after disgorging and before the addition of dosage. 'Champagne tends to be very abstract and acidic at this stage,' she states, 'but California sparklings taste like Chardonnay and Pinot Noir.' The wines achieve balance, elegance and rich creaminess from extended ageing, but it is the fruit that marks them as different.

THE ERA OF CUSTOM-CRUSH

Probably one of the most transformative events in recent years for California's sparkling wine has been the development of a large custom-crush facility called Rack & Riddle. Originally built as a small facility in Mendocino County by partners Rebecca Faust and Bruce Lundquist in 2007, within just a few years of business, it had doubled in size. Its services include making custom sparkling wine for wineries – with that winery's grapes or still wine – using the *méthode traditionale* (secondary fermentation in bottle). They blend, age, riddle, disgorge and add dosage – all according to winery specifications. In addition they also sell 'shiners' (literally shiny bottles, with no labels) so wineries can add their own label and offer bubbles as a new selection to winery customers.

Rack & Riddle was so successful that it had to expand to two facilities in Sonoma County, and by the end of 2019, its annual production had climbed to 750,000 cases. According to executive director of winemaking, Penny Gadd-Coster: 'We created the opportunity for small and large wineries to make sparkling wines in the traditional method so they could add them to their portfolios or expand their production. Still wine wineries don't usually have the right facilities, so we provide not only state-of-the-art equipment but seasoned expertise as well.' Indeed, their services are in such high demand, that even some of the large French-owned wineries are outsourcing ageing and dosage work to Rack & Riddle.

THE FUTURE OF CALIFORNIA SPARKLING

While wildfires and the Covid-19 pandemic have certainly put a wrinkle in production and sales during the past few years, most producers are very positive about the future. Several believe that there is room for growth, as consumer behaviour and perspectives change. Gary Heck at Korbel is one: 'In America we are a bubbly consuming people – think about Coca-Cola and soda pop. In a restaurant, if we see someone order a glass of sparkling wine, we often ask what the celebration is. Even though some of us drink it all the time, it is still considered the wine of festivity and joy. It is, in the end, a happy beverage.'

NOT TO BE SNIFFED AT

Bob Thompson and Hugh Johnson follow Sauvignon Blanc's tentative route to California stardom, explaining that at its smoky, herbaceous, aromatic best, this wine can take on a 40-clove chicken and garlic casserole with consummate ease.

BOB THOMPSON AND **HUGH JOHNSON** (1976)

First-rate vineyards of Sauvignon Blanc have been growing since the early days of wine in California, admired in a lonely kind of way by a few growers and winemakers.

Sauvignon Blanc was one of the early varietal wines, but unheralded. More than that it was eminently ignored by the public even after Dr Maynard Amerine of the University of California, Davis, went on record saying this wine is fine in California even more consistently than is Chardonnay. Only in 1971 when the uncanny Robert Mondavi rechristened a dry wine from the grape as Fumé Blanc did the variety begin to command real attention. As others followed his lead it became obvious that there is something in a name. There also may be something in the shape of a bottle. The Fumé Blancs that go to market in Burgundy-style bottles seem to move more quickly than Sauvignon Blanc by that or any other name in a Bordeaux-style bottle.

Even as the Mondavi coinage rescued Sauvignon Blanc from a sagging fate, it also led to a confusion in wine names as great or greater than the one surrounding Chenin Blanc, the other grape Mondavi rescued from oblivion with an inspired choice of name. In addition to Sauvignon Blanc and Fumé Blanc, the recent roster of varietal wines from the one grape includes Blanc de Sauvignon, Fleur de Sauvignon, Blanc Fumé, Pouilly Fumé, Sonoma Blanc and Château Beaulieu (subtitled Sauvignon Blanc).

Sauvignon Blanc as a variety deserves at least two names for its wines. The dry ones are more austere than Chardonnays, but sweet ones turn all soft and fruity in a remarkably complete metamorphosis. Further, the two basic names have legitimate origins in French wines of vastly different characters and styles.

Most if not all of California's Sauvignon Blanc vines are descended from cuttings made in Sauternes and Graves during the last two decades of the 19th century. A considerable number of them came from Château d'Yquem to a Livermore Valley grower named Louis Mel, who had family ties to Yquem's proprietors. Sauvignon Blanc is the minority grape in Sauternes, where it adds some resolve to the supple character of Sémillon. It is the majority partner in the blends of Graves, especially dry ones.

The use of Blanc Fumé and assorted variations arises because the wines of Pouilly-sur-Loire and Sancerre are made from a grape known there as Blanc Fumé, Sauvignon Blanc and Savagnin de Jura. The UC Davis says that Pouilly Fumés and Sancerres are indeed from Savagnin, but that Savagnin is not the Sauvignon of Graves and Sauternes. Be the botanic specifics what they may, enough similarity links a Pouilly Fumé made from Savagnin to a California Fumé Blanc made dry from Sauvignon Blanc to explain Robert Mondavi's adaptation of the name.

When Maynard Amerine and Vernon Singleton drew up their cosmonology of flavour associations to help pinpoint varietal characteristics, they found in Sauvignon Blanc reminders of the taste of olives. They also thought the wines herbaceous, as the red Cabernet Sauvignon also is. (Most back labels say 'spicy', but that is a cop-out on herbaceous.) Others have added to the list green grass – not lawn grass, but the tall, jointed kind that is so fresh and juicy to chew in wet, early spring. The French think of smoky as a flavour association. *Fumé*, the word, translates as 'smoky'.

Hardly neutral flavours, those, and a dry wine of Sauvignon Blanc can offer them in abundance. In an old technical bulletin for winemakers, the university observed that the distinctive flavour of the grape is carried over 'and even increased in the wine'. The bulletin goes on to say: 'The distinct aromatic flavour is so strong that in some regions and years it may have to be blended with a more neutral-flavoured variety to achieve consumer acceptance.'

As much as all of the flavour associations suggest dry wine, Sauvignon Blanc has the curious capacity to change its stripes the more sugar is left unfermented. Made sweet, the wine develops a soft, round character well suited to the role. If a mitigating dollop of Sémillon or some such slips into the blend, the transformation is even greater.

At this point the names are not reliable guides to dry versus sweet. Most wines with names that turn on the word Fumé are bone-dry, or just off-dry. Those called Sauvignon Blanc cover the gamut, though with a greater tendency to be sweet.

An old recipe of Jim Beard's called Chicken Forty Cloves of Garlic provides a gastronomer's measure of the herbacity or smokiness of a dry Sauvignon Blanc. The dish destroys any wine that vacillates, but is companionable to an uncompromised varietal wine from this grape. The weakness of the test is that it can be made only when no important engagements are scheduled for the next day or two. Forty cloves of garlic will linger on a body (though not as much as you might think; the manner of cooking tames it surprisingly).

Under mortal circumstances dry Sauvignon Blancs are recommended by their makers to go with fowl, shellfish, light meats, cold cuts and dishes covered in cream sauces.

The sweet Sauvignon Blancs, in the conventional wisdom, go with ham or poultry, or, better, chilled fresh fruit. Sweet, in their case, means the degree of sweetness typically found in a Chenin Blanc, a Vouvray or perhaps a Graves, but not the unctuous riches of a true Sauternes. Botrytis is not a part of their making, nor are they left to grow overripe on the vine.

Dry Sauvignon Blanc does not demand deep chilling. Most are cool enough after 40 minutes in the refrigerator, especially if they have five or six years of age. Sweet ones are far better colder when young. In this case, too, bouquetish oldsters do not deserve to be diminished by deep chilling.

As befits a botanic cousin of Cabernet Sauvignon, Sauvignon Blanc yields wines that will age handsomely for four, five, a dozen years, depending on how sturdily the winemaker rigged them to start. The Wente Bros, to cite one example, made a sturdy 1937 that is still in good form. There should be vintage charts but, alas, the obscurity of its fame has kept the wine from being made in vintages by enough wineries to give a clear picture.

Excerpt from *The California Wine Book* by Bob Thompson and Hugh Johnson, William Morrow and Company Inc (New York) 1976. Reproduced here with kind permission of the authors.

ALL HAIL ZINFANDEL, PRINCE OF CALIFORNIA!

Quaffer, chiller, alcoholic monster or majestic keeper? Paul Draper charts the mysterious but noble lines of the versatile grape that California made its own.

PAUL DRAPER (2021)

The noble lines of California's Cabernet Sauvignon, Chardonnay and Pinot Noir stem from their aristocratic forebears in Europe. Scions easily adapted to the benign climate of the Golden State, *La California* – the imaginary earthly paradise of the 16th-century novelist Garci Rodríguez de Montalvo. Like any other children of famous parents, they seem destined always to be compared with their European progenitors.

Enter Zinfandel, the Horatio Alger of varietals, the 'True American'. Born of peasant stock somewhere in Europe, Zinfandel did not make its name or fortune in its native land. It did not come to the attention of its monarchs nor was it tutored and polished by the English wine trade until worthy of knighthood. Not until it was planted on the hillsides of California's cool North Coast did it find its ideal soils and climate. By the 1880s it was recognized in California as the variety of choice for making the best dry red wines. The orphan had found a home where, properly handled, it could produce wine of such quality that it might some day stand beside the noblest varieties of the world.

THE MYSTERY

Zinfandel had long been referred to as the 'mystery grape', and at least one of its leading students, Dr Harold Olmo (1909–2006) of the University of California at Davis, thought it might be best if we continued to consider it a mystery until all the research was done. He may have been reacting to the various theories, often mentioned in the press, for which no historical or scientific sources were quoted. For simplicity, the mystery of Zinfandel might be divided in three parts:

1 Where precisely did it originate?
2 How and when did it reach the East Coast of the United States?
3 How and when did it reach California and achieve broad distribution?

ORIGINS

In 1967 Dr Austin Goheen of UC Davis made the chance discovery when visiting a colleague in Puglia, in southeastern Italy, of a grape variety, Primitivo, that looked like Zinfandel. Isozyme 'finger printing' showed the two to be identical. Goheen's graduate students who had visited vineyards to collect samples of Primitivo were told by some of the older growers that it was a foreign grape. Research has shown that it was not known in Italy until around 1860.

In the mid-1980s, a California winemaker of Croatian descent claimed to have solved the mystery of the origin and that Zinfandel was identical to the principal red wine grape of Croatia, Plavac Mali. Dr Carole Meredith of UC Davis, a grape geneticist and leader in the use of DNA for grape identification, was intrigued. She had earlier made the somewhat surprising identification of Cabernet Sauvignon as a cross between Cabernet Franc and Sauvignon Blanc. (There is no record of Cabernet Sauvignon until the early 19th century when it began to replace Malbec as the dominant variety in Bordeaux.) Meredith began testing several of the examples of Plavac Mali in the Davis collection, with mixed results. She then decided to travel to Croatia in the spring of 1995 when she was contacted by a professor of genetics at the University of Zagreb, Ivan Pejić. He asked for her help with a government project to identify Croatia's indigenous grape varieties. Along with Pejić's colleague, Edi Maletić, professor of viticulture, the three traveled the islands and the Dalmatian Coast collecting over 100 samples of Plavac Mali.

When Meredith returned to Davis and ran the DNA on the samples, she found they were not Zinfandel at all, but their genes shared either a parent or offspring relationship with it; it was not clear which. She continued to test Croatian varieties in the Davis collection in the hope of finding one that solved the Zinfandel-Plavac Mali relationship. At last she found what she was looking for: an old Dalmatian variety, Dobričić, that partnered Zinfandel as the second of the two parents of Plavac Mali.

From 1998 through to 2000 professors Pejić and Maletić continued their search for a surviving Zinfandel vine in Croatia, but with no success. Then, in the spring of 2001, they found a vine in a 2.5-acre replanted vineyard in the region of Kastela that looked like Zinfandel. In December 2001 Meredith confirmed that it was indeed a match. The Kastela region is named after the series of old castles along the coast. When the vine was identified as Zinfandel, the owner of the vineyard and local growers, none of whom had any real depth of knowledge of old Croatian varieties but were naturally interested in promoting their region, came up with a name for the vine that had no historic precedent in Croatia. Because this was the first Zinfandel vine to be found, the press immediately took up their name for the grape, *Crljenak Kaštelanski,* which simply means a 'red grape from Kastela'. This name has persisted in many write-ups as a synonym for Zinfandel, with no real historic justification. Subsequently, so many unauthorized cuttings were taken from this famous vine that it died.

Maletić and Pejić continued their search and the following year visited a series of small cliff-side vineyards overlooking the Croatian coast. They stopped for lunch at a tiny café where their table stood on packed earth under two large spreading vines. Gazing upwards during lunch, they noticed that the leaves of these old vines looked very much like Zinfandel. The villagers identified the vines as Pribidrag, saying that it had been extensively planted in the area in the past. Samples of both vines were sent to Dr Meredith and she subsequently identified them both as Zinfandel.

Research then found that the historic name for this Croatian grape – which did indeed date back centuries – is Tribidrag, a simple phonetic variation of Pribidrag. As these vines were much older than the Crljenak sample and their name was known historically, this was found to be the preferred name.

Cuttings of all three vines have since been cleaned up using shoot tip therapy[1] and planted in several California vineyards. At Ridge Vineyards, we planted all three – as well as an excellent clone of Primitivo – alongside our existing old California clones in our search for those that produce the finest wine.

Zinfandel from the three Croatian clones and from heritage California clones has been planted in a number of areas in Croatia. Clearly the mystery of Zinfandel's origin is a mystery no longer.

ARRIVAL ON THE EAST COAST

In 1820 George Gibbs, a horticulturist on Long Island, imported 28 vine varieties from Europe. Five were from the kingdom of Hungary. Croatia had been part of the Habsburg Empire since 1527, and had shared a monarch with Hungary since the late 11th century. In turn, these countries became part of the newly constituted Austrian Empire in 1804. There is no record of Gibbs having travelled to Europe to select those vines. He would have bought his collection from a nursery, most likely in Austria, as it included the five Hungarian varieties.

In the early 1800s a Hungarian horticulturist, Demeter Görög, established a nursery in Grinzing, the well-known grape-growing suburb of Vienna. His collection included varieties that he had assiduously collected from all over Hungary,

---

[1] Shoot tip therapy is a disease elimination technique whereby tiny pieces of the vine's apical growing point are cultured in a sterile growth media apart from the plant.

which included Croatia. As the Austrian Empire had only just been formed, the Imperial Botanical Garden in Vienna would probably not yet have included many Hungarian varieties. The Görög nursery could have provided Zinfandel to a nursery Gibbs might have worked with.

There seems to be only a partial list of the vine varieties included in Gibbs's purchase of 1820. Those named do not include Zinfandel, although it's possible that when the shipment arrived there were cuttings identified as some version of the name 'Zinfandel', which had not been on the list.

Gibbs was a serious horticulturist and a respected friend of William Prince, the well-known owner of the first commercial nursery in America. Over the years, his nursery had earned an excellent reputation for high quality in America and Europe. He was not someone who would have invented a fictitious name for a grape variety. Research has found a Hungarian variety listed in an etymologic work of 1797 spelled 'Cinifadl'. The 'C' is pronounced 'T', Tzinifadl, and is described as a black grape. The Merriam Webster dictionary lists the name Zinfandel as probably a modification of the obsolete Hungarian word 'Tzinifandli'. Görög's collection of vines from the kingdom of Hungary could have mistakenly attached that Hungarian grape name to cuttings of a quite different variety such as the Tribidrag of Croatia. In any case it seems likely that cuttings in Gibbs's 1820 shipment carried a version of the name 'Tzinifadl', which he may have written as the more pronounceable 'Zinfindal'. This seems a possible explanation for the source of the name.

In 1829, when Gibbs brought in a second shipment of vines he made a point in a note to Prince that 'you can depend on them as genuine, as this time they came from the Imperial Botanical Garden at Schoenbrunn'. In 1830, one year after Gibbs received this collection, he attended the annual meeting of the Massachusetts Horticultural Society in Boston. He presented a fine display of his foreign vines, which included the Zinfindal, and offered cuttings for sale. It does not seem possible he would have had time to grow up the cuttings received in 1829 in time to show vines and have cuttings for sale in 1830. They would have had to come from the 1820 shipment.

In 1830 Samuel Perkins, a leading nurseryman in Boston, bought cuttings from Gibbs which included the one he called Zinfindal. Shortly after that the Perkins Nursery offered 'Zinfandal' cuttings for sale. At that time, William Prince bought Zinfindal cuttings from Perkins to add to his collection. Confusingly, earlier, in 1830, Prince had mentioned in a 'dialogue' that Gibbs had brought in a grape variety called 'Zinfardel' from Germany and Prince had listed it in his catalogue. He described it as medium-sized, round, black, with a thick bloom and a large, double-shouldered cluster. This is a good description of the grape we know as Zinfandel. As Germany did not yet exist it was clearly a reference to a German-speaking land, in this case Austria.

In 1839, a 'Zinfindal' won a prize in the collection of Otis Johnson of Lynn, Massachusetts. J Fiske Allen, the leading New England authority on grape culture in the 1840s and '50s, described Zinfindal in his *Practical Treatise...on the Grape Vine* in 1848; his description is very close to what we know today as Zinfandel.

Allen's description of another variety, Black St Peter's, is virtually identical to that of the Zinfindal. In a footnote, Charles Sullivan mentions an English report of 1857 that describes a particular Black St Peter's variety as a vine raised from seed in 1775 by a certain Daniel West in St Pancras (London), and notes that it became popular in England. In 1789 a William Speechley in London lists a St Peter's grape whose description is quite similar to our notion of Zinfandel. We will see later that there was a reason for Sullivan's footnote.

ARRIVAL AND DISTRIBUTION IN CALIFORNIA

In New England the established nurserymen had developed what could be called the standard New England collection of grape varieties, which they consistently offered in their catalogues. Some of those included table grapes that could serve for winemaking as well. The list typically might have offered names like Black

Uniquely suited to California, the Zinfandel grape yields everything from delicate rosé wines (from cooler sites and younger vines) to serious 'claret-like' reds. The grapes of Summit Lake Vineyard, Napa (*left*), and old vines of Rattlesnake Acres, Calistoga (*right*), yield deeper, richer styles.

Hamburg, Muscat of Alexandria, Golden Chasselas, Black St Peter's, White Malvasia, Syrian and, occasionally 'Zinfindal'.

In the 1850s, a number of people in California were interested in the possibilities for viticulture and horticulture. Two of the most often noted were Captain Frederick W Macondray and J W Osborne. Macondray, the first president of the California Agricultural Society, had brought in his collection of vinifera grapes from New England on one of his sailing vessels. J W Osborne, also a mariner from New England, and the owner of Oak Knoll Farm north of the city of Napa, was instrumental in distributing Macondray's cuttings. In 1857 both men entered exhibitions of vinifera grapes at the Mechanics Institute Fair in San Francisco with the standard New England collections, which included 'Zinfindal'. In 1859 Osborne sold two wagonloads of cuttings from Macondray to a Sonoma vineyardist, William Boggs. The cuttings were again a standard collection and included 'Zinfindal'. Boggs showed the variety to General Mariano Vallejo's winemaker, Dr Victor Faure, who asked for cuttings; in 1862 he reportedly produced a small amount of wine from the first crop of the vines and thought it a good 'claret'.

During the same period, Antoine Delmas, a member of the large colony of French growers in Santa Clara County, was cultivating and selling vinifera cuttings, among which were the Zinfindal look-alike from New England called Black St Peter's.

Delmas stated that he provided the Black St Peter's to General Vallejo. Boggs did note that Vallejo had some vinifera vines that resembled Zinfandal, called Black St Peter's, which could have been the vines sold to him by Delmas. In 1858 Delmas made a red wine that was judged best at the 1859 California State Fair. The young 'claret' had been made from foreign grapes that 'had been selected more as table fruit than for winemaking'. Supposedly this was the Black St Peter's version of the Zinfandal.

The variety was widely known to nurserymen and growers in the Sacramento area at an early date. A P Smith had exhibited it at the State Fair in 1858, and the official record spelled it 'Zeinfindal'. He is reported to have gotten it as early as 1855 from the New Englander Wilson G Flint. James Nickerson, another established Sacramento nurseryman, exhibited Black 'Zinfandal' at the Fair in 1859, as did Smith, and by 1860 Smith was reportedly making good 'claret' from his vines. By 1861, growers James Marshall of Grass Valley and Charles Covillaud of Marysville had written in approval of the variety. In the same year, Colonel James Warren found 'Zinfandel' (note current spelling) at Covillaud's ranch and praised this 'rare variety', which he thought came from the Rhine Valley. By 1865, Benjamin Bugbey of Natoma Vineyard had selected Zinfandel as one of the five best for the future of California winemaking. Four years later, Nevada City winemaker F Seibert won one of the first awards given for pure Zinfandal, and George West of Stockton produced the first successful white Zinfandel. Back in Napa Valley, Jacob Schram praised the 'Zenfenthal' as perhaps the best grape available for red wine. By the time of the vast grape plantings of the 1880s, the name is consistently spelled Zinfandel and is at the top of the list of the most suitable red varieties.

At this point it seems essential to quote historian Charles Sullivan's research, which refutes a false but often repeated story of Zinfandel's arrival in California:

> *In spite of the fact that he has often been credited with bringing Zinfandel to California, Agoston Haraszthy has not been mentioned here as a part of its history. There is no evidence from the period that he had any role in its introduction or dissemination. Haraszthy was a prolific writer and the greatest publicist for California wine that the industry has ever had, yet in all his writings, including his many reports published in the* Journal of Alta California *and the* California Farmer, *he never mentioned Zinfandel, let alone any role he had in its history, and he is not reported to have been a modest man.*
>
> *It appears that his son, Arpad Haraszthy, writing 32 years after the key event he describes, claimed accomplishments for his father for which there is no evidence. At the time of which he was writing, Arpad was a boy of 11 who had been sent off with his mother and sisters to live in New Jersey and receive a proper education. He returned once for two months in 1857 before leaving for Paris to study civil engineering. Instead he learned winemaking with special emphasis on sparkling wines, and returned in 1862 to take over production at his father's winery.*
>
> *In 1886, 17 years after his father's death, he wrote a four-page statement claiming that Agoston had imported the Zinfandel to his Crystal Springs nursery just south of San Francisco in 1854. Two years later, he changed his story and claimed that his father had imported Zinfandel direct from Hungary while in San Diego in 1852. No documentary proof can be found for these claims other than Arpad's statements, which were heatedly disputed when they were published.*
>
> *One of the most detailed rebuttals came from nurseryman William Boggs in a letter to the* St Helena Star *dated June 8th 1885. Boggs had been one of two directors, and Agoston Haraszthy president, of the Sonoma Horticultural Society, for which Boggs in 1859 had purchased the Zinfandel cuttings mentioned earlier. This was important as there were virtually no vinifera vines in Sonoma County except the Mission variety, and Agoston never claimed any connection with the purchase or dissemination of these vines. Arpad repeated his claims again and again until a myth grew that still influences some less knowledgeable journalists today.*

Zinfandel's arrival and distribution in California is well documented. The now standard spelling Zinfandel appeared as early as the 1860s. George Husmann's often mentioned quote in his *Grape Culture and Wine-Making in California* (1888) states that Zinfandel is 'one of the most valuable grapes for red wine in good locations, and properly handled. I have yet to see the red wine of any variety, which I prefer to the best samples of Zinfandel produced in this state'.

The relative quality of these early wines can probably best be attested to by the enthusiastic acceptance of the variety. In addition, it is difficult to believe that some of the exceptional Zinfandels produced traditionally just after Prohibition in the 1930s were the first efforts of the winemakers who made them.

I had the opportunity years ago to assess the quality of a group of Zinfandels from the 1930s with several knowledgeable tasters. The standouts were the 1937 Larkmead from Napa County and the 1939 Fountain Grove from Sonoma. Both were in excellent condition, but their astounding freshness, especially that of the Larkmead, would probably argue for the inclusion of a fair percentage of Petite Sirah in these Zinfandel 'clarets'. On another occasion, again with a group of seasoned tasters, a Bordeaux wine merchant and I were treated to a blind tasting of the 1935 Simi Zinfandel and the 1924 Château Margaux. Both were in excellent condition and there were no signs that either was beginning to fade. We agreed that one of the wines was an old Médoc, but the group was evenly split on which one. The Simi had developed into a lovely 'old claret' with great staying power. I have not found Zinfandel vintages of this quality from the 1940s and '50s, but I did again in tasting wines from the '60s and early '70s. These latter wines from several small producers presaged the arrival of the best Zinfandels of today. The finest, most complex examples of this former 'orphan' have now joined the nobility.

Bibliographic Note
Historian Charles Sullivan's essay on Zinfandel's arrival on the East Coast and in California provided essential background for this essay. *See* Charles L Sullivan, 'Zinfandel: A True Vinifera', *Vinifera Wine Growers Journal*, Summer 1982, 71–86, and 'A Man Named Agoston Haraszthy', *Vintage Magazine*, February 1980 (part I), 13–19; March 1980 (part 2), 23–25; and April 1980 (part 3), 11–17.

BRAINS, BOFFINS, WHIZZ-KIDS AND SCHOLARS

California's pioneer thinkers have aided the rapid trajectory of its wines from bundled vine cuttings on their sea journey from Europe to wines of mesmerizing beauty on the tables of the White House. Here's how they pave(ed) the path to success.

KELLI WHITE (2021)
The Boffins, from Hilgard to Amerine

RANDALL GRAHM (2021)
California Dreamin'

BOB THOMPSON (1984)
California and the Critics

WARREN WINIARSKI (2021)
Good Words Make Better Wines

THE BOFFINS, FROM HILGARD TO AMERINE

'Boffins': scientific experts, especially those involved in technological research. Behind every great wine ambition, from the defeat of phylloxera to the choosing of the next varietal champion, there has been a great intellect bent on smoothing the path to success. Kelli White introduces the men who sought to tame the chaos of California's early wine years.

KELLI WHITE (2021)

Energy, character, terroir, authenticity. Californian winemakers traffic in intangibles, seeming to spend as much time debating lofty concepts as they do winemaking techniques. This is a luxury made possible by the strong foundation of knowledge that underlies the California wine industry today. Contemporary winemakers can take for granted that varieties are planted in suitable places, are farmed sensibly, and that there are known solutions to any problems they might encounter. This security is intellectually and creatively freeing. It is also a relatively recent phenomenon.

The California wine industry only got its bearings round about the 1960s. Prior to that, it was locked in a perpetual adolescence, its maturation thwarted by infestation, oppressive politics or its own ineptitude. Thankfully, a handful of leaders emerged to guide California wine forward. And though winemaker-torchbearers could be found (André Tchelistcheff and Joseph Heitz come to mind), much of this work fell to a succession of scientific researchers, or boffins, affiliated with the University of California. Armed with both intellectual rigour and middle initials, these men sought to tame the chaos of California wine's early years.

The first of these boffins arrived in 1875. His name was Eugene Woldemar Hilgard and he did not come to make friends.

ACT ONE: THE BEFORETIMES

'The foreign guest at our principal hotels,' Hilgard wrote in an 1889 editorial called 'Plain Talk to the Wine Men', 'might be aghast at having the claret cork fly at him, followed by a significant puff of smoke, and a liquid resembling sauce rather than wine and of uncanny odour.'

Published in the *San Francisco Examiner*, the piece went on to condemn what Hilgard regarded as the typical Californian winemaking practices of the day. 'After crushing promiscuously grapes sound, mouldy, green and sunburnt,' the winemaker 'allows his fermenting tanks to get so hot as to scald the yeast, and then wonders why the wine has "stuck"; permits the "cap" to get white with mould and swarming with vinegar flies and then cheerfully stirs it under so as to thoroughly infect the wine with the germs of destruction.'

Though his satirical skills are undeniable, E W Hilgard was primarily revered as a geologist and chemist. Born and educated in Germany, he received his doctorate in flame chemistry under Professor Bunson of bunson burner fame. He then spent several years working in the east and middle west of America before moving to head the University of California's College of Agriculture in 1875.

By the time of his arrival, wine in California was fairly well-established. Though vinifera had been introduced via Spanish missionaries as far back as the late 1700s, it was the Gold Rush of 1849 that truly got things started. The promise of quick riches had attracted people from all over the world, and the state's population swelled. Prospecting being thirsty work, vineyards quickly followed.

While much is made of the significance of Europeans among California's founding winemakers, little is recalled about how they often fumbled in the hot, dry climate. According to historian Charles Sullivan: 'A good part of the California problem lay in the tendency to harvest grapes too late... This tendency came partly from a European tradition in which cool fall weather led producers to let their grapes hang as long as possible.' The lack of chilly autumns and naturally cool caves also meant that, in this era before refrigeration, fermentation temperatures would soar unchecked, making for clumsy, inferior wines. Hilgard railed against these practices and also advocated improved cellar hygiene, better grape selection and more thoughtful vineyard locations. He was strongly in favour of hillside sites, pointing to Schramsberg, one of Napa Valley's most celebrated wineries and the first to cultivate mountain slopes, as proof of the concept.

With little idea of what would grow well where, California's early farmers grew everything everywhere. Because of this, much of Hilgard's long tenure was dedicated to varietal studies. Between 1881 and 1893 he conducted a remarkable experiment, fermenting hundreds of small lots of wine from all over the state. The alcohol, acid, sugar, solids and tannin of each batch were logged along with tasting notes, a quality assessment and ampelographic information for the variety. The result was an invaluable library of information that Hilgard and his colleagues used to advise the industry. And while this research may seem mundane viewed through 21st-century eyes, it was truly groundbreaking at the time. According to Dr Austin Goheen, a later boffin of the University of California: 'Professor Hilgard is probably the first scientific viticulturist in California, and he may well be the first viticulturist anywhere in the world, who held a scientific interest in comparing cultivars in a systematic way.' But questionable cellar techniques and poor site selection would prove the least of Hilgard's concerns. Shortly after his arrival in California, he was called upon to deliver an unwelcome diagnosis: phylloxera had arrived and was coming for everyone.

Though he was dismissed as doomsayer in many circles, Hilgard knew the truth. In both lectures and written reports, he attempted to warn California grape

Eugene W Hilgard (1833–1916): University of California 1875–1904.

Frederic T Bioletti (1865–1939): University of California 1889–1935.

William V Cruess (1886–1968): University of California 1910–54.

farmers about the inevitable devastation and educate them as to the evolving European techniques used to combat the louse. Of the various remedies (which included chemical asphyxiation and flooding), he wisely placed the most faith in grafting onto resistant rootstocks. And while phylloxera did ultimately lay its waste, Hilgard and his colleague Hayne's proselytizing did much to salvage the Californian wine industry.

Hilgard was aided in his work by Frederic Theodore Bioletti, who had joined the budding University of California wine team in 1889. According to the recollection of Harold Olmo, Hilgard hired Bioletti to help him communicate with the many Italian growers that dominated the vineyards of Napa and Sonoma. This was news to Bioletti who was born in Liverpool and spoke no Italian. Both men were embarrassed by the mistake, which was rectified several years later when Bioletti ultimately mastered the language.

Bespectacled, mustachioed and small, Bioletti would go on to play a critical role in the history of California viticulture. His phylloxera work was especially significant, prompting André Tchelistcheff to describe he and his colleague, Frenchman Pierre Viala, as 'two of the most important figures in the history of viticulture, who saved the world from phylloxera'. Bioletti also introduced the Guyot training system to California which was first applied to the Thompson Seedless variety; the resulting increase in fruitfulness graduated this grape from wallflower to prom queen practically overnight.

Bioletti also conducted important research into the development of equipment to help cool fermentations, and into ampelography, sulphur dioxide and

Albert J Winkler (1894–1989): University of California 1921–63.

Harold P Olmo (1909–2006): University of California 1931–77.

Maynard A Amerine (1911–1998): University of California 1935–74.

yeast. Pure dried yeast strains had first been developed in Denmark in the 1880s and Bioletti began experimenting with them in 1893. Excited by the control they offered the winemaker, he sent packets out to wineries around the state. Later, he established the University's grape-breeding programme.

Bioletti's work was particularly impactful through his rich connections to the industry. He could regularly be found manning the 'University car' – a wheeled appendage that hooked onto railcars and was outfitted with maps, charts and vineyard equipment. Travelling this way, he was able to meet the farmers in their fields, or at least the nearest train depot, rather than attempt to lure them to the campus.

When Hilgard retired, Bioletti replaced him as director and soon hired William Vere Cruess to assist him in his research. Cruess proved the perfect partner, for as Bioletti's true passion lay in botany, Cruess was truly a master of the microscopic.

Cruess' contribution to the California wine industry may be less lauded than his fellow boffins (thanks, Prohibition) but by the time of his retirement he had published over 400 works, including five books. He was among the earliest scientists to apply a sophisticated understanding of microbiology to the study of fermentation, wine preservation and spoilage, and his detailing of the importance of sulphur dioxide proved essential in the dirty days that followed Repeal.

Cruess was fascinated by ambient yeasts and especially flor, a preoccupation that contrasted with his fellow faculty members' interest in commercial strains. He carefully catalogued a range of moulds, yeasts and bacteria which formed the basis of a collection that is still utilized by teachers and students to this day. Indeed, this is the research that occupied his time right up to the point a certain constitutional amendment rendered the study futile.

On December 31st 1918, Cruess published an article entitled *The Fermentation Organisms of California Grapes*; 17 days later, Prohibition was ratified.

ACT TWO: AMNESIA

Prohibition was a 13-year period in American history (though some states stayed dry longer) in which it was illegal to produce and sell alcohol. Viewed on the national timeline Prohibition seems brief, but it lasted long enough to have a profound cultural impact. On account of this 'Great Experiment', America got many of its classic cocktails along with the more dubious gifts of organized crime, NASCAR and the Miss America pageant. Unsurprisingly, it also landed a near-fatal blow square on the wine industry's jaw.

During Prohibition there were a handful of ways a winery could stay in operation – the production of sacramental wine was most common – but the vast majority of wineries simply closed.

Our boffins also led unfermented lives during this time. Bioletti turned his attention to table grapes and olives while Cruess spearheaded the development of a new field of research – food science and technology. Therein, he made enormous contributions to the American kitchen and is credited with the invention of the canned fruit cocktail, which fought food waste by providing a syrupy home for bruised peaches and pears.

And then suddenly everything changed again.

Nineteen thirty-three should have been a banner year for California wine. Prohibition was repealed; the Golden Gate Bridge was completed, providing a more direct link between San Francisco and the northern wine counties; and the European wine industry was still recovering from phylloxera (France's *Appellation Contrôlée* system would debut two years later), which theoretically should have been a bolster to domestic wine sales. And yet it was a disaster.

After 13 years of neglect, wineries were in terrible condition. Rusted iron and copper equipment had infused that year's production with a hazy, sometimes dangerous sediment and poor sanitation led to severely acetic wines. Per the recollection of André Tchelistcheff: 'Carloads of wines came back to the winery to be dumped as not suitable beverages for human consumption... There was a re-fermentation in the bottle, there was a breakdown of mineral salts in the bottle, wines mucky, muddy in the glass...' In short, with very few exceptions, winemakers had forgotten how to make wine.

Enter the boffins.

'Cruess basically saved the American wine industry single-handedly and got everyone going again post-Prohibition,' winemaker Tegan Passalacqua explains. Because the most immediate concerns involved chemical instability and microbial spoilage, Cruess and his Food Science team were uniquely poised to help.

A big part of Cruess' efforts involved resuscitating his old research, especially on sulphur dioxide, and the rapid publication of *The Principles and Practice of Wine Making* in 1934. The classes he conducted were also immensely important and many of his students went on to make history. Peter Mondavi began his work on cold fermentation under Cruess, and Myron Nightingale would later become a pioneer of botrytis at Beringer. For all of his efforts and impact, Cruess would eventually be awarded the Legion of Honour medal by the French government.

Bioletti and Cruess provided an essential bridge of knowledge that spanned Prohibition and hastened recovery. But the generation of boffins that followed would prove just as significant.

Albert Julius Winkler's first assignment under Bioletti was to study the effects of pruning, leaf removal and crop thinning. Although this was 1921 and the middle of Prohibition, area under vine was actually increasing in California. Home-winemaking, which was sort of softly legal under the Volstead Act, had become extremely popular and grapes were being shipped by railcar all over the United States. Winkler's work not only provided a foundation of knowledge that continues to inform contemporary pruning practices, but also demonstrated for the first time how carbohydrates are stored in and move throughout the grape vine.

Following Repeal, Winkler dedicated himself to the restoration of California's vineyards. During the 1920s and early '30s, nearly all of California's acreage was converted to either table or raisin grapes, or so-called 'shipper varieties', predominately black grapes that were sturdy enough to survive a cross-country journey without spoiling. In preparation for this task, Winkler spent time in Alsace, which was also going through a journey of varietal self-discovery, after being reunited with France following World War I (it had been relegated to bulk wine production under German rule).

When Bioletti retired in 1935, Winkler was tapped to replace him. Leaving Cruess and his food scientists behind in Berkeley, he moved the still-tiny viti-culture and oenology department northwards to the remote Davis campus. He brought with him Harold Paul Olmo, a promising geneticist he had hired in 1931, and soon added Maynard Andrew Amerine to the team. These three men, plus a handful of colleagues, would be the captains that would skilfully steer the indus-try through those rocky first post-Prohibition decades.

ACT THREE: REGROWING PAINS

'Let's call it Winkler,' Lodi grape grower L K Marshall suggested, to honour the venerable professor. Olmo, as he recounts in his oral history, hesitantly acceded to the idea, and so this mystery grape briefly bore his predecessor's name. Like Bioletti and Winkler before him, Olmo was an accomplished ampelographer. One of his primary objectives following Repeal was to sort out what was actually growing in California's vineyards. Sometimes it was as easy as determining that a variety widely known as 'Gamay Beaujolais' was actually Pinot Noir. Other times the confusion was more elaborate.

First introduced as West's White Prolific, the grape temporarily named Winkler had been more commonly referred to as Barbero across California. This was a broadly planted variety, especially in the San Joaquin Valley, so Olmo made a special effort to discover its true identity. Eventually he realized it was Colombard, the popular Cognac ingredient. 'But then we had another difficulty . . . we had a variety misnamed already in the Napa Valley called Colombard. So the problem was solved . . . simply by saying that this is French Colombard.'

In addition to unmasking disguised grapes, Olmo studied clonal variation within varieties, developing, among others, Clone 4 Chardonnay, one of the most widely planted in the state; he also worked to improve pest and disease resistance through cross-breeding. One of the fruits of this research, O39-16, remains the rootstock of choice for sites with heavy nematode pressure. He also developed entirely new varieties such as Ruby Cabernet, Rubired and Emerald Riesling, which have faded in and out of fashion over the years.

By many reports, Olmo was a kind man and a bit of a rascal. Dinner guests might be surprised to discover a whoopie cushion under their seat and students in need might suddenly find their tuition covered. In a similar sense, he not only cared about the health of the vine (his collaborative achievements, too many to list, include the early identification of virus and the creation of virus-free stock) but about the overall health of the industry. Olmo was disturbed by the constant boom-and-bust cycle of the grape market, thinking it damaging for winery, grower and consumer alike. In a 1954 assembly he publicly suggested that there ought to be contracts between grape farmers and winery owners in order to establish trust and consistency. Perpetually ahead of his time, Olmo was laughed off the stage.

While Olmo was figuring out which vine was which, Winkler and Amerine were determining where they should be planted. To accomplish this, they effectively restarted Hilgard's old varietal research, but paid extra close attention to climate. During the course of their multi-year study (1934–42), these boffins divided the state of California into five zones (now known as the Winkler Scale) with Region I being the coolest and Region V being the hottest. They then compared the climate data to the wine chemistry and noted that wines made from cooler climates tended to be higher in acid with deeper colours, while warmer regions resulted in softer structure and higher sugars. This observation resulted in varietal recommendations for the various zones.

They must have made quite the pair. Winkler was Texas-born and apparently something of a teetotaller (his wife was head of the Davis chapter of the Woman's Christian Temperance Union) while Amerine was a celebrated gourmand. According to Axel Borg, longtime wine librarian at UC Davis, Amerine was a formal, elegant man. 'Even on the hottest days of summer, he always had a sports coat on,' Borg recalls, 'and he always sent thank you notes.' Apparently, these cards arrived so fast that his friends joked that Amerine must travel around with a stack of them already filled out in his car.

While on the road, Winkler and Amerine continued to play Hilgard's Greatest Hits, imploring growers to plant better and climatically-appropriate varieties, to improve harvest practices and winery hygiene, to control fermentation temperature and to stop bottling generic wines such as Chablis, port, sherry and claret. Their success on these counts was mixed.

Though varietal bottling and vintage-dating began to gain more traction during the 1950s, the concept that growers should not plant their vineyards with a mishmash of disparate varieties was slower to take hold. According to Amerine's oral history, despite the population boom in California that followed World War II and led to a rising interest in wine, there wasn't a widespread commitment to quality vinifera varieties until the mid-1960s.

This long delay between Amerine's ideation and the industry's execution left our boffin in despair. Per his recollection: 'As late as 1965 I couldn't see very much influence of that work. If I had found the right biochemical job, I would have left the university at that time because I felt I'd wasted all those years as far as application of our results was concerned . . . 25 years of my life were gone and I didn't see any planting [of the recommended varieties] . . . But some time in the 1960s, around 1965, they began to plant the better varieties. And before they had finished, they had planted 400,000 acres. An enormous change in the variety picture.'

EMERITI

Happily, Maynard Amerine never did take that corporate gig, as he went on to pioneer many important academic initiatives, including a number within the burgeoning field of sensory science. By the end of his career, he had published several hundred works, including multiple books, and had lectured all around the world. Upon his passing in 1998, Amerine was considered one of the most significant wine scientists to have ever lived. Many in the industry credit him, at least in part, with their success. As Robert Mondavi is quoted as saying in Amerine's obituary: 'I built my whole business on Mr Amerine's books on winemaking. If you followed that, you could not help but do an outstanding job. I used (them) as my Bible.'

In 1962, Albert Winkler published *General Viticulture*, another seminal work to come out of UC Davis. This book was so influential (it was translated into Russian, Spanish, Hindi, Greek and more) that it won the author a Legion of Honour medal to match that belonging to Cruess. Harold Olmo only finished one of the books he started, *A Survey of the Grape Industry of Western Australia* (1956), but his influence lives on in other ways. During the long arc of his career, he was a Guggenheim fellow and Fulbright scholar, consulted with the United Nations for 20 years, and conducted viticultural research all over the Middle East, India and South America.

But though our boffins are profoundly accomplished, their most important contribution is arguably in the training of the next generation. Renowned grape geneticist Carole Meredith replaced Olmo upon his retirement, Ann Noble of the Aroma Wheel fame succeeded Amerine, and Beth Forrestel is hard at work expanding and refining the scope of the Winkler Scale – a mighty undertaking that should be of great consequence to the industry.

The California wine scene is very different now than it was 50, 100 or 150 years ago. Most wineries have their own laboratories and chemical instability is (for the most part) a distant memory. If a wine is unpalatable today, it is likely by design. Even a UC Davis student might have no conception that 'Hilgard' is more than just the name of a lecture hall; that 'Bioletti' has significance beyond his eponymous 'Way'. Science is slow, memory fades fast, and we have a propensity to take ideas for granted once they enter the public domain. So much of what we now perceive as common knowledge – be it cane pruning, grape contracts, adding sulphur at the crush pad, or simply not planting Pinot Noir in the desert – went through a cycle of presentation, criticism, refinement and application/rejection.

I do not begrudge today's winemakers their art. But it is important to remember that science is the scaffolding upon which it hangs. Long live the boffins!

Special thanks from the author go to Axel Borg, Tegan Passalacqua, Jeanne Olmo and Dan Petroski.

CALIFORNIA DREAMIN'

Writer, philosopher and winemaking maverick, Randall Grahm, describes his pursuit of new and more fascinating grape varieties – and through them, the pathway to true sustainability and distinction in California.

RANDALL GRAHM (2021)

For as long as I've been thinking about making fine wine I've always been intrigued by the question of how, in the New World, in California specifically, one might find one's true and lasting place on the global stage. In the last 40 years California wines have been particularly successful in their domestic market, somewhat less so internationally, but as the world gets smaller and the wine business grows infinitely more competitive, the California wine industry, especially the fine wine segment, will have to come to terms with its true value proposition. What might we have to offer that is truly unique, valuable and in some very real sense, sustainable?

If we look at California's success to date, I believe that it may well have been down to felicitous timing and perhaps exquisite luck. California wine really began to gain acceptance in the early to mid-1970s as the US prospered economically and Americans became more urbane and adventurous. I believe that there were essentially three main factors that contributed to its success. Most importantly, at least as late as the 1970s, many European wines still had a taste profile that was not particularly cordial to the American palate; prestigious Bordeaux wines – the ones you were told you really *should* appreciate – were often quite austere, if not green, tart or hard, whereas California wines, produced in the land of abundant sunshine, were typically softer, riper, fruitier and more attractive to the still evolving American palate.[1]

The Chardonnays were likewise softer, riper, fruitier; the comforting flavours of vanillin (from oak) and buttery diacetyl from the malolactic fermentation seemed as American as apple pie. Then if you add in the pride of place and the fact that Napa and Sonoma were beginning to grow as vacation destinations,

---

[1] Global climate change and advances in winemaking technology have greatly obviated this particular issue in recent years, effacing to some extent the obvious stylistic differences between Old World wines and New; again, the shrinking world enhances competition for all parties.

Some know him as the 'Willy Wonka' of wine; others as California's voice of reason. Says Randall: 'In the Old World you have all been given the news: what grows well where... In the New World we are making it up as we go along, and there are more ways to stuff it up than get it right.'
wineanorak.com

thus building the rudiments of brand loyalty[2], it is not surprising that California wines became as well accepted as they have been. Thirdly, there was the element of label simplification where the New World handily won out over the Old World. You only had to remember the variety of grape that you liked, sometimes not even more than a single syllable – Cab, Chard, Zin, etc, with no unpronounceable foreign words or the possibility of non-pronounced consonants – and perhaps just one other directional vector point (eg Napa or Sonoma) and you were guided in for a safe landing.

I might argue that 'fine wine' has existed for a long time in California, but in recent years, significant technological advances and a greater understanding of the mechanisms for manipulating certain accepted signifiers of wine 'quality' have enabled certain winemakers to more consistently achieve greater commercial success, but, alas, I fear, at the cost of a certain loss of originality and distinctiveness. The fact that the wine business – largely by virtue of the enormous cost of entry – has become in many cases first and foremost a business, has imparted an enormous amount of self-consciousness (and cynicism) about the wines that we produce.[3] The California wine industry, like the American film

[2] A concept very cordial to the Boomer generation; significantly less interesting to succeeding generations.

[3] Not that many years ago, winery owners had minimal expectations of great fame and fortune in the wine business and still maintained the quaint notion of producing wines to please themselves. 'If nobody wants to buy the wine, then @#$% them, I'll drink it myself,' they would exclaim. Nowadays, nobody says that because the wine has become far too expensive to drink oneself.

industry, seems to have a strong financial motivation to play it safe; I would, however, argue that in an overcrowded and possibly shrinking market[4], following the herd is the least safe thing you can do. The real answer, I believe, is to try to find a unique and viable market niche based on fundamental structural features (like a unique terroir), not ephemeral ones like the endorsement of a rap star or the presence of an unholy amount of residual sugar or *goût de* charred bourbon barrel in the finished wine.

Personally, I am not paying much attention – perhaps it would actually serve me better to be a little more tuned in – to what most of my California colleagues have lately been up to. Frankly, it has been challenging to see past the Pet Nat wines, the orange wines, the 'clean' wines, or whatever fashionable *plat du jour* is being served up, to discern through the fog of (wine) war, who in fact is doing the truly important work that will be able to propel us into the future.[5] I have no illusions that the work that I'm currently planning and doing will tangibly change anything or anyone in California; I'm just trying to find my own niche of sustainability, which, if achieved, would be no mean feat.

CALIFORNIA, THE POSITIVES

I think that I may have hit upon a couple of approaches to producing unique and distinctive wines in California. I'm honestly not sure if this methodology will work for anyone – myself included – but there may be some lessons to be learned along the way. My rationale is an argument based on first principles, primarily trying to grasp what possible natural advantages California might enjoy relative to its competitors.

Here's what I think we have going for us in California:

1 There is still virgin land available (in parts). This might enable one to pursue certain viticultural strategies (at least for a while) of direct plantation, ie, no rootstock, which could be useful in the discovery and production of certain unique planting stocks. Own-rooted vines (where feasible) are believed by some to impart

---

[4] I believe that there is an important distinction to be drawn among wine collectors as to the real connoisseurs and the simple amassers of trophy wines. It is my unscientific contention that we are perhaps living or have recently lived in a trophy wine bubble, with too much discretionary income chasing a non-trivial number of 'rare' wines that are more or less indistinguishable from one another. As economic conditions become more strained, as they most certainly will, I would bet that there will be more structural pressure for rare and fine wines to truly exemplify special and distinctive qualities.

[5] I don't wish to come across as dismissive; there are indeed some small producers in California who are bucking the dominant trends and doing very interesting work with alternative varieties and methodologies, even taking a look at radically unfashionable varieties like Mission, Carignane, Palomino, Mondeuse, etc. There are even a few brave souls who are committed to dry-farming in California, who are putting it all (meaning their vineyards) on the line to a far greater extent than am I.

a unique expression of the variety itself. (Own-rooted vines are also generally more vigorous and drought tolerant than virtually all rootstock.)

2 California is blessed with an exceptionally benign climate, with significantly less vine pathogen pressure, allowing for a far more hands-off approach to disease control and for the possibility to produce a more 'natural' or uninflected wine.[6,7] In many parts of the state one can find a preternaturally long growing season, allowing for the ripening of certain varieties in climes significantly cooler than where they have historically been grown.

3 Most significantly, California has a cultural openness to innovation and experimentation and for the most part is blessed to have great regulatory tolerance for plantation of unique varieties and farming approaches, at least in comparison to our European *confrères*. We are only limited by the natural constraints of the site itself (and, one might argue, those limits confer the wine's unique frame).

4 Access to market. California 'wine country' is an exceptionally attractive tourist destination, pandemics and wildfires notwithstanding. The ability to visit the actual sites of production can generate a unique intimacy with the customer and potentially create a stronger affinity[8]. This is particularly useful if one is attempting to convey a fairly complex storyline, and as always, 'showing' is a lot more powerful than telling.

I have argued elsewhere that, at least at first blush, we in the New World are at some great disadvantage in our identification of optimal planting material (grape variety and rootstock) in that we've not had the benefit of centuries to iterate and carefully observe the vinous results obtained on our individual sites. How might we possibly find a match of a given grape variety to a particular site as exquisite and congruent as say Pinot Noir and the Côte d'Or, Nebbiolo and Barolo, Syrah/Sérine and Côte-Rôtie, as examples? Certainly, if we were considering a relatively stable climate, the New World would not have as great a chance to achieve the

---

[6] Many clones or biotypes (such as Sérine in Côte-Rôtie or Vaccarèse in Châteauneuf-du-Pape) have been eschewed for their tight clusters and susceptibility to bunch rot, but these issues are non-problematic in much drier California.

[7] It is a cardinal belief of mine that tricked-up, spoofilated wines will never have long-lasting appeal. Wines of natural beauty, made *sans maquillage*, are the only ones that have a chance at long-term sustainability.

[8] From a regulatory standpoint, planting vineyards in new viticultural areas is orders of magnitude more straightforward in the New World.

congruency of the Old. However, the epic disaster that is global climate change would seem to level the playing field in a sense, and should soon – if it hasn't already – cause grape growers throughout the world to rethink the suitability of their practices and varietal choices. We in the New World may not have soils that are quite as distinctive and interesting for grapes as those of the Old World, but as far as new plantings are concerned, we have the advantage of being able to grow varieties in areas significantly cooler and possibly in climates arguably more appropriate than are currently being exploited in the Old World.[9,10]

Châteauneuf-du-Pape, for example, with a few notable exceptions, has now, I'm afraid, become a *climat* increasingly problematic for the varieties it has grown successfully heretofore. Grenache, the backbone of the Châteauneuf 18-grape blend, has been virtually impossible to harvest at an alcoholic degree of under 15% in recent years; growing grapes there and elsewhere in classic appellations without supplemental irrigation is also now verging on the impossible. The prospect of continuing climate change is particularly ominous for some of the greatest *crus* of Europe. It is a tragedy beyond comprehension to imagine a world where much of the Côte d'Or may no longer be suitable for Pinot Noir. (Which gives no joy to this would-be New World competitor.) But this unfortunate reality might well create some opportunities for emergent wine regions both in California and elsewhere in the New World. Nevertheless, it is my personal opinion that the real opportunities for California may well lie beyond traditional grapes, and might better be found in pursuing unique, 'oddball' varieties or perhaps in the creation of altogether new varieties and possibly suites of unique, complex blends of these new *cépages*.

In a previously 'normal' world, one with a more or less stable climate, growers could rely upon Nature to create, either through plant mutation or epigenetic variability, discernible phenotypic differences in vineyards. The observation and selection of favourable agronomic plant and fruit characteristics for a given site we know as *sélection massale*. Alas, I believe that the climate is changing too rapidly and the natural variable processes are too slight and slow for this practice to be of much practical use for vignerons in California.

[9] This may be a bit of a subjective impression, but it seems that when I started in the wine business 40 years ago, I imagined there were opportunities for California to grow novel grape varieties to more complete maturity/balance than was then achievable in the Old World. Forty years later, the opposite opportunity seems to present itself. Ruchè, an extraordinary, fragrant Piemontese variety grown in the Castagnole Monferrato appellation, is regularly harvested at 15%. Tannat, from the Madiran appellation in Gascogne, has a similar issue with skyrocketing potential alcohols. These unique and compelling grapes grown in California could be introduced with a different and possibly as compelling a presentation as compared to the Old World paradigms.

[10] I would frame the challenge moving forward both for Old World and New: how to find or create vinous elegance and complexity in a world that is for the most part growing ever drier and warmer?

WITH A BIT OF FINE TUNING…

In my own vineyard, Popelouchum, near the town of San Juan Bautista in California's Central Coast, I've taken up the idea of self-crosses or what I fancifully call 'varietal auto-tuning'.[11] Normally, mind you, self-crosses are not the obvious best way to create stronger, more appropriate biotypes. In fact, because grapes are heterozygous, one finds the expression of recessive genes and instances of genetic weakness in the offspring – metabolic or growth disorders, sterility, failure to thrive, parthenocarpy, etc.[12] So, while the substantial majority of offspring of self-crosses are less interesting than their parents, this technique can create a substantial amount of variability in a trial and with it, the possibility of discovering biotypes that might be better suited to the unique conditions that present themselves.

Obviously, it is crucial to grow the new self-crossed seedlings side by side with the original parent to observe the phenotypic differences and note whether any significant improvements have been achieved. We have begun work self-crossing both Sérine and Rossese (a Ligurian grape variety, aka Tibouren in Provence), and the results so far are enormously encouraging.[13]

The opportunities afforded by self-crossing may be particularly useful under the following conditions:

1 Presence of debilitating virus Happily, grape-vine viruses are not transmitted through seeds, and the ability to eliminate virus while at the same creating variability of phenotypic expression represents a great opportunity for California

---

[11] It's important to note that a self-cross of a given grape variety is no longer, in fact, technically the same grape variety. A Grenache x Grenache cross, for example, while likely tasting very Grenache-ish, could, strictly speaking, no longer be called 'Grenache'. I am afraid that even thinking about this sort of issue will be enough to melt down the responsible American regulatory agency (TTB).

[12] Parthenocarpy, or seedlessness, may in fact be very useful in creating particularly intense and flavourful, small-berried grapes, albeit of very shy yield. If one, for example, is working with a variety like Nebbiolo which typically produces hard seed tannins, some component of seedless grapes in the blend might well be useful to achieve a stylistic objective. Identifying a biotype that produces fewer seeds than normal will also be useful in producing a smaller-clustered, smaller-berried variant, particularly in varieties that have a tendency to generate a substantially proportioned cluster. While the benefits of shrinking the size of a large clustered variety are patently obvious, there appear to be benefits in identifying smaller-clustered variants of small-clustered varieties such as Pinot Noir as well. This is perhaps an over-simplification, but a more favourable surface area/volume ratio of skin to pulp seems to create a sensory threshold above which the typicity of the variety begins to emerge.

[13] There is perhaps a far more compelling case to be made for self-crossing Rossese/Tibouren in comparison to Sérine. Rossese ripens quite variably; its cluster size can run from reasonable to enormous. Its suitability for producing red wine in California is yet to be determined, but its potential for elegance under California's quasi-Mediterranean conditions seems quite promising.

and indeed for the Old World.[14] Debilitating grape viruses create a certain cloud over a given variety, often daunting perhaps all but the most quixotic growers.[15] Viral issues can express themselves in many ways – delayed or uneven ripening, erratic fruit set, grafting incompatibility, sudden vine decline, all features that drive potential champions of exotic varieties slightly crazy.[16] It is ironic, but as mentioned earlier, historically Old World vineyards would often struggle to ripen their grapes in many years, sometimes due to viral issues. While achieving full ripeness these days in both New and Old World is typically a lot easier in the changed climate, finding unique biotypes that develop ripe flavours at lower potential alcohols is now perhaps the more relevant objective.

2 Improved winemaking quality/flavour intensity and complexity There has been no historical inevitability for growers the world over to feel compelled to choose particular clones/biotypes for their ultimate winemaking quality potential. Far too many clones have been selected for their thriftiness and general utility, ie, disease resistance, reliability of production, etc, rather than for their winemaking potential. But more to the point, varieties have been selected over time for their suitability to their particular place of origin, which is not necessarily relevant when they undergo relocation. In Côte-Rôtie, Sérine, a genius grape, will reliably produce a significant titer of rotundone, the molecule responsible for the variety's peppery typicity, but why should the same variety necessarily produce prodigious levels of rotundone under California's conditions? The variability found in self-crosses might well lead to the discovery of a high rotundone producer under brighter and drier California conditions. Nursery trials that revealed smaller bunches and berries[17] would likely suggest grapes of potentially higher

[14] The Old World regulatory bodies will have to wrap their heads around the technical issue of nomenclature. A self-cross is technically not identical to its parent, but presumably if it is both genotypically and phenotypically 'close enough' to the platonic ideal of the variety (at least as that is imagined), it should pass muster. In Calabria, the self-crossing experiments were successfully done with the grapes Gaglioppo and Magliocco, resulting in significantly 'improved' versions from the extant plant material.

[15] It's interesting to note that Viognier itself was in this category in the 1970s and came close to near disappearance for its viral issues.

[16] The US Department of Agriculture, responsible for phytosanitation, is generally unhappy with the idea of releasing new plant material that tests positive for any known grape virus; alas, its suggested 'cure', heat-treatment or thermo-therapy, can be fairly draconian, often resulting in the unintended consequence of the disappearance of the originality of the phenotype. In some cases, the virus had inhibited the yield; in some cases, it inhibited the sizing of the clusters. Withal, something important is often lost in these more productive 'improved' vines.

[17] A particular biotype's seed productivity would appear to be the dominant factor in determining berry size, and a seedless variant should by all reckoning produce a particularly intensely flavoured wine.

qualitative potential.[18] Apart from flavour considerations – which of course are primary, relevant phenological differences – bud-break and maturity dates, grape chemistry, etc, would be of great interest.[19]

3 Complexity Self-crossing represents a unique opportunity to create complexity through diversity and thoughtful selection. While many of the self-crosses will likely be far less interesting than their parents, often just slightly duller variations of their dad/mom, one might look for the 'outliers' for distinctive characteristics. In the case of Syrah/Sérine (itself the product of a mixed marriage, viz Dureza and Mondeuse Blanche), I've already found among the seedlings several white grape offspring, which I imagine might offer some interesting aromatic complexity. Needless to say, I'm looking carefully at the smaller-clustered biotypes as well as those that appear to be the pepperiest (by rotundone assay) and, of course, anything that looks and tastes particularly odd and distinctive.[20] A new plantation assembled from a blend of these unique biotypes could have singular complexity and nuance.

Working out the ideal percentages of seedless 'Sérine' in the blend, and how much 'Sérine Blanche' might be optimal, will be exceptionally satisfying work. At the very least, it seems to represent a potential path to a unique interpretation of Syrah/Sérine under California conditions.

LET TERROIR SPEAK ITS TRUTH

As I mentioned at the outset of this article, California's commercial success lay partially in its simplification of wine's terminology, making varietal rather than geographical designation primary in the presentation of the wine. But the

[18] This point is perhaps too important to footnote, but perhaps the single most useful application of the self-crossing technique would be to consider its use on what are typically considered to be large clustered grape varieties – with Grenache, Cinsault, Rossese, Nebbiolo, Sangiovese as examples, especially those with the tendency to form 'wings'. All things being equal, large berried, large clustered and winged grape biotypes are typically less intense than their smaller variants. Vignerons working with extant clones are often compelled to do significant thinning work to achieve the flavour intensity that they seek to produce great wine.

[19] One last note on Syrah/Sérine: The Holy Grail, at least for me, with this variety would be the creation/discovery of a unique biotype with significantly better stomatal regulation, crucial for both drought, wind and heat tolerance. Alas, unless one could iterate tens of thousands of self-crosses, the genetics of the regulation of stomata are almost certainly too complex to find the unique biotype in Syrah/Sérine with this improved functionality. But, it is not unreasonable to perhaps discover superior drought or heat tolerance in other varieties with less complicated genetics, ie, absence of multiple gene regulation.

[20] I'm told that the appearance of pink variants is exceptionally rare, but they hold particular fascination for me. With so many vinifera varieties the pink or lesser pigmented variant often has the most intense fragrance and expresses unique complexity.

American wine business has matured to the point where, I believe, customers are beginning to seek additional dimensionality in how wines are identified and certainly, more importantly, in how these wines are actually experienced.

The expression of terroir[21] or the unique qualities associated with place of origin, I believe, is the element that we California winemakers must seek in order to elevate our wines to an appropriate level of seriousness on the world stage. But this will perhaps require a significant amount of unlearning of our common typical modern viticultural practices – those that rely upon a strong level of stylistic or authorial control, as it were, of the process.

This is a much longer conversation, but if wine growers could learn to leverage Nature's gifts to a greater extent – the potential flavour and textural contribution of the site itself, as a good example – our wines would be infinitely more interesting and compelling. Notably, certain farming practices conduce to the more articulate expression of terroir[22]: dry-farming, restricted yields, no-tillage, organic and biodynamic farming, harvesting fruit at appropriate maturity levels, sensitive and gentle extraction of musts; these are all strategies that work towards allowing the inherent, unique qualities of the site to emerge as a prominent element and to speak its truth, in current parlance.[23]

The fashion for grape breeding comes and goes, and as a practice is generally deployed to solve a perceived problem: an individual grower or perhaps an aspiring region that would prefer a grape less prone to bunch rot, or something more winter-hardy, a grape that ripens earlier or later, one more consistent in yield, etc. It's not obvious that many grape breeders embark on the more open-ended project of searching for pure vinous beauty or originality. But I believe that grape breeding offers a special opportunity to help in our quest for greater congruity of variety (or more aptly, multiple varieties) for a given site, along with an opportunity to create unique taste profiles as well as possibly unique complexity to a grape blend.

The most unorthodox initiative being undertaken at Popelouchum is the ambitious project of attempting to breed 10,000 new cultivars from two different

[21] One must begin by planting one's vines in a distinctive/articulate terroir, ie, one with discernible soil characteristics that can be expressed by a grape variety or perhaps multiple varieties appropriately congruent to the site.

[22] At Popelouchum, we've adopted the use of biochar as a soil amendment. While it might certainly be argued that the use of any soil amendment represents a sort of deformation of terroir, biochar uniquely aids in the plant's extraction of existing soil minerals, thus acting as a sort of terroir amplifier.

[23] Near complete control of the wine-growing process is a hallmark of New World winemaking – from the insistence on standardized clonal material, to drip irrigation, to the use of stylistic enhancers in the winery: cultured yeast and bacteria, enzymes, fining agents, organoleptic tannins, pigments (MegaPurple, the grape juice concentrate, etc).

In pursuit of a site-match as exquisite as Pinot Noir finds on Burgundy's Côte d'Or, Randall Grahm is seeking out the cultivar that suits his vineyards best. This is the Pinot's eye view from the heights of Popelouchum, Central Coast, California.

Vitis vinifera varieties. By creating such a vast multitude of new germplasm, there certainly exists the possibility of discovering a new and exciting variety or two with unique flavour and useful agronomic characteristics. But, looking at the initiative through a very different lens, and considering what might result from a field blend composed of a set of genetically distinctive, individual biotypes, there might be the special opportunity to reflect the unique inherent qualities of the site itself.

By using a vast number of genetically distinctive biotypes – though all derived from common parents, so each with a familial resonance – one has essentially effaced the expression of varietal characteristics. As a Gestalt problem, this would allow the more subtle elements of the wine – the expression of soil character or terroir – to emerge. The outstanding question is: *Might the use of a very large set of genetically distinctive individuals represent an opportunity to create a wine of unique complexity and nuance that could not be achieved by any other means?*

At Popelouchum, I've finally settled on a choice of parents for what I hope will be a long vitaceous lineage. Perhaps there will emerge a few individual offspring with noteworthy and compelling characteristics. But, qualifying these characteristics *a priori* in an altogether new variety is not an obviously straightforward process, and indeed might only be possible when one encounters the new varieties for the first time with no preconceived expectations.

I wouldn't necessarily be looking for or expecting 'haunting fragrance', for example (though would be very pleased to discover that, were it to emerge), or for preternatural levels of fruitiness. (Indeed, that latter element would be a distraction.) Rather, I believe I would focus on the qualities in the grape that suggested both complexity of flavour and aroma, as well as exhibiting a persistence of flavour. I'm not quite sure how to properly characterize this in physical terms, but I'd also be looking for a sort of 'openness' on the palate, such as one finds in grapes like Pinot Noir and Nebbiolo, sufficient to allow other elements, in particular soil characteristics, to emerge.

In fact, I believe there has been a sort of category error in how most of us think about wine – principally as a beverage composed of definable grape varieties, noble or common, as platonically pure *monocépage* expressions of the noblest (Pinot Noir, Nebbiolo, Syrah, Chardonnay, etc), or as artfully composed varietal blends (Bordeaux, Côtes du Rhône) of the perhaps slightly less noble. But if we somehow began to think of grapes less for their own distinctive flavour contribution but rather instead as potential transmitters or carriers of other important information – say, the unique qualities of a given (and special) viticultural site – we open the possibility of a new world of original flavours and conversations. We might now better focus on the qualities that differentiate one vineyard site from another. In California, this may well represent an opportunity for it to begin to find its own unique voice, rather than being an imperfect echo of a possibly static Old World paradigm.

CALIFORNIA AND
THE CRITICS

In a prophetic article from 1984, Bob Thompson –
affectionately known by his fellow wine scribes as
'the Sage of St Helena' – takes a look at the emerging
cult of the wine critic and finds his arteries hardening
towards 'novelty wines' and the uneven commentary
that surrounds them.

BOB THOMPSON (1984)

In the most perfect of all possible worlds, a wine bibber would live by the counsel of a wise wine merchant. Glimpses of the ideal may be had from old literature, above all George Saintsbury's *Notes on a Cellarbook* (1920), the most gentlemanly record of wine buying and wine drinking to be found anywhere. At each of his posts, Saintsbury found a merchant he trusted and with whom he could deal man to man. The merchant, for his part, did his homework at both ends. He learned which were the reputable producers, learned Saintsbury's preferences, and put the two together. Merchants and merchants alone stood between the good professor and the men who made the wines.

As Saintsbury also records, in some parts of the world hierarchies of consumers and producers have sometimes gotten so rigidly established that buyers need only ask for a correct label to keep their social feathers preened. Check the vintage charts for a superior year, check the roster of Firsts, Seconds and Thirds (or *Grands* and *Petits*), check the wallet for maximum allowable expenditure, and bingo! The best money can buy. If anyone drinks with long teeth, it is the drinker's fault, not the wine's. Sooner or later the reluctant learn to like what they are supposed to like, and the hierarchy grows stronger.

In the 1950s and '60s, California was something like that. Form players could, and did, coast through the era knowing to a surety that a baker's dozen of labels yielded every fully pedigreed bottle a collector had to have. Beaulieu Vineyard, Inglenook, Charles Krug and Louis M Martini had all the Napa Cabernet Sauvignons one needed until Souverain Cellars and Heitz Cellars joined the lists. Almaden, Buena Vista, Concannon, Hallcrest, Paul Masson and Martin Ray had to be watched for an occasional memorable example of Cabernet. For Chardonnay the knowing bibber went to Hanzell, Heitz, Charles Krug, Stony Hill, Wente Bros and, towards the closing hours of the 1960s, Chalone. On the occasions when Pinot Noir rose to the heights, the bottles came from Beaulieu, Chalone, Hanzell, Heitz and Martini. Even less often, Martin Ray would join the list. Oh, the rare surprise would come from elsewhere, but a collector could earn full marks for thoroughness as well as skill by sticking with that short list year after year. A true believer would round out the cellar with some Johannisberg Rieslings, Zinfandels and the odd Barbera, but not at the expense of adding any different labels. The ultimate hobbyist knew enough to harbour some Livermore Sauvignon Blancs from Wente and Concannon.

By 1982 Napa's wineries had become 110, and its 10,000 acres of vineyard 25,000. Sonoma nearly paralleled that growth. Monterey County had gone from a single, episodic winery to a dozen, and from 30 acres of vineyard to 32,000. And so on, through San Luis Obispo, Santa Barbara, Mendocino, Lake, the Sierra Foothills, Temecula and, I fear, someplace I have yet to hear about.

Where does the confident collector of 1968 turn 15 years later? In circles. The old certainties were based on a stagnant market rather than mature development of the state's vineyard lands, and they have been drowned by a single wave of new optimism. In the turbulence, a newcomer wins a competition against a well-regarded older hand, and puts his price up accordingly. Sometimes a price is set because somebody has built a jewel-box winery full of state-of-the-art equipment using money rented at 24 percent. Sometimes it is only the wish to be one of the best that causes a fledgling proprietor to position himself at the top, as the marketing people say. The old hands must elect to play in the new game, or sit tight and wait for the bubble to pop.

A high-school track coach I knew once launched tryouts by lining up all his new hopefuls and firing his starter's pistol without a word of explanation. He thought the natural sprinters would take off while the distance men hung back, thus sorting themselves out on the first day. What he learned was that in a race of no known distance, the only place people feel safe is in touch with the leaders. Like the novice trackmen, California's wineries find themselves running in an uncertain, but wildly hopeful, bunch. While would-be connoisseurs wait for class to tell in the various distances, the question will not go away. Which are the wines to buy? The question before that is, what advice to heed?

The answer ought not to be hard, but it is. Prohibition decimated the ranks of wise wine merchants to such a degree that there are not yet enough to go around. The good ones that do exist cannot keep up with the scores of new labels that have appeared in each of the past several years. But this is not the main difficulty. With wine more than with most products, people with guests want to do the right thing, which is to say bring to their dinner tables only the best. In a winner-take-all society, that means Number One, the Super Bowl winner. (I have heard a restaurant diner reject a bottle of Third Growth Médoc on the grounds that he was not having any third-rate anything.)

The truth is that at least a hundred California Cabernet Sauvignons, about the same number of Chardonnays, and smaller numbers of each of the other varietals and the generics are perfectly acceptable. If all were right with the world, huge numbers of people would buy a dozen or so cases of wine a year, more or less as Saintsbury did. The roster would include several bottles each of a pricey Cabernet Sauvignon or Pinot Noir for grand occasions and slightly larger supplies of a less costly one for regular company. There would be a similar pair of Chardonnays or Sauvignon Blancs, some White Riesling or Chenin Blanc for weekend sipping, some sparkling wine, a few bottles of a dry sherry-type for evenings, and a few bottles of a port-type for the winter fire. (In addition, there would be considerable amounts of a daily red and daily white. Saintsbury took his regular meals in a common room, and did not need to lay in daily stocks.) All would be bought on the advice of a merchant, who would suggest an occasional trial bottle to see if greater satisfaction might be found with something different. Smaller numbers – those of us who use wine more as a hobby than as a beverage – would buy more widely so we could fret over nuances in the wines and the critics.

This is not going to happen soon, if ever. It has gotten into the national psyche that there can be a Super Bowl wine. Even before the Super Bowl syndrome developed, it had gotten into the national mind that wine is a matter for experts. The question thus remains, what advice to heed? For those who will not, or cannot, put their trust in a good merchant (or, better yet, themselves), the fragile choices are three: the laws governing labels, which are decades away from defining much; awards from county fair and other competitions, which only point to benchmarks; and published critics, who also only point to benchmarks and who are a growth industry themselves and thus extremely uneven as advisers...

...By now it should be abundantly clear that I have the touch of megalomania required of all critics. It should be equally clear that my critical arteries are hardening in the direction of conventional, conservative style rather than novelty. High-alcohol Zinfandels have an audience in this world, mostly of people in wine clubs who taste them comparatively. But that audience does not, and will not, include me, because inky colours, searing tannins, the fires of 14 and 15 percent of alcohol, and dense aromas of raisins and wood too often have come, all of them at once, in wines that age gracelessly in my cellar when they are not overwhelming good food on my dinner table. My only standard in wine is how well it fits what I eat. We critics, all of us, are transparent, easier to solve than commuter crossword puzzles.

Some of us look at wine only as a food. Some only want the tasting game. Most want a little of each. In any case, for critics and normal people alike, wine comes down to a handful of points that make us each and every one an open book. Those points, a majority of them common to many foods, are: alcohol, sugar-acid balance, tannin, fruit flavours and, latterly, wood flavours. Alcohol is prominent enough to light its characteristic little fire in the back of the throat, or not. A good many people want the sensation. A good many do not. Most lean one way or the other consistently. Sugar can be tasted as sweet, or it cannot. It may be the number one factor in the choices of a majority of all wine drinkers, who, again, tend to be habitual in liking a little or not wanting any in their dinner wines. Because of wine's acids, it may remind one of the feel of grapefruit juice at one extreme, or be as flat as yesterday's cola at the other. Some people like tart, some like bland, most like the middle road.

The puckering powers of tannin divide the world of red wine drinkers into two camps in the same way as sugars and acids. Forcible amounts of oak evoke yes or no responses, too. This much is simple and steady. Fruit flavours are harder to be categorical about. Some pungently aromatic varieties – Gewürztraminer and Sauvignon Blanc – are sought or shunned on their basic character. In most cases, though, the sum of the parts wins or loses on the tongues of critics, connoisseurs and beginners. The excuses all come later.

Excerpt from *The University of California/Sotheby Book of California Wine* (1984) edited by Doris Muscatine, Maynard A Amerine and Bob Thompson. Reproduced here with kind permission of the author and publishers.

'The Grape Crusher' by Gino Miles, at Vista Point, Napa Valley. Sitting high above Highway 29, this statue is three times lifesize and visible to all who arrive in the valley.

Such aspects of wine 'anatomy' were important not only to wine writers speaking about fine wine, but also to the winemakers, who began to modify the descriptors in the winery for the wines that were being made.

While there may be some difference of opinion on the meaning of these terms, most would recognize them and acknowledge that they represent distinct and important aspects of fine wine analysis.

We have spoken about the basic, even primitive character of the categories in the quantitative form of the 20-point system. Because we tend to take them for granted now, it is difficult to remember that in an early era in our modern wine-making capability, those basic standards were like targets in the sky. They had then an educative function – they were a step that led to other ascending steps – but they are like grammar and spelling to us now. The Davis 20-point system led us out of the wilderness, but good words led us to the promised land… where we try to write poetry in our glass!

And so, we come to a final thought: what are the wines of the promised land? These words, the 'promised land', show us the limitations of words, for they are but a metaphor – not for a place or a thing – but for something we humans seek but cannot find in ourselves. If we consider this thought as it relates to wine, we might also reflect on an older way of looking at things which suggested that to truly understand something, you must get to know it at its best. For, when something is at its best, it is mostly truly itself. Wine at its best, then, can give us a sense of *completeness* – meaning, it has a beginning, a middle and an end. As humans, we are by our nature incomplete. Completeness is something we long for, but do not possess. And yet, we are able to possess it 'somehow' by sensing it when we experience wine at its best. It is then we are aware we have been, momentarily, lifted beyond ourselves… Only a thought.

7

BRING OUT THE BIG GUNS

The mightiest grape comes under scrutiny. The most influential regions reveal their unique quality. And the biggest players impress us with everything from crowd-pleasing quaffers to top-dollar style icons. These are the wines that lead the way.

NAPA vs SONOMA

Elin McCoy compares and contrasts California's two iconic wine regions – Napa exuding style, celebrity and top-dollar Cabernet, Sonoma the heartland of relaxed rural living and delicate Pinot Noir – and asks which of these neighbouring wine enclaves is better prepared to face the future?

ELIN McCOY (2021)

Glitzy vs laid-back, stretch limousines vs SUVs, Cabernet vs Pinot, polished vs rustic, big celebs vs local winemakers – for a deep dive into the differences between Napa and Sonoma, California's two most famous wine regions, their annual wine auctions are a handy place to start.

That was my thinking in 2019 after I attended both events, before the global pandemic put everything on hiatus. Napa's four-day spectacle in June featured pop star Katy Perry belting out her hits *Firework* and *Roar* for an audience of 900. Confetti fluttered down, caressed by purple lighting. One auction lot included dinner with the Rothschilds at Château Mouton Rothschild. The final take was nearly $12 million.

All of it reinforced the long-held view of Napa as the land of glamour, money, architectural statement wineries, posh tourists and big deal, $200 and up Cabernet Sauvignon blends.

Sonoma's more down-to-earth weekend in September was smaller, with a community-first vibe; a pre-auction tasting on the lawn included Sonoma cider as well as wines, and vintners gave speeches. Some 400 attendees raised $6.1 million. It reflected the prevailing vision of Sonoma as a slower, more rural (some say more authentic) wine region, with dirt roads, descendants of Italian grape growers, young experimental winemakers, the foggy coastline and coveted Pinot Noirs that aren't nearly as expensive as Napa's Cabernets.

Yet neither picture tells the whole story, especially today.

There have always been similarities between the two regions. Confusingly, Napa, like Sonoma, is the name of a county, a valley and a city. Sadly, both regions have experienced devastating wildfires in the past few years. Given climate change, these are sure to continue. Historically, both wine spots north of San Francisco have 19th century roots.

But the contrasts in geography, size, diversity, grapes, culture, tourism and prices are wider than you might expect for two neighbouring regions separated by a mountain range and a mere hour's drive apart.

THE REPUTATIONAL DIFFERENCE

In terms of global attention and prestige, Napa has been the winner ever since its modern glory days began in the 1970s, back when there were no Ferraris parked on St Helena's Main Street and tasting rooms poured wine for free. Why did Napa get all the love?

Prohibition hit both regions hard, but Napa's wine industry bounced back much more quickly than Sonoma's. The 1976 Paris tasting (the famous Judgement of Paris), where Stag's Leap Wine Cellars and Chateau Montelena beat out top Bordeaux and burgundies, boosted Napa's reputation and helped establish Cabernet Sauvignon as the key grape at a time when Bordeaux reds ruled the wine world. And Napa had savvy marketer Robert Mondavi, who acted like a one-man public relations machine for the valley. He travelled the world extolling the greatness of its wines and virtually single-handedly created a wine and food culture modeled on Europe's. When the Bordelais wanted to expand into the New World, they headed to Napa (and they still do), adding more buzz. The wine auction itself – roughly copied from Burgundy's annual Hospices de Beaune event – was a Mondavi idea.

The cult Cabernet boom that began in the 1990s ushered in an era of wines that aimed to be just as good and expensive as First Growth Bordeaux. Their rarity and three-digit prices – $100, $200, $300 and up – not to mention the struggle to get on the mailing list of the latest hot name, guaranteed more prestige for the valley.

For decades Sonoma was the also-ran, the little brother or sister, despite the fact that the northern California wine rush began there when Russian fur traders planted vines near coastal Fort Ross in 1817. Colourful pioneers like the mysterious Hungarian wheeler-dealer Count Agoston Haraszthy, who established California's oldest commercial winery in Sonoma in 1857, set an early renegade winemaker tone. Only over the past two decades has Sonoma finally grabbed serious attention, especially as a hotspot for Pinot Noir and a paradise for the relaxed rural lifestyle.

GEOGRAPHY IS DESTINY

Napa has the simpler, more cohesive image, partly because of its emphasis on Cabernet, partly because of its compact, easy-to-understand geography. Two north-south roads, one with towns and traffic (Highway 29) and one without (Silverado Trail) traverse this narrow valley cupped by two mountain ranges. Its 16 American Viticultural Areas, or AVAs, lie on the valley floor or on hillside slopes right above it. The whole valley is bound by a billboard message: 'Welcome to this world-famous wine-growing region, Napa Valley', with author Robert Louis Stevenson's quote: 'And the wine is bottled poetry.'

Its grape diversity used to be more like Sonoma's and you can still find 40-odd varieties planted, from esoteric Refosco to familiar Sauvignon Blanc. But the high prices wineries can charge for bottles of Cabernet have meant that more vineyards replanted to the grape. As wine and grape prices escalated, so too did the cost of land. Today, vineyard land in top Napa spots sells for $300,000 to $400,000 an acre compared to a third to half that for Sonoma.

On the other hand, Sonoma's landscape sprawls. The region lies at the western edge of the continent where it meets the Pacific Ocean and the San Andreas Fault and is three times bigger than the Napa Valley. Its 18 AVAs are a patchwork, spread over hillsides and ridges, next to meandering rivers, in pastoral valleys and along an 88-kilometre (55-mile) long coastline. Microclimates range from sunny and warm to cold and foggy. Petaluma Gap – the most recently added AVA – is distinguished by wind. That diversity extends to some 60 grape varieties.

As Napa zeroed-in on one key varietal, Sonoma's narrative has been the rediscovery of its old vine history and the hunt for which sub-regions are right for which grapes. History lives on in the largest concentration of century-old vineyards in the state, with a mix of varieties like Zinfandel, Alicante Bouschet, Petite Sirah and many others more mysterious. Morgan Twain-Peterson MW of Bedrock Vineyards, a vocal advocate for saving these older vines, once told me that field blends produced from these grapes made California's most authentic wines.

The warm, dry Alexander Valley turned out to be a disaster for fine Chardonnay, but ideal for Cabernet, as is Moon Mountain AVA in Sonoma Valley. Warm Dry Creek Valley gained a reputation for Zinfandel, and Pinot and Chardonnay found ideal homes in spots once thought too cold to ripen grapes. This fragmentation resulted in a complicated image for Sonoma, but may be its most important attribute for the future.

Sonoma's Pinot and Chardonnay makers were bottling dozens of single-vineyard wines long before the vineyard-designated wine trend hit Napa. In my view, an awful lot of them don't yet show the kinds of distinctive differences you see in, for example, Kistler's single-vineyard Sonoma Chardonnays, or for that matter, burgundy. But they have played a key role in Sonoma's rise, encouraging a new focus on the vineyard rather than the wizard winemaker in the cellar, a view that's now the thinking in Napa too. And with cheaper grape prices, it's easier for young experimental winemakers who can't afford to buy land to get into the wine game there by buying grapes. What drew many of them was the dream of Pinot Noir – also known as 'the heartbreak grape'.

THE RISE OF PINOT NOIR

The recent surge in demand for Pinot Noir really benefited Sonoma, despite the fact that Chardonnay is the region's most widely planted grape and there's almost as much Cabernet as Pinot. Its single-vineyard Pinots gave the region a claim to fame distinct from Napa's. While Cabernets from several Sonoma AVAs, like Moon Mountain, Chalk Hill and Alexander Valley, can be stellar, they haven't gained the acclaim of the best in Napa.

It's hard to remember that Pinot Noir wasn't all that popular in the US until the 21st century. When Hanzell Vineyards planted it in Sonoma Valley in 1957, most growers thought it was too finicky to be commercial. Change came when a pack of burgundy-loving winemakers staked it all on cool climate viticulture. When interest in Pinot Noir exploded after the 2004 film *Sideways* (*see* page 52), the region came into its own. The first winemakers zeroed-in on the Russian River Valley, but the latest buzz vineyards are on the west Sonoma Coast where maritime chill and Pacific winds make wines that are sleeker, higher in minerality and lower in alcohol, with layers of bright flavours. Their rise coincided with a new wine consciousness and fatigue with high-alcohol cult Cabernets.

Given the recent prices of the best red burgundies compared to red Bordeaux, you might think Sonoma's top Pinot Noirs would be selling at the same level as Napa's Cabernets, but you would be wrong.

Ironically, the cool Napa AVAs – like Wild Horse Valley and Los Carneros – planted to Pinot Noir and Chardonnay haven't yet attracted as much attention as those of Sonoma.

THE ESTATE VS THE FARM

Driving around the two regions, you immediately notice how many Napa wineries fit the grand château mould. Some are historic ivy-covered stone cellars like Chateau Montelena and Inglenook, others are grand Tuscan villas and sleek statements of modernism by famous architects built by the billionaires streaming into the valley. There's even a castle with a dungeon.

Yes, Napa still has down-home wineries that more resemble farms or small domaines in Burgundy. The weathered barn, farmhouse and biodynamic vineyards of Matthiasson in Oak Knoll is one. It reminds me of many boutique-y wineries in Sonoma, such as Ted Lemon's biodynamic haven Littorai in Sebastopol, in the Sonoma Coast appellation.

This page, top left Napa's Chateau Montelena – built (in 1882) by Alfred L Tubbs, who made a fortune in the rope business during the Gold Rush.

Top right Inglenook's striking Napa 'château' (completed 1887) incorporated the strong cable used in San Francisco's cable cars to stave off earthquake damage. Purchased by Francis and Eleanor Coppola in 1975.

Centre The striking Dominus winery completed in 1997 by Christian Moueix of Pomerol (Yountville, Napa), and (*right*) modelled on a 'Tuscan castle', Castello di Amorosa in Calistoga, Napa.

Facing page. Top The Donum estate, incorporating wine and art; the sophisticated side of Sonoma.

Flowers winery (*right*), capturing the wilder side of Sonoma's Coast: the rugged vineyards matter most. And (*left*) the Dehlinger Vineyard, Russian River.

But nothing is simple in Napa vs Sonoma comparisons. Sonoma, too, has its grand estates – though these still feel like exceptions. The first built-from-scratch example was Jordan winery in Alexander Valley, founded in 1972, with the aim of making Cabernet in the model of Bordeaux. Its tile-roofed, ivy-covered mansion with yellow walls and bright red shutters could have been transported from France, and brought a new European sensibility to small-town Sonoma. Chateau St Jean, Ferrari-Carano and Francis Ford Coppola's winery – all have some of that Napa castle flair. And let's not forget the dominant force in shaping the county's AVA boundaries has been brought by its two biggest landowners, Kendall-Jackson and the Gallo family. But Sonoma's smaller vintners have been the ones to set the direction of the region's quality wines, just as they did in Napa in the 1970s and '80s.

And then there's tourism. Ten years ago, public relations professional Tom Wark described Napa Valley as a 'wine Disneyland', and Sonoma as a 'wine region'. The situation isn't all that different today. Go-with-the-flow Sonoma has bucolic back roads, better biking trails, glamping (the glamorous form of camping), and casual outdoor dinners at hip places like Scribe Winery – all appealing to a younger generation. Napa has sophisticated restaurants and five-star luxury hotels, with more on the way. Both offer serious yoga and spas.

Has Napa's oenotourism become over-tourism? Some critics say Napa is losing its soul and tight community while others worry it will destroy the region's rural beauty. The region may be showing the world where the limits of oenotourism are.

CLIMATE CHANGE AND THE FUTURE

Today, no wine region can escape the effects of climate change, which brings me to imagining what Napa and Sonoma might become in the future. Which region will be the winner in the face of global warming and increasing drought?

Right now Sonoma's diversity gives the region more flexibility. Its proximity to the ocean means at least some AVAs may not suffer that much as the planet warms. The old historic vines, with their deep, deep roots, are varieties that have managed to survive for more than a century, yet the region's current star, Pinot Noir, is the grape most sensitive to changes in temperature. Will other grapes become more important in the future and change Sonoma's current image?

Napa has always been hotter and drier than most of Sonoma. Many have blamed higher alcohol levels in its Cabernets on global warming, though choice of rootstock and clone and later harvest dates are also factors.

Forward-thinking wineries like Larkmead and Spottswoode are already planting experimental plots of other red grapes that withstand heat and drought better than Cabernet. In 50 years, will Napa be synonymous with Touriga Nacional instead of Cabernet? We'll see.

HOW THE GALLOS DID IT

Ernest and Julio Gallo founded their company at a time when America had no need of wine, nor did the brothers have any knowledge of how it was made – few people did. Elaine Chukan Brown charts the rise and rise of an empire that began with nothing, but now has everything, sustainability included.

ELAINE CHUKAN BROWN (2021)

In early January 2021, E&J Gallo closed its acquisition of more than 30 wine brands and five additional wineries from the beer giant Constellation. The transfer of assets took almost two years to finalize as the purchase moved such a substantial market share to Gallo that the Federal Trade Commission of the United States forced changes to the deal in order to limit Gallo's gain. Even after the adjustments to the original purchase, the final sale stands as one of the largest wine acquisitions in history.

The brands acquired largely include wines on the less expensive side (many $11 per bottle and under), wines that in the United States are commonly called 'grocery store brands' for their prevalence in stores across the country. Gallo now represents almost one of every three bottles of wine produced in the state of California. According to the 2021 survey carried out by *Wine Business Monthly,* Gallo has an 88-million case sales volume in the US annually, and a global case sales volume of 100 million[1].

When asked about the acquisition from Constellation, chief marketing officer and granddaughter of co-founder Ernest Gallo, Stephanie Gallo said the purchase presented a unique opportunity for Gallo to 'bring new customers into the wine category'. A friendlier variation of her grandfather's famous comment: 'We don't want most of the business. We want it all.'

Today, Gallo is not only the biggest winery in California (no small feat as this is the fourth largest wine-producing region in the world), but it has been since at least the 1990s.

[1] *Wine Business Monthly* (February 2021).

BUILDING AN EMPIRE

The end of Prohibition was still in view when brothers Ernest and Julio founded their eponymous winery in 1933 in Modesto. The 13-year ban on alcohol sales across the United States meant they were beginning a new venture in a country with a depleted winemaking knowledge, no obvious wine market and no real distribution network.

Indeed, the brothers themselves had no winemaking experience. But thanks to their parents' short-lived grape-growing business, followed by another enterprise selling boxed grapes to home winemakers around the country, the brothers did have a sense of both farming and distribution. (During Prohibition, it was legal for heads of household to make up to 900 litres of home wine per year. Many also made more, illegally, to sell to bootleggers, making grape boxes an important commodity for the country.)

As the story goes, the brothers initially taught themselves winemaking from a pre-Prohibition era pamphlet they found in the basement of a local library. But over time, Ernest began collaborating with scientists at the University of California, Davis, to advance their efforts, and the duo quickly founded their own research vineyard and winery to keep the lessons gained comfortably within the business.

In the first years of E&J Gallo, the wines made were sold in bulk for others to bottle and label under their own company names. Such was the nature of the wine market at the time. By the late 1930s, though, the brothers had taken the bold step of bottling and labelling wine under their own name. They also established their own unique sales team whose entire job was to sell Gallo wine to key markets around the country. It was an approach not seen before in the United States and it successfully changed both the marketing and status of wine in the nation. Prior to the Gallo effort, wine took a backseat to spirits on store shelves. By sending wine specialists into the market and offering buyers special deals for greater purchases, Gallo began to change how wine was placed, establishing more visibility for it in stores. To increase business stability, the brothers only expanded into a new market once their foothold and dominance in current markets was secured.

Any financial gain Gallo aquired through its revolutionary marketing efforts was immediately poured back into the business. The brothers steadily expanded production volume as they took more market share across the country, buying more grapes from growers to meet demand.

But rather than simply expanding volume, Gallo also expanded into the areas that supported its business. At the same time as it began bottling wine under its own name, it also purchased its own bottling facilities. A few years later

Purchased by Gallo in 2017, the 600-acre Stagecoach vineyard straddles the Atlas Peak and Pritchard Hill AVAs; it represents the largest contiguous vineyard in the Napa Valley. For Gallo, this purchase affirms its committment to the luxury wine sector.

it invested in its own label production and design team. Once the brothers had established market recognition of the Gallo name for wine, they trademarked it (famously even protecting the Gallo name from use by other family members' businesses). In the 1950s, they built their own glass production facility to both make their own bottles and sell them to other producers as well. Eventually they also bought the sand mines needed to make the glass. (Today, Gallos owns the largest glass plant in North America – also in Modesto, in California's Central Valley.) By the 1950s, Gallo was the largest wine producer in the United States, and it started its own advertising team as well. In the 1960s, it established its own trucking company to transport its wines around the country. The consolidation of resources meant Gallo could also capitalize on economies of scale.

Gallo successfully lowered costs by scaling production to build both greater efficiency and bring almost every aspect of the wine business under Gallo ownership. The reduced cost translated not only into greater savings for their own business but also greater value for the customer. Over time, the combination won them even greater market share as customers came to see the quality of Gallo brands as exceeding that of similarly priced competitors. By the 1990s, Gallo was the largest winery in the world. The brothers then began expanding into the fine wine market.

Having successfully established themselves across more affordable categories, the Gallos then began looking to cover every price tier, creating fine and luxury wine brands and establishing their success with international critics. They planted and purchased their own high-end vineyards in the prestigious North Coast regions of Sonoma County and Napa Valley, and began expanding their offerings on brands owned by but not associated with the Gallo name. By the late 1990s, Gallo-owned brands were winning top wine awards in the United States and beginning to gain international recognition as well. In 2000, Gallo was named the 'Best American Wine Producer' at the prestigious London International Wine Challenge, and the following year its wine was named 'Best Chardonnay in the World' by the International Wine and Spirits Competition. In the 2000s, it continued to expand by buying already established, highly respected and high-end wineries.

Gallo's unique business practices changed the American wine industry. It was the first winery, to establish itself through vertical integration. Before the Gallo brothers, the wine industry was segregated – one person grew grapes and sold them to someone else who made the wine, who sold it to someone else who bottled it. It was then distributed on someone else's trucks and sold to stores by someone else's sales teams. But the Gallo brothers instead took control of literally every aspect of their business from vineyards all the way through to its placement on store shelves. The approach made Gallo dominant, but it also re-invigorated public interest in wine, opening the way more broadly for others to gain wine sales as well, even if not to the same enormous degree.

THE STATE OF THE EMPIRE

The success of the Gallo brothers makes them easy to criticize. The general assumption seems to be that for the company to be so large, it must also be evil. Its history is not without faults.

The United Farm Workers Union has carried out multiple boycotts and strikes against Gallo from the 1970s through to the 2000s, asserting unfair labour practices and poor representation. Local accusations of price gouging over grape prices for growers without a Gallo contract have followed the company for decades. But at the same time, growers with long-term contracts consistently laud the company for their treatment. In the 1980s, Ernest and Julio sued their own brother Joe to keep him from using the Gallo name to market his cheese company. At the same time, Gallo's notoriously secret business practices contributes to the criticism. As a private company it has no obligation to disclose records, making it hard to assess the validity of the rumours.

Today, Gallo is led by second- and third-generation family members. Still entirely family-owned, Gallo stands as one of the largest family-owned businesses in the world. Newer generations appear intent on bolstering environmental efforts, and employee confidence in the company, as shown by the generally good retention rate and multiple awards from outside groups, grows.

Gallo has made a public commitment to sustainability efforts. It was the first winery in the United States to receive the ISO 14001 certification – the international standard providing criteria for an effective environmental management system and performance requirements. It reduced both water and energy use in its wineries and glass plant by dropping overall water need and adopting ultraviolet-based water treatment systems to recycle most of the water in use. At its research winery it has successfully converted grape must and other MOG into biofuel to streamline energy use, and has also integrated solar power into its systems. At the glass factory it converted furnaces to oxygen-fired systems, thus drastically reducing smog emissions. It also created a glass recycling programme that is now responsible for 30 percent of all glass recycled in California. In vineyards, farming practices have steadily shifted to reduce chemical inputs. Employees also collaborate in international environmental partnerships to develop and encourage performance protocols that make sustainability practices more economically viable.

Recent years have brought multiple sources of recognition to Gallo for positive employee treatment. Glassdoor – an online platform that allows current and former employees to anonymously rate employers – has awarded Gallo 'Best Place to Work' in the United States for five years in a row, from 2017 through 2021. The Human Rights Campaign gave Gallo a '100 Percent Corporate Equality Index' eight years in a row for LGBTQ+ inclusive workplace policies. The average score among Fortune 500 companies is 76 percent. In 2021, Diversity Jobs, an online assessment platform that scores employers for how well they support diversity and inclusion in the workplace, named Gallo one of their top employers.

Today, the company includes 15 active family members in the business and more than 6,500 employees worldwide, with its wines represented in more than 90 countries. It is also the largest exporter of California wine. With its recent acquisition from Constellation, Gallo increased its operational footprint by adding production facilities in California, Washington and New York states. It is also separately acquiring Nobilo, a New Zealand Sauvignon Blanc-focused winery, from Constellation. Whatever the criticism or positive recognition the winery may continue to garner, the company designed itself to both expand and stay stable. The largest winery in the world is here to stay.

THE ESSENCE OF NAPA CABERNET

Cabernet Sauvignon is the most 'Hollywood' of California's grapes – glamorous, adored, with top-dollar performance and perfect ripeness. But Harry Eyres thinks that as the Napa Valley enters a new era of thoughtfulness, it's high time this grape returned to its classic roots.

HARRY EYRES (2021)

In late September 2020 the Glass Fire raged through the northern section of the Napa Valley and parts of Sonoma, wreaking havoc on vineyards, wineries, houses, restaurants and other establishments. I was sad to read of the damage to producers such as Newton Vineyard, Sterling Vineyards, Behrens Family Winery, Burgess Cellars, Hourglass Winery and others. But what tore most at my heart was the razing to the ground of much of the beautiful Meadowood resort, hidden in its side-valley off the Silverado Trail near St Helena. I've been lucky enough to stay at Meadowood on a number of occasions. What I've always loved is its closeness to nature, the way its clapperboard cottages nestle in among the woodpecker-haunted live-oaks, madrones and mossy boulders. Now nature seems to have turned against it, or against us all.

Meadowood historically was not a luxury resort but a sleepy country club which also served as a meeting-place for Napa residents and vintners. When Bill Harlan and his partners bought it in 1979 he had the idea – partly seeded by Robert Mondavi – of making it into a common ground for the Napa Valley, and a site for the annual Napa Valley Auction. (This has since become a glitzy event and has raised more than $200 million for charity.)

Days after the fire, Harlan said, with typical undauntedness, that he and his partner Stan Kroenke would rebuild Meadowood. Beyond the tragedy and destruction, he told me, he saw 'an exciting new chapter. We'll make it even better than we did 36 years ago'. I found myself hoping that the new chapter might in some ways look back to the past. In Napa, the glitziness has sometimes obscured the essence. That essence for me is the astonishing natural beauty, a talented and resilient community, the commitment to agriculture enshrined in the 1968 Agriculture Preserve (protecting 23,000 acres of the valley) and – most importantly – the classic wines that this most prestigious American wine appellation has produced, especially from Cabernet Sauvignon, for 150 years and more. Gastronomy and hospitality have grown naturally and organically out of all these things.

Here, I want to talk about the essence of Napa Cabernet itself. I somehow feel this was better understood a few decades ago. Early enthusiasts and evangelists included Hugh Johnson, who used his poetic pen to sum up the elusive character of 'Rutherford dust' in *The World Atlas of Wine* (1971), and, perhaps surprisingly given his allegiance to Bordeaux, Michael Broadbent. Steven Spurrier hosted his famous Judgement of Paris tasting in 1976 (*see* page 70), when perhaps as much by accident as by design the Napa wines were not as extremely ripe and high in alcohol as some later became. In earlier days I don't believe that sheer power and heft were the prime hallmarks of Napa Cabernet. Researching a book on the grape in the late 1980s I spoke to André Tchelistcheff, the undisputed dean of Napa Cab and maker of the great Beaulieu Vineyards Georges de Latour Private Reserves of the 1940s, '50s and '60s; he stressed balance and elegance above power. Certainly those were qualities not just of his wines but of others such as Inglenook.

I remember drinking two fine Napa Cabernets from the 1978 vintage with Bill Harlan and Robin Lail some time in 2008. One was a Joseph Phelps, the other from Stag's Leap Wine Cellars. What I recall was nothing big or bold or brash, but a lovely and linear fruit purity, enveloped in warmth.

Cory Empting, director of wine growing at Harlan Estate, Bond and Promontory, confirmed my hunch. He regularly tastes classic Napa Cabernets from the 1950s, '60s and '70s and finds in those wines a 'beautiful acidity, which brings tension'. With the Inglenooks from that time in particular: 'There's generosity of fruit with acidity. And sometimes the alcohol level is higher than quoted.' At some point in the mid-1990s, especially from 1997, he notes 'an inflection point: acidity no longer features'. It also needs saying that some of the acidity came from added tartaric acid; the (entirely legal) practice of regularly acidifying Napa Cabernets was discontinued at many properties in the 1990s.

The pursuit of ripeness – picking later and at 23.5 or 24 Brix rather than 21 or 22 – was not without benefits. Empting believes the 1980s mark something of a low point, not just in Napa but in agriculture more generally, with overuse of chemical fertilizers and bloated yields, and sometimes more focus on the work in the cellar than in the vineyard – but this is true in Burgundy and Bordeaux as well as Napa. Some of the Napa Cabernets of that period were austerely tannic, and simply not very enjoyable to drink. A reaction in the 'hedonic' direction or 'the pursuit of something softer and rounder, more approachable', as Empting puts it, was entirely understandable.

This clearly went too far, even though the diplomatic Empting wouldn't put it quite that way. And the typecasting of Napa Cab as big and lush rather than long and elegant was associated with Robert Parker, even though Parker made no secret of the fact that he liked lush and ample wines from Bordeaux as well as from Napa – so this was more a matter of Parker's palate than anything specific to Napa.

Typecasting can be infuriating (as the late Christopher Plummer would have agreed) and extremely hard to shake off. And the characterization of Napa Cabernet as being more about ripe fruit and soft tannins than enduring bone structure is not only erroneous but quite recent. All the same it seems to have become embedded.

The best Napa Cabernets are, of course, quite powerful wines, the product of unfailingly ripe grapes, often weighing in at more than 14.5% alcohol. But alcohol levels in Bordeaux in the last five or six very warm vintages have been similar. It's also the case that the Cabernet harvest in Napa, especially on the hillsides, often extends well into the second half of October or even November – so these can be later-ripened grapes than the Cabernets of the Médoc. What's even more important to my mind is that the classic Napa Cabs have always been graceful – structured as much by acidity as by tannin – as well as powerful. Gracefulness translates into drinkability, whereas sheer power wins points but not true friends.

Is there a way back – or a way forward which is also a way back? There are some in Napa, such as Dan Petroski of Larkmead, who believe the region may soon be too warm for some of its best-known varieties, including Cabernet and Merlot, to thrive. Petroski is busy planting Touriga Nacional and Tempranillo. Empting believes there is another way, and it's based on farming. 'As the vines get older you get better acidity, and the confidence to pick earlier.' He's joined by others in Napa, such as Steve Matthiasson, Cathy Corison and Aaron Pott, who maintain that (natural) acidity has always been a key feature of Napa Cabernet.

I've been speaking in very general terms about Napa Cab, but of course there is quite a bit of variety – no fewer than 16 nested AVAs within the broader Napa AVA, in fact – reflecting topography and geology. In particular there are distinctions between valley floor wines and hillside wines, between sedimentary and volcanic soils, between different sub-zones. More concentration, complexity and character is to be found in wines from hillside vineyards, most would agree; certainly that is Bill Harlan's strong conviction. Hillsides bring deeper, darker, more mysterious overtones. The tannins can also be harder to tame.

Thinking back to those classic 1978s, my feeling was that those wines seemed to reflect the landscape of Napa itself; a kind of North American idyll, grand but also gentle, with Mediterranean echoes. Civilized, even classical, but with haunting pan-pipe sounds from the rugged hills. What makes the greatest Napa Cabernets so special, to my mind, is the perfect balance of the civilized and the wild.

First published in *The World of Fine Wine* (2021) and reproduced here with kind permission of the publishers.

SCREAMING EAGLE

The rarity and expense of this renowned and sought-after Napa Cabernet blend means few have ever tasted this wine, let alone been granted entry into the winery. Adam Lechmere managed to do both.

ADAM LECHMERE (2012/2021)

The first thing you notice on turning off the Silverado Trail at the leaning mailbox that signals the entrance to Screaming Eagle is its normality.

I don't know what I expected. I suppose I thought the vines would be gilded, or perhaps the little groups of pickers standing around would be clad in gold braid and grey gloves, like hotel doormen. But it's all very normal.

Nevertheless, there was a certain magical quality in the air at 7.30am on this Monday in late October. Mist hung in the valley, a soft white fleece over the vineyards; it sat in pockets on the deep, red soil of the tiny Oakville property – what the founder Jean Phillips called her 'beautiful ranch with my precious little winery' – and all was rather fetchingly serene as I drove up in my rental car. Screaming Eagle isn't the most famous winery in the world, but its wines are certainly among the most sought-after. The simple reason for the renown of this 49-acre plot of Cabernet Sauvignon, Cabernet Franc and Merlot is the sheer rarity of its wines: the vines can yield a maximum of 850 cases each for its Cabernet Sauvignon and its newer Merlot-based wine, The Flight. (The first vintage, 1992, saw fewer than 200.)

The fact that Phillips guarded her privacy, giving no tastings and discouraging visits (to this day there is no sign on the property, the website gives nothing away, and we were asked not to photograph the entrance for fear of aiding its identification) only added to the mystique. There are dozens of great wine properties with a pedigree stretching back to the Middle Ages, producing arguably greater wines, but it's not impossible to visit any of the top names of Bordeaux, Tuscany or Burgundy. Finally – and it seems no Napa success story is complete without him – US critic Robert Parker gave the first vintage a perfect 100 points. Very quickly Screaming Eagle went from small hobby winery to an American sensation. Parker's notice also propelled Phillips' winemaker, Heidi Peterson Barrett, who was also working at Dalla Valle Vineyards, from respected consultant to seer.

ALLURE AND MYSTERY

Phillips sold Screaming Eagle in 2006 (for an undisclosed price estimated at around $30 million) and it is now wholly owned by US property billionaire Stan Kroenke, who has a majority share in London's Arsenal football club, as well as a clutch of basketball, hockey and American football teams (the NFL LA Rams and NBA Denver Nuggets among them). He was estimated to be worth $8.5 billion in 2018 and is listed by *The Land Report* magazine as the US's ninth-largest land owner. Also part of his portfolio is the 600-acre Jonata vineyard in the Santa Ynez Valley, which produces six high-end wines in the $50–170 range, The Hilt (185 acres) in the Sta Rita Hills for stellar-priced Pinot Noir and Chardonnay, and the prestigious Burgundy estate Domaine Bonneau du Martray.

At Screaming Eagle, Kroenke has augmented the tiny brick fermentation shed with a new winery building with 45 stainless-steel fermenters and barrel cellar. He's also undertaken a comprehensive survey of the land, but otherwise things continue much as they did. The price of Screaming Eagle is $1,150 a bottle, released mostly to the property's private mailing list, on strict allocations of three bottles per person. (People tend to drink one, cellar one and sell the third.) The estate Merlot, The Flight, reaches $550 a bottle. There is no second wine: what doesn't make the top Cabernet and Merlot blends is poured down the drain.

The wine quickly finds its level in the secondary market. As soon as they get to retail, bottles have doubled and tripled in price. The average price of the 2018 vintage in the UK is currently £2,685, while older vintages can fetch upwards of £15,000 a bottle. At auction, the wines tend to go in large format. Three magnums of Screaming Eagle 2015 went for $40,000 at Zachys in February 2021. Charity auction prices can be distorted but at the 2008 Auction Napa Valley a Chinese billionaire spent $500,000 for six magnums of the 1992.

The combination of Screaming Eagle's rarity and expense makes it one of the least-known wines in the world. Many of those who sell it have never opened a bottle. The directors of London merchant Fine & Rare, which holds about 30 bottles from various vintages (worth more than £33,000), have never tasted it. It's amazing how many people – veteran wine writers, sommeliers at world-class restaurants – have neither tried it nor visited the winery. A sommelier from Spain's El Bulli (a five-time winner of the World's Best Restaurant, closed in 2011) told me he'd been turned down for a visit, and had never even sniffed the wine. Even American rapper Jay-Z couldn't get an invitation. 'We'll happily meet him and show him the wine,' says general manager Armand de Maigret, 'but we prefer to do that elsewhere, not at the winery.'

For Screaming Eagle winemaker, Nick Gislason – who has been at the property since 2010 – science isn't enough. Flavour and mouthfeel are the most important factors in perfecting his wines, and these can only be judged by humans, not machines. Screaming Eagle has been a farm and vineyard in Oakville since the early 20th century.

PRIDE OF PLACE

Screaming Eagle is the archetypal Napa cult wine. But just as you don't hear the word 'garagiste' in St-Emilion anymore, the word 'cult', with its overtones of excess, now seems old hat. 'No one calls us that any more,' de Maigret says. 'We're a grand cru – a Napa first growth. Cults are wines that show the winemaker's hand. But here it's not the winemaker making the wine, it's the place.'

The place is Oakville; the soils rich, deep red, volcanic, and dotted with the sizeable rocks they call corestones. On the top of the hill these are pulled out of the ground as big as truck wheels, but down in the valley they are more manageable. Oakville soils are notably varied, and the Screaming Eagle terroir is no exception. 'The main sub-classes of soil include Perkins Gravelly Loam and Bale Clay Loam, comprising igneous alluvium,' explains winemaker Nick Gislason, who came from Craggy Range in Marlborough, New Zealand, via Harlan Estate down the road in Oakville. 'There is a considerable gravel and clay content, going from cobbles and gravels on the east side of the property to loam and clay on the west.'

This is some of the finest Cabernet land in Napa, and the team – de Maigret and Gislason (who directs both viticulture and winery work), David Abreu, who is on hand for vineyard emergencies, and Bordeaux's Michel Rolland who visits two or three times a year for blending – control the vines with forensic attention.

SELECTION IS KEY

The 46 acres of vines – Cabernet Sauvignon, Merlot, Cabernet Franc and some Sauvignon Blanc – are planted across all soil types, at an average density of 2,800 vines per acre. Merlot and Cabernet are planted on gravel and clay-based soils. 'Parcels from both sides, as well as the middle, make the blend,' Gislason says. Final yields range from a tiny one to three tons per acre, depending on the block.

AND THE WINES?

The 2008 (88% Cabernet Sauvignon, 7% Cabernet Franc, 5% Merlot) has a fresh spearmint nose with plum, blackcurrant, hints of smoke and musk. All repeated on the palate: bright and juicy with spice, lifted black fruit, liquorice, sandalwood and Parma violets. Fine, earthy and chilli-spiced tannins are perfectly integrated with fresh acidity. Very long.

The 2009 (tasted just after bottling) is the exact same blend. Dense aromas of blackcurrant, with hints of mint and capsicum. This weight follows through on the palate with powerful tannins giving a serious edge to the fruit. There is a note of spice and cedar, but the overall impression is of great precision allied with perfumed fruit. Hugely complex and very young. I wouldn't touch either vintage until at least five years have elapsed.

(At neighbouring Mondavi/Rothschild joint venture Opus One, they reckon on between two and three.) 'The blocks are so small and variation within them is key,' says de Maigret. They are picked in up to five different passes. 'We pick on taste, and use the refractometer [a tool to measure grapes' sugar levels] afterwards to confirm what we're tasting.'

The estate is divided into 45 parcels, each with its own fermenter. That way, 'we can select just the top lots for the blend, and are never forced through logistical constraints to combine lots earlier in the process'. So they select, and select, and select, from vineyard to barrel to bottle. 'By definition, blending lots too early results in an average,' Gislason says. 'And here, average simply will not do. We are looking to select only the top end of that bell curve, and that's only really possible after the true character of each plot has revealed itself.'

Tasting the 2010 vintage in barrel (the wines spend about 20 months in 75 percent new French oak), the different soil types come through. Cabernet from different blocks runs the gamut from blackcurrant, earth and tar to cedar, sandalwood and Parma violets. Gislason reckons Cabernet performs particularly well on 'the more clay and loamy soils, giving floral tones, a lot of cedar, and firm backbone with extraordinarily fine-grained tannin, and holds acidity remarkably well'.

With Merlot, the difference between the east and west side is pronounced: the west (more clay, picked a day after the east in 2010) is rounder and lighter than its gravel-grown sibling, its tannins more giving. 'The best Merlot typically comes from the gravelly east end of the property, and it's very atypical in character for Napa Merlot,' says Gislason. 'On that site, it picks up amazing floral characters and minerality, and seems to have a spirit that lies somewhere between the minerality and perfume of Bordeaux and the richness of Napa.'

The result is a wonderful wine. Whether it's worth even its release price is another question. I've certainly had wines quite as good for a fraction of the cost. But that's beside the point. What I was not prepared for was the elegance – 'cult' and 'Parker' seem linked with 'blockbuster'. It is perfumed and delicate, with a deep mineral backbone and splendid, exotic fruit. The outlandish sister of the more bookish Opus One, perhaps. As a confection of Napa and Bordeaux it is pre-eminent. All great wines aim to capture the spirit of place, but to find a wine that seems to contain the essence of two great regions is gratifying. Two great wines for the price of one. It's almost a bargain.

First published in *Decanter* magazine (2012); reproduced here with permission of the author and publishers.

THE POST-PARKER RECALIBRATION

Echoing Harry Eyres' call for a return to a classic style, Margaret Rand argues that far from being stuck in the steroidal era, makers of Napa Valley Cabernet are already embracing diversity and welcoming back 'bone structure' in their wines.

MARGARET RAND (2021)

Ten years is enough to change the perspective – or at least to detect that it is changing. The last 10 years in Napa have seen wine styles evolving against a roller-coaster of climate extremes: the rains of 2011, the long drought of 2012 to 2015, the floods and rains of 2017 and the heat of 2015, 2016, 2017 and 2019, culminating (at the time of writing) in the heat and fires of 2020, a year in which many top red wines were not released because of smoke taint. Remarkably, winemakers still find the energy to reflect on how they got here.

Where is 'here'? Even this is open to question, as instead of having one Napa style we have many; we have a degree of evolution in even the weightiest, most opulent Cabernets; we have a young generation of winemakers that can't afford $300 or $400 wines, and which doesn't buy into that world (most, it's true, are making wine in parts of California outside Napa, but not all, by any means); we have acceptance that Napa wine, even Napa Cabernet, does not have to be just one thing to be accepted. That's not bad for 10 years.

Steve Matthiasson of Matthiasson Wines, when I spoke to him, said: 'We drank Stag's Leap 1977 last night; it was 13% alcohol. That would be considered avant garde now, with its core of bright red fruit. But back in 1977 it was normal.' He's not the only one to look back a lot further than 10 years for a definition of what is modern. Brothers Graeme and Alex MacDonald of MacDonald Vineyards were brought up on Napa wines of the 1960s, '70s and '80s and love them so much that at Graeme's bachelor party: 'I wanted to drink nothing younger than I was, and a friend turned up with bottles from the 1970s and 1980s.' The only snag was that each bottle had to be finished before he would open the next, but that's another matter.

But ascribe the more diverse styles of Napa now to the influence only of a new generation, and Rory Williams of Frog's Leap Winery will not agree. 'My family has been blowing the trumpet for lower alcohol and higher acid for a long time, including during the steroidal era. Quieter voices like my parents' – like Cathy Corison and others – are now getting hot again.'

And Cathy Corison? What does she say? 'I had this wine fully formed in my mind 35 to 40 years ago, and I had to go to Rutherford Bench to find the grapes to make it… I hope I'm better at it now, but I'm still doing the same thing.

'It would be easier now to find acceptance. Not that my style has changed, but there is more diversity worldwide. Wine criticism is more democratic, and there are more voices. When I first released my wine in 1990, with the 1987 vintage, big, overblown styles were not really established. After a while they became dominant. There was a time when it was very difficult.'

The perspective now focuses on asking how this happened, and why. It's not just a matter of blaming Robert Parker. Nor, says Chris Phelps of Inglenook, did winemakers 'suddenly say, bigger is better'. Chris's view is that 1990 was the turning point: 'Suddenly we were astonished at the Brix levels we were getting' – which meant alcohol levels rising to 15% and over. Climate had a role in this, but so did the new clones planted after phylloxera. Says Graeme MacDonald: 'Almost all vines in that [previous] era had leafroll (*see* footnote on page 134). The chemistry of those early wines, the pH, was similar to today, but the alcohol was much lower… those very virused vines couldn't get above 22–23 Brix. They were far less "sugar machine" than vines are now.' Phelps adds that: 'Clones in Bordeaux are typically selected for early ripening, and we were all very proud in Napa to have

Voices for calm. Cathy Corison (*left*) makes age-worthy, elegant Cabernet that speaks of its place. At Frog's Leap, the Williams family harvest (*right*) to achieve lower alcohol and fresher acidity.

these carefully selected Bordeaux clones. They ripened earlier, and doubled down on the new style that was evolving. It was a double whammy: climate change, new clones and the embracing of a new style. Writers were taken by it, the public was enamoured, and it became Bigger is Better.'

And still is, sometimes. There has been no wholesale rejection of that style, even if the wines are less pruney and jammy than they were. There is still a market for big wines. Says Chris Howell of Cain Vineyard: 'People talk about change, but changes at the root – and the wine trade mechanism is very slow.' Producers in the luxury goods category are reluctant to risk change and, says Howell, 'wines that are in a given space create a culture in themselves. Drinkers are used to it, and like it.' He adds: 'It might take another decade for the most iconic wines to evolve slowly, but they will.' Matthiasson agrees: 'There's no reason why Napa can't continue to evolve, but the time isn't quite yet. Cutting-edge restaurants and wine shops can't move all this [newer style] wine yet. Steak houses, country clubs, fine dining, classic-style restaurants, still outnumber the cutting-edge ones. The path of least resistance, still, is to make what people expect.' And as Alex MacDonald says: 'The cost of entry in Napa is extreme. If big corporations come in, they make decisions on style based on economics. Or millionaires who've made money elsewhere and want a passion project or a glory project and hire top consultants – they have to protect their investment, and they want something safe.' There's a move towards other styles, but it's not a tsunami.

Picking earlier is part of it, though picking early is not. 'We want complexity via the perfect picking decision,' says Alex MacDonald. 'If you pick too early, you get simple flavours. Too late, and they're stewed. The lowest ripeness gives you wintergreen flavours; then bell pepper, sage, black olive. Then red fruit, raspberry and red cherry. Then black cherry, then violets, then prunes.' (We are talking about Cabernet here, obviously.) It is fair to say that wintergreen flavours – fragrant, even medicinal from this small, heather-like plant – are not a Napa objective: this is a place that naturally offers good ripeness, what Williams calls 'seamless texture and generosity of fruit at the core that can last for decades. It is uniquely Californian; it is something that Napa gives us'.

But that generosity of fruit should not be taken to mean that extreme alcohol and overripeness are part of Napa's terroir. Matthiasson briskly knocks that one on the head. 'All someone has to do, to achieve change in one vintage, is get a new winemaker in.' And what might that new winemaker do? Aron Weinkauf of Spottswoode points out that: 'In the end, winemaking is about intent... If people change what they're working for, they will change the winemaking.'

In the vineyard, you can address canopy management. 'St Helena is a fairly warm appellation, one of the two warmest in Napa Valley,' says Weinkauf, 'so we need shielding of fruit. We have a large, open, wide trellis, 75–100cm across. It has a vertical orientation but it's spread over a metre, so it's very shading. We leave the shoots on a bit longer, and there's no de-leafing on the afternoon sunny side. We use shade cloths on a quarter to a third of the vineyard. We had a misting system installed in 2012, and it worked really well, but we walked away from it because water is a finite resource, and it did more to keep the plants hydrated than to reduce the temperature.' Rows can be oriented for greater freshness; different rootstocks, different clones can be used; these things are for the longer term, but they cover a big part of the freshness picture.

In the cellar, just abandoning the addition of concentrate [to fill out the flavour and colour profile] is a big step, and one that not all the iconic wines have taken. As Phelps points out, concentrate adds not just to the weight of a wine but to its colour and sweetness, too. 'If wines are too smooth to be true, they probably are. And by "true" I mean honest. There is something devious about sweet wines. But Americans have a sweet tooth.'

The next 10 years, obviously, will see more changes. Some are looking to grapes other than Cabernet Sauvignon: Matthiasson grows the Italian red grapes Refosco and Schioppettino; the new generation at one major property is said to have wanted to plant Sicily's white Carricante grape, though wasn't allowed to do so. The MacDonalds say that 'you see a lot of places planted with Cabernet where Sauvignon Blanc should be, because they can charge $100 for Cabernet rather than $50 for Sauvignon'. A lot of the iconoclastic energy that looks to champion different grapes and different styles is in lower-priced parts of California: the Sierra Foothills, perhaps, or Mendocino, or Lodi. But not all. Some young winemakers come to Napa and buy grapes; some join their family companies in Napa and then have to decide whether to follow the established style or branch out. At Harlan Estate, son Will is now in charge of Promontory, a much fresher and more elegant wine than Harlan's proprietary red – though it was actually his father, Bill, who started the Promontory ball rolling.

The climate is likely to hand out more extremes, and become even less predictable. But Weinkauf points first to the 'incredible buffering capacity' of the Pacific. 'The offshore flow of wind is diminished, but it's still there. There will be radical extremes, but we will have better tools, and being able to react will be vital. We'll have more shade cloths, different irrigation, different cover cropping; all these will be tools that all will need and all will have to figure out how to apply. In some years they'll work for us, in other years they'll work against us. But the finances of Napa mean that this region can better sustain itself than less well-endowed appellations. When you can afford to improve your tool kit, you have more chance of surviving catastrophe.'

A

OF CALIFORNIA WINE

Snippets, snapshots and historical tidbits – an alphabetical selection of impromtu wine bites collected from some of our favourite authors to enhance this picture of California wine.

OC = Oz Clarke
HJ = Hugh Johnson
BSP = Brian St Pierre
BT = Bob Thompson
CT = Clare Tooley MW
SK = Susan Keevil

AVA (AMERICAL VITICULTURAL AREA)

A designated grape-growing region with unique geographical and climatic traits. Its wines will have consistent regional characteristics but – in contrast to the stricter French *Appellation Contrôlée* rules – they can be made from any grape variety. In California there are 139 AVAs, and counting... SK

BELLE & BARNEY, BOB & MARGRIT

A nod to the power couples that got it going. Belle and Barney Rhodes, and Margrit and Bob Mondavi (*see* 'M') pushed the tide of acclaim set in motion by the Judgement of Paris and spread word of Napa and its world-class wine across the globe. SK

CARNEROS, FOGGY ENOUGH FOR FIZZ

The southern end of Sonoma drifts away into what used to be a hillocky, hummocky sprawl of dun-coloured land slithering off into San Pablo Bay, good for little but grazing a few sheep or cows. And it is poor stuff – heavy, unfriendly clays, most of which spend half the summer shrouded in fog. Even the sheep need gloves and galoshes. And there's the magic. This is Carneros, slung across the bottom of Sonoma and Napa ... it was the first area to be developed in the 1970s and '80s, when wineries were looking for cool conditions to make Pinot Noir and, in particular, sparkling wine. OC

DISNEYLAND This well-known tract of southern California wasn't always a theme park; in the late 19th century it was home to a utopian-socialist vineyard cooperative, settled by German freethinkers who wished to escape the dirt and debauchery of gold-infested San Francisco: they christened the land Anaheim. At its peak, it made more than four million litres of wine annually, before a bacteria-bearing bug – later identified as Pierce's disease – killed off all the vines. Orange groves followed, earning the name Orange County. Then came the funfair crowds. (Something similar occurred to the north, when the abundant vineyard area of Santa Clara was replaced by a different sort of theme park: Silicon Valley.) BSP

FOG Let's talk about fog. Let's talk about ice-cold Arctic currents on the Pacific Coast. Let's talk about how you don't go swimming off San Francisco unless you're coated in goose fat and wearing a wetsuit. Why? San Francisco is on the same latitude as southern Spain, so swimming should be a breeze. But then it should also be too hot to grow decent wine grapes. It's the Arctic currents. These are 7–9°C colder than the surface waters off the coast. They well up during the summer and cause mighty fog banks that can be truly frightening. I've driven towards them and felt I was approaching the edge of the world, with hell just a gear change away to the west. OC

EAST OF... The importance of the east-west dynamic cannot be overstated, underpinning as it does Californian wine's diversity and potential for absolute quality. To the west, Santa Barbara, Sonoma and Mendocino are naturally cooled by their proximity to the Pacific Ocean. Further inland transverse wine valleys like Edna, Santa Maria and Ynez take full advantage of their east-west orientation to plant varieties that favour cooler climate as they funnel the ocean breezes from west to east. To the north, natural corridors like the Petaluma Gap do the same, with sea air bringing a fierce chill even on the hottest summer day. CT

GUILLAUME GRAPEVINE NURSERY California's growers get it right today. Long gone are the pre-Prohibition days of misidentification – mistaking a Durif vine for Petite Sirah, a Riesling for a Sylvaner – or planting on the wrong rootstock and dicing with the devastations of phylloxera. Guillaume is the *pépinière* to the stars, providing baby vines (own-rooted or otherwise) to all who wish to plant their vineyards anew. Aided by the University at Davis, down the road. SK

HANZELL A picture-perfect little winery in Sonoma, modelled on the Clos de Vougeot in Burgundy. Founded in 1953 by James Zellerbach, a rich Francophile, who imported California's first French oak barrels. His wines fooled French experts, who thought they were from Burgundy, thanks to the oak. The wines and barrels were sold to Joe Heitz in 1961, establishing Joe as a leading winemaker and creating a craze for French oak barrels. (Which endures.) BSP

ITALIAN SWISS COLONY A utopian co-op intended to give work and eventual ownership of vineyards to immigrant Swiss and Italians, who farmed a large swathe of vineyards (1,500 acres) along the Russian River in Sonoma. In 1885, Italian vines were brought in, introducing Barbera, Nebbiolo and Sangiovese to America; the wine became the first and most important brand from California. BSP

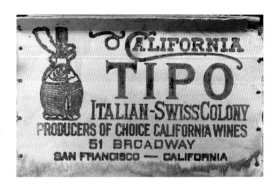

JUDGEMENT 'Chateau Montelena Chardonnay 1973: This is the wine that trounced the white burgundies at Steven Spurrier's blind tasting in Paris in 1976 and shocked the French! At seven years old: pronounced yellow; broad, sweet buttery nose, very much my style of Chardonnay; medium dry, fairly full-bodied, fine, rich, meaty nose, very good acidity.' *Michael Broadbent, writing in 1991.*

KRUG, CHARLES German newspaperman and freethinker who was taught winemaking by Agoston Haraszthy and established a winery in Napa in 1859. He made the best wine in Napa for more than a decade (earning the moniker 'wine king of the Napa Valley') and organized the winemaking community into an effective force in business and politics, then eventually went bankrupt. His winery and vineyards were bought and restored in 1943 by the Mondavi family. BSP

LONDON, JACK World-famous author, innovative farmer, passionate adventurer, proud socialist: he bought land in Sonoma County when he got rich, built a mansion ('Wolf House') and planted vineyards in what he called the Valley of the Moon – they're still there and still producing some of California's best Zinfandel. BSP

MENDOCINO A couple of hours' drive north of San Francisco, this is one of the state's oldest, and most famously offbeat, counties: it was the first to vote to decriminalize marijuana; first to ban genetically modified organisms; created its own language ('Boontling') and culture based on marijuana, microbreweries, artists' colonies, beautiful beaches, fishing and wine. Twenty-five percent of its wine grapes are farmed organically; all but a few of its 97 wineries grow first-rate Pinot Noir, and its sparkling wine is a notable standout, led by Roederer Estate and Scharffenberger (now owned by Roederer), both of which have been instrumental in setting a high standard since the early 1980s. BSP

OPUS ONE The meeting of two legends, Baron Philippe de Rothschild (Pauillac) and Robert Mondavi (Napa), who joined forces to create an exemplary Bordeaux blend from Napa Valley grapes. The striking winery (pictured below) reflects the prestige and ambition of the wine. SK

NEBBIOLO This is a grape variety that its supporters ecstatically describe as the finest in the world, yet which most wine drinkers have never dared to approach. It's the biggest question of all. What do we do with Nebbiolo?

Well there was a fellow to the south of San Francisco who knew just what to do. Jim Clendenen (1953–2021) was a great, straggly haired, jovial wine wizard who cheerfully made his own way down in the Santa Maria Valley. Pendulums swinging wildly from ripe to raw, from too much oak to not enough. Jim just got some chalk and wrote his maxim up on the wall: 'Say no to fads. Don't forget the past. And if you spill use salt and soda water.' And he could make Nebbiolo. Nebbiolo seems to love a mixture of sun and fogs. That's what it gets in Barolo's best vintages at home in Italy. That's what Jim got every year in the Bien Nacido Vineyards. The Santa Maria Valley's fogs are notorious. They blanket the vines so thickly each morning the vineyard workers need helmet lamps, but the fog always clears, the sun always comes out and Jim makes truly delicious Nebbiolo – sweet and sour, bitter and soft, as though the skins of damsons, black cherries and sloes have been squeezed dry. Jim left this in the barrel for five years – that's old school for you. And Jim said: 'If you have terroir, it's a miracle. I don't say I don't want terroir to dominate. But if terroir creeps out of the soil, it's a miracle. It's a dark and devilish plot.' OC

PARADISE CIRCA 1970 Napa is an American Indian word for plenty. The upper part of the Napa Valley, where civilization barely seems to have penetrated, is a sort of earthly paradise, so fruitful and green, so sculpted from the hills for protection and privacy and peacefulness does it seem to be. The broad valley floor is planted for mile after mile with vines, interrupted only for a big stone winery building in a grove of gigantic oak trees, or a quiet white house with sprinklers hissing arcs of water on a green lawn. The hills on either side are covered mainly with oak, or pine, or sometimes the bushy manzanita with its blood-red limbs. Only occasionally has the high ground been cleared to make way for a ramp, or a mound, or an amphitheatre of vine plants, which stand each on its own, not wired into hedges as they are in France. There is evidence, nonetheless, that the hills may give the best wine. HJ

QUAKES! On April 18th 1906, a massive earthquake, followed by fire, destroyed a third of San Francisco's buildings. Much of the 1905 vintage, stored in large barrels in waterfront warehouses, was used to help put out the flames... The great operatic tenor Enrico Caruso was staying at the Palace Hotel and was so traumatized by the event that he fled the city and never returned. BSP

RHÔNE RANGERS The name given to a group of young winemakers, mostly from Santa Cruz and the Central Coast, who champion wines made from Syrah, Grenache, Carignan, Mourvèdre and other Rhône grapes – Randall Grahm, Gary Eberle, Sean Thackery and Bob Lindquist exuberantly affirmed this counter-cultural movement in the 1980s and '90s. 'Fine wine that wasn't Cabernet Sauvignon or Chardonnay? The Sixties gave us permission!' BSP

SURVIVOR! Anyone sane would have knocked it down and built it again, but the 6.0 earthquake of 2014 wasn't going to defeat the Trefethens. Their 128-year-old, pumpkin-coloured barn for them symbolized the strength of family winemaking in Napa and refurbishment was the only option. It took 33 months and 'somewhere between $1 and $10 million' to get the job done. SK

TCHELISTCHEFF, ANDRÉ Born in Moscow in 1901, André was given a vineyard in Crimea on his first birthday. His family left Russia during the 1917 Revolution but André returned to fight with the anti-communist White Army during the Civil War. He was left for dead after being machine-gunned on a Crimean battlefield but escaped to Paris where he took up study at the Pasteur Institute with the fermentation and microbiology of wine on his mind. In 1938 he was invited to California by the founder of Beaulieu Vineyards, Georges de Latour, and

began to make history: his Cabernet Sauvignon 'Private Reserve' became a benchmark red that was regularly served at the White House. André advised in the making of some of California's most distinguished wines, with Robert Mondavi, Warren Winiarski, Mike Grgich, Rob Davis, Louis Martini and Rodney Strong counting him as their mentor. He became known as 'America's most influential post-Prohibition winemaker'. He died in 1994. SK

UC DAVIS The University of California's department of viticulture and oenology was established back in 1880, when its founders recognized the rich potential of the state for wine growing. The Davis campus came later, in 1935, quickly becoming a pivotal centre of wine learning as the country shook itself free of Prohibition. UC Davis is now also home to 'the greatest wine library in the world' (Hugh Johnson) with 30,000 rare books and manuscripts, valuable archives of research data and historic records in over 50 languages. SK

VINTAGES Years ago, the California wine industry devised a slogan to the effect that 'every year is a vintage year'. It has been pilloried ever since... I began harbouring unkind thoughts of my own about this sweeping claim when the Louis M Martini Pinot Noir 1958 did not turn out at all like its silky forerunner from 1957 . . . 'Every Year is a Vintage Year' had its genesis in a climate that ripens grapes for winemaking far more reliably than that in any part of Europe. [But] In Europe, a region and a grape variety are substantially synonymous. If the season is good, it is good for everybody, or almost everybody, within a region. In California, the erratic climate patterns have led to interplantings unthinkable in Europe. So for all who missed the 1957 and 1958 Pinot Noirs, almost any two consecutive years of any ageworthy variety will teach the practical lesson just as well! BT

WILD WEST WINE Paso Robles, California's fastest-growing AVA (with over 150 wineries installed since 2000), has a history stacked with outlaws, innovators and rule breakers (the bank robber Jesse James gets a mention) and that's very much the spirit in which its wines reach the market today. Expect rich, ripe reds, from brambley Zinfandel to textured Rhône varietals and peppery Cabernet blends. SK

XYLEM Forever conscious of drought and with necessity being the mother of invention, California's wine industry continues tirelessly to adopt sustainable viticultural practices and pioneer technology relating to water and its flow from soil through root and upwards through the vine's xylem (its internal water transport system). Finding the sweet spot between irrigation and evapotranspiration is the goal. (No stone is left unturned to achieve a balance, including rootstock experimentation, adjusting row orientation, managing soils, adopting new trellising and pruning techniques, dry-farming as well as the development of state-of-the-art sap sensor equipment and data collection.) CT

GEORGE YOUNT Beaver trapper and California pioneer, Yount was the first Euro-American settler in the Napa Valley. He planted Napa's first vineyard in 1839 and later gave his son-in-law, T L Rutherford, a land grant at Rancho Caymus as a wedding present – the land was immediately planted to vines. Both men created towns named after themselves: Yountville and Rutherford. BSP

WHITE ZINFANDEL California's dubious addition to the world's oversupply of indifferent rosé began as a wayward fermentation at Sutter Home winery and became wildly popular, probably because it was slightly sweet and not called 'rosé'. Cruder, sweeter versions soon abounded – a cloying pink apocalypse, the latest in a line of indignities inflicted on the grape, which had already been pushed into ersatz 'nouveau' Beaujolais, pulled into high-alcohol port-style sweeties,

squeezed into tannic, muscle-bound brutes hoping for bundles of points from the weary palates of critics, and (mercifully, only briefly) sparkling wine. Most of the confusion of its versatility has finally fallen away; the tide of White Zin may yet ebb, leaving Zinfandel as Mother Nature intended, red, deft, fine and inviting, lightly tart and companionable in every way (*see* Paul Draper's eloquent essay on pages 145–52, for a revealing rationale). We can also hope that some day the next generation may be able to celebrate a small but extraordinary irony: treated with care and respect for the grape and for consumers, Zinfandel actually makes a fine rosé! BSP

8

TERROIR...
THE DIRT MATTERS!

It was climate, in all its
Pacific-influenced permutations,
that first informed and guided
California's vine sites, but as
the state's relatively young wines
evolve, so the shape of the land,
its geology, elevation, aspect and
soil structure gain more sway.

JOHN SZABO MS (2021)
A Volcanic Tour of
California's North Coast

**ELAINE CHUKAN BROWN AND
LARRY WALKER** (2021)
Gold in Them Thar Hills

ELIN McCOY (2021)
Finding Napa's Top Terroir

A VOLCANIC TOUR OF CALIFORNIA'S NORTH COAST

Earth sciences are rarely, if ever, simple and the geologic tale of Northern California – as rich in events as a 19th-century Russian novel – is particularly stirring. The wines emerging from this mottled geology are themselves worthy of an epic chronicle, so sit back and hold on tight, while Master Sommelier John Szabo takes you on the seismic wine adventure of a lifetime.

JOHN SZABO MS (2021)

The most agreeable way to reach volcanic wine country is to head north out of San Francisco on Route 101. From downtown head towards Russian Hill (named for the 19th-century Russian ships that used to dock there), veer left towards the Presidio Park and the southern foot of the Golden Gate Bridge, then, as you head over that iconic crossing, you'll catch a glimpse of Alcatraz Island to the right and the wide expanse of the Pacific Ocean to your left… that is, if the thick, pea-soup fog that streams through the mouth of the bay with Swiss regularity doesn't obscure the view. Your best bet is to go mid-afternoon, after the morning fog has burned off and before late-afternoon breezes draw the cool, moist air back inland.

THE DEADLIEST FAULT…

Several kilometres into Marin County, take a detour towards the Pacific where Highway 1 splits westward and out towards Bolinas. Then northwest up the coast to Point Reyes and Bodega Bay. You'll be driving up a valley with hills rising to some 300 metres on either side, though the valley floor is not a flat trough like most; it's crisscrossed here and there by low ridges which break and fall, disrupting streambeds and sending their waters in opposing directions before running haphazardly into the low hills. There seems to be no logic to the landscape, no reason for ponds to be sitting halfway up hillsides and on the tops of low ridges.

But this is no ordinary valley; you're driving along the San Andreas Fault. Arguably the world's most famous fault line, geologists explain its notoriously deadly potential as the result of a 'triple junction': an area where three tectonic

It looks peaceful enough now, but Mount Konocti (*left*) sits atop a massive underground volcanic complex, the threat potential of which is classified as 'high'. Chunks of volcanic glass, obsidian (*right*), litter the surrounding vineyards, some as large as a VW Beetle.

plates converge. Not only is the Juan de Fuca plate sliding under the North American plate, but beginning some 25 million years ago, another joined the fray: the northward-drifting Pacific Plate. The three plates first met in southern California, at which point subduction – one plate sliding under another – was partially replaced with translation, one plate sliding laterally past another, giving rise to an unstable fault line; San Andreas is the major (but certainly not the only) fault line on the west coast of North America. The junction reached northern California some seven million years ago.

The volcanic activity in what are now Napa, Sonoma and Lake Counties must have been apocalyptic during this era, if the mute remnants of the astonishingly diverse volcanic ashes, tuffs, pyroclastic material, lahars (volcanic mudflows) and lavas have been properly read. Wave after wave of eruption from multiple vents in the earth's crust covered the entire region in a thick fiery outflow. There was no single, classically drawn volcanic cone – like Mount Etna or Mount Fuji – but rather larger, elongated fissures in the earth that threw up huge curtains of lava. Although it's tempting to look at, say, Mount Veeder atop the Mayacamas Mountains, or the perfectly shaped, truncated cone of Mount St Helena at the northern end of the Napa, as classic stratovolcanoes (conical-shaped volcanoes, built up from multiple hardened layers of lava over successive eruptions), neither was thus formed. Indeed, neither ever 'erupted' in the proper sense. These mountains, like the coastal ranges of Sonoma, the Mayacamas as well as the Vaca

Mountains on the western edge of the Napa Valley, and the hills further inland, are the result of 'up thrusts': crinkles in the earth's crust caused by pressure from the Pacific plate. Then a massive eruption covered northern Napa, Sonoma and Lake Counties – if the carbon dating on the trees of Sonoma's Petrified Forest is accurate, this was around 3.4 million years ago.

And since then, every few decades or so, as the tension between plates builds beyond what frictional resistance can hold, a correction is needed to release the pressure, and the earth heaves and shudders like a rumbling giant. In the San Francisco earthquake of 1906, the San Andreas Fault slipped nearly five metres, wreaking a havoc scarcely imaginable and virtually destroying the entire city.

And volcanic activity continues too. North of Napa and Sonoma, in Lake County, the 'Clear Lake Volcanic Field' features some of the youngest volcanic soils in California as well as two bona fide stratovolcanoes: the 1,440-metre Cobb Mountain and 1,306-metre Mount Konocti (*Koh-nock-tie*), both of which are home to vineyards. Mount Konocti (300,000 years old) last erupted as recently as 11,000 years ago – a geological blink of an eye – and its vineyards are littered with the remnants, including pieces of obsidian (volcanic glass) ranging from tiny stones to pieces the size of a Volkswagen Beetle. Konocti is officially listed as 'dormant', although sporadic, pre-eruptive-type earthquakes occur, and indeed the entire area sits on a massive underground volcanic complex, whose colossal magma chamber powers the world's largest geothermal power plant, producing enough energy to supply nearly a million homes. *The Volcano Hazards Program* of the US geological Survey lists Clear Lake as a 'high' threat potential.

WHAT IT MEANS FOR THE GRAPES, IN RUSSIAN RIVER...

But volcanoes alone don't tell the full North Coast story. For a view of other earth processes, leave San Andreas behind and turn back inland up the coast on Highway 116 from Jenner, where the Russian River meets the Pacific, and head towards Sebastopol (more nods to the Russians). Three million years ago, you would have been sailing in the Wilson Grove Sea, which gives its name to the formation of marine sandstones that now underly a large part of the Russian River Valley and environs. These sandstones have been weathering for millennia into the locally famous, sandy-loam 'Goldridge' soils, long favoured by wine growers for the creamy, silky Pinot Noir and Chardonnay they effortlessly yield. You'll find these wines from the cool, fog-prone, Pacific-influenced AVAs such as the Sonoma Coast, Russian River Valley and Green Valley. Sonoma does these varieties better, in more quantity and with more consistency, than any other region in California. Bottlings from the likes of David Ramey, Walter Hansel, Joseph Swan, Rochioli, Gary Farrell or Dutton-Goldfield will help convince.

...IN SONOMA

But then again, three million years ago, your attention would surely have been drawn to those erupting volcanoes to the east. From Mount St Helena south to San Francisco Bay, and extending from the east side of the Santa Rosa plain to the east side of Napa Valley, numerous volcanic cones and fissures were erupting not only dark fluid lavas, but also explosive plumes of ash. Sonoma's Chalk Hill AVA, for example, has no chalk at all, but instead is moored on whitish volcanic ash. Here, white grape varieties are particularly successful, especially Sauvignon Blanc and Chardonnay, though drinkers of more elegant-style Cabernets will also find happiness. This is not the cool finesse that comes with vineyard elevation – Chalk Hill's vines sit mainly above the fog line and thus experience more sunlight and warmth, plus longer days than those on the valley floor, and ripeness is rarely an issue – it is the intense varietal aromatic character with a balancing measure of acidity that is imbued by well-drained soils that allow a slow build of character. Wines from Chalk Hill Vineyard, Rodney Strong and Arnot-Roberts bear witness.

More of the so-called 'Sonoma Volcanics', the official name for the white ash formation, become evident as you drive towards the town of Sonoma itself, nestled in the valley between the Mayacamas Mountains to the east and Sonoma Mountain to the west.

Viticulture in the Moon Mountain AVA above Sonoma town is truly 'mountain viticulture'. To reach these hillside vineyards you'll climb off the valley floor along a narrow, windy road lined with oaks and fragrant laurels, past meadows, canyons and ridges, eventually sighting vines near the top of the Mayacamas range at nearly 700 metres above sea level on the Sonoma side of Mount Veeder.

The view is splendid: a sweeping vista of the entire Sonoma Valley. To the southwest you'll see the rare stretch of flat land that interrupts the Coastal Range; this is known as the Petaluma Gap, and sea-chilled air funnels in through this 25-kilometre (16-mile) break with branch-breaking urgency each summer afternoon. Wind is converted into wine in the recent (2017) Petaluma Gap AVA, featuring edgy Pinot Noir, steely Chardonnay and peppery Syrah from the likes of Kosta Browne, Keller Estates and Sojourn Cellars. In the distance, the skyline of San Francisco can be made out on a clear day.

Though also breezy, Moon Mountain is defined by its volcanics, in fact it is the only entirely volcanic AVA in Sonoma. The petition to gain AVA designation, granted in 2013, hinged on a three-million-year-old lava flow of andesite, basalt and rhyolite mixed with ash. The iron-rich red soils are most obvious in the historically significant Monte Rosso vineyard, now owned by Gallo, in which the oldest Cabernet Sauvignon vines in the United States – well over a century

The Moon Mountain AVA (*left*) is the only entirely volcanic AVA in Sonoma. It's iron-rich soils at the Monte Rosso Vineyard (*top right*) are home to the oldest Cabernet Sauvignon vines in the States – at over a century old, these vines provide valuable parent material for the country's top Cabernet heritage clones. In contrast, the weathered sandstones of the Sonoma Coast (*lower right*) are where Pinot Noir and Chardonnay vines thrive.

old – reportedly still root. Elsewhere, veins of white volcanic ash and rhyolite can be clearly seen. Erich Bradley of Repris Wines, who has been making wine on Moon Mountain since 1999, describes Cabernet Sauvignon grown on rhyolite as having both higher pH and higher acidity consistently, and more sour red cherry and carob flavours, while the Cabernets from basalts will have a darker and riper fruit character.

Directly west across the valley from Moon Mountain is the Sonoma Mountain AVA, where similar volcanic geology unfolded. The major difference here is aspect:

Sonoma Mountain vineyards mostly face east and thus capture the gentle morning sun above the fog line; they then rest in cool, late-afternoon shadows when vines across the valley are still weathering the penetrating rays of the sinking sun. Cabernet Sauvignon from here tends to have a firmness and tight structure not frequently found elsewhere in California, while the even cooler microclimates harboured in the irregular folds and crevices of the mountainside, especially on the western flank cooled by wind and fog from the Petaluma Gap, are well suited to white grapes such as Chardonnay, Sauvignon Blanc and Sémillon. Benziger, Laurel Glen and Kenwood wineries are notable residents.

You'll enter the Knights Valley AVA further north along Highway 128 above Calistoga in the morning shadow of Mount St Helena. This remote region is essentially a northern extension of the Napa Valley, separated only by a low gap in the Mayacamas Range. Continue on the 128, over another set of low-lying hills, and you'll descend into the Alexander Valley AVA, Sonoma County's most planted, which runs diagonally southeast-northwest along the upper Russian River.

As in the Napa Valley, the vineyards on the valley floor in both of these appellations root in mixed alluvial-sedimentary soil. But the vineyards that creep up into the hillsides, especially on the western flanks of each, trade topsoil for dark volcanic rocks and occasionally lighter rhyolitic stone and ash.

The Knights Valley's protected bowl shape, and the Alexander Valley's distance from the cooling Pacific, explain the relative warmth of these regions. Fog does not penetrate this far inland and summer temperatures creep up into the 30s with regularity, even at the higher elevations. This is mainly Cabernet and Zinfandel country, with a few exceptions from the southern (slightly cooler) end of the Alexander Valley where richer Chardonnays and barrel-aged Sauvignons perform well. Kendall-Jackson's dramatic Stonestreet Mountain Vineyards, Silver Oaks' Sonoma outpost and Clos du Bois are classics to visit, while prominent names with Knight's Valley labels include Ehret Family Vineyards and Napa-based Beringer and Peter Michael.

...AND IN NAPA

Leave Sonoma County behind on the 128 south from Knight's Valley and head into the Napa Valley towards St Helena: the road eventually becomes the famed Highway 29 – the Fifth Avenue or Champs Elysées of the wine world – where one grand winery after another lines the highway. Each building is a marvel of architecture, from classic French château to medieval Tuscan or renaissance palazzo, Persian palace, gothic German schloss, Mission-style ranch, or more contemporary variations on wood, glass and steel – the styles are as varied as the origins of the immigrants who have established the California wine industry here over the last two centuries.

It's easy to see what attracted early settlers here, and what makes the vines they brought happy. Even in January, the sharp mid-winter sun still casts warm light across the valley, first awakening the Mayacamas Mountains with its gentler morning rays before turning its attention towards the Vaca Mountains with its more energetic afternoon glare. Cheerful, yellow mustard flowers light up the rows between vines, as though to signal to the vines that another growing cycle is soon to begin. Meanwhile up in the hills, the sun fights its way through the thick overhead canopy cast by massive redwoods, alders and oaks, then bonsai-perfect, life-sized models of Douglas Firs and myriad pines, before finally dappling its light on the lower-lying shiny red wood of the manzanita trees and fragrant laurels.

For all the fashionable talk of 'cool climate pockets', the Napa Valley is a very warm and pleasant place to be year-round. People, and vines, clearly like the dry Mediterranean climate, where sunshine and warmth are rarely lacking. Thick vines grow happily in the rich soils of the valley floor, washed down from the hills over millennia by the Napa River. But the most compelling wines come from the hills, where volcanic soils meet other formations in a seemingly haphazard mash-up.

'Mountain wines', grown on poor, stony volcanic soils have a markedly different character than valley floor wines. Why? Well, paradoxically, volcanic soils, at least the best ones for wine growing, are relatively infertile. Despite lavas generally having a generous amount of the major macro- and micro-nutrients required by plants (potassium, calcium, magnesium, sulphur, iron, etc), they're not readily available to root systems. They must first be weathered into an available form, and then made soluble in water to be taken up nutritiously. But hillsides don't hold water, rainfall is low, and these relatively young soils/rocks are not ready to give up their nutrients just yet. The situation is compounded by the fact that little else can grow in dry, rocky, infertile soils, so there's very little build-up of organic matter that could otherwise store water and furnish nutrients.

In the end, the vines get a broad and balanced diet, but in small quantities (low fertility but without particular deficiencies), which triggers them to focus on ripening fruit – the raison d'être of a vine – rather than growing shoots and leaves. Simply put, semi-parched, semi-starved vines struggle, produce less fruit, smaller bunches, thicker grape skins (where most aromas and flavours are stored), and

A break in California's coastal mountain range necessitates one of its most famous bridges, the Golden Gate (*top left*). Through this 'gateway' pour the cooling fogs that soothe the vines as far north as Spring Mountain, to the northwest of Napa Valley – seen here at the Philip Togni Vineyard (*top right*) – and east of Napa town, the Coombsville caldera (*right,* with the cone-shaped Mount Veeder pictured centre). Both these vineyards are important for their volcanic bedrock and their resulting top-flight volcanic wines.

result in more deeply coloured, concentrated and structured wines with a broad range of flavours. They age magnificently. For a vine it's probably hell. For a winemaker, and wine drinkers, it's much closer to heaven.

NAPA AT ITS MOST ORGANIC

In broad terms, the most 'volcanic' regions in the Napa Valley are found in the AVAs of Coombsville, the upper slopes of the Stags Leap District, Atlas Peak, Howell Mountain, Spring Mountain, Diamond Mountain District and Calistoga, as well as an unofficial region, Pritchard Hill.

Coombsville lies in an ancient caldera to the east of the town of Napa, where variations of compacted volcanic ash alternate with solid basalt bedrock, as can be clearly seen at Caldwell Cellars. 'Shit, all we did for the first 10 years was haul solid rock out of here,' John Caldwell recalls of the early stages of developing his vineyards in the 1980s. Just west of the property is a still-active basalt quarry where hard rock is mined for the construction industry. Caldwell's underground cellar itself was carved into the hillside, and considering the difficulty in planting vineyards, he thought the construction company 'was going to have a hell of a time digging it out'. They quoted him by the metre rather than by the day, which he thought was idiotic on their part. 'But turns out they knew more than I did. The whole mountainside here was pure compacted volcanic ash, easy to dig. They got through four metres a day,' he smiles. 'They made good money off of me!'

It's easy to recognize the Stags Leap AVA north of Coombsville with its arresting palisades, the towering cliffs of pure basalt shaped like the pipes of an organ that rise above vineyards. The vines planted higher up in these foothills of the Vaca Mountains dig right into the weathered basalt, as seen at Shafer's Hillside Select, Cliff Lede's Poetry, Silverado or the Stag's Leap Wine Cellars' vineyards, yielding broad-shouldered, dark and sumptuous Cabernet.

Further east above the Stags Leap AVA at the top of the Vaca Range is Atlas Peak AVA, where some of the highest and most rugged Napa vineyards are planted, at over 800 metres. There are only two access roads to this noticeably cooler and isolated area: Soda Canyon Road, which runs up from the Silverado Trail, and a bit south, Atlas Peak Road, off Hardman Lane. Both twist and turn for some 25 kilometres (15 miles) up into the mountains flanked by red-tinged basalt soils. Atlas Peak is home to the Krupp Brother's (now Gallo-owned) Stagecoach Vineyards, one of Napa's most celebrated and extensive sites, which supplies grapes to many wineries. Italy's greatly admired Piero Antinori also chose Atlas Peak to establish his Napa outpost, Antica Napa Valley.

North of Atlas Peak at the top of the Vaca Range are two more eminently volcanic regions. Pritchard Hill lies above the Silverado Trail and here such revered vineyards as Colgin, Dalla Valle, Ovid and Continuum stand proudly. At the very top of the hill, at Ovid, there's virtually no topsoil: hard volcanic bedrock breaks through the surface like rugged islands of basalt in a shallow sea. Echoing John Caldwell, Ovid's winemaker Austin Peterson recalls the difficulty of planting a vineyard where the topsoil is measured in centimetres and 'hundreds of tons of volcanic rock had to be removed just to get vines in the ground and allow tractors to plough without constantly breaking down'. The vineyard for another of Napa's most sought-after wines, Screaming Eagle, sits below Pritchard Hill down towards the valley floor, though the magic of this site is explained by the slice of volcanic bedrock that sloughed off the mountain at some point in the distant past, creating a slightly raised patch of rocky land above the richer alluvial valley soils.

Howell Mountain, just North of Pritchard Hill, is likewise a difficult place to access, rising up to 700 metres above the valley. That's high enough to be above the inversion layer (a common deviation from the normal decrease of temperature with altitude, in which a higher layer of the atmosphere instead becomes warmer). This means cooler days and warmer nights than the valley floor, ensuring a long, slow, even ripening period. Soils are split between volcanic ash and tuff, and weathered, iron-rich red basalt. Although Howell Mountain sees twice as much rain as the valley floor, these soils are incapable of holding much water, ensuring that the vines struggle (they have to dig deep to quench their thirst) and that wine growers can micro-manage irrigation to obtain small, concentrated berries. Arkentstone, Cade, Cakebread, Duckhorn, Dunn, Robert Craig are just some of the celebrated wineries with vines on Howell Mountain.

Across the valley in the Mayacamas Mountains at the northern end of Napa Valley, Spring Mountain District, Diamond Mountain District and Calistoga are also sources of top-flight volcanic wines. This side of the valley is noticeably cooler and greener, thanks to its eastern-facing flanks that welcome the gentler rays of the morning sun. The flora is conspicuously different: tall, moss-covered redwoods and pines contrast with the ground-hugging, scruffier, desert-like shrubs of the hotter, west-facing side of the valley. Spring Mountain is named for several natural springs that provided water for the residents of St Helena in the 19th and early 20th centuries.

The AVA counts upwards of 30 wineries, sharing just 740 acres. Most, thus, are small, family-runs vineyards. Not all are on volcanic soils; some lie on marine sediments – the so-called Franciscan Formation – like Cain Vineyard, while others lie on undulating hills or terraced slopes carved out of andesite volcanic rock, announced by Andesite Vineyards. Other prominent producers include Barnett, Price Mountain, Smith-Madrone, Spring Mountain Vineyard, Stony Hill and Philip Togni.

Diamond Mountain gets its name from the bits of crystals of volcanic origin that are mixed in with red basaltic soils and white volcanic ash, AVA features touted most conspicuously by Diamond Creek's Red Rock Terrace and Volcanic Hill vineyards, respectively. Neighbouring Dyer Vineyard's tiny 2.3-acre site sits on rhyolitic tuff. Although two dozen or so Diamond Mountain District-labeled wines are produced annually, only about half a dozen wineries are located on the mountain itself, including Schramsberg's J Davies vineyard, Reverie and Von Strasser.

The entire Calistoga AVA sits on volcanic bedrock, with the lower slopes characterized by more alluvial soils and the upper slopes more purely volcanic. Magnesium- and calcium-rich geothermal hot springs in the area reflect the past, and continuing, volcanic activity beneath the earth's surface. It's often believed that Calistoga is the warmest region in the Napa Valley, and while the valley's hottest spot is indeed near Bale Lane at the AVA's southern boundary, there is some respite. A gentle gap in the Mayacamas allows cooler, marine-influenced air from the Russian River to funnel in, dropping afternoon evening temperatures to acid-retaining levels. Araujo, Bennett Lane, Clos Pegase, Chateau Montelena and Storybook Mountain Vineyards are some of the prominent locals making rigidly structured, ageworthy wines.

End your journey with a soak in one of Calistoga's myriad natural hot pools, whose magical waters have been enjoyed by the area's original residents, the native American Wappo tribe, for thousands of years. Calling the land *coo-lay-no-maock* (the oven place), they would steam and soak in the hot springs, believing that the geysers had healing powers. As you heal, you might reflect on Northern California's tumultuous geological past, and what a rich palette of soils it has left behind for contemporary vintners. And enjoy the current calm; we know it's only temporary.

GOLD IN THEM THAR HILLS

Elaine Chukan Brown and Larry Walker explore the lesser-known terroirs of the San Francisco Bay Area, Lodi and the 'Gold Rush' foothills of the Sierra Nevada, discovering inland wines that still breathe in the icy air of the coast and lay their own claim to cool-climate fame.

ELAINE CHUKAN BROWN AND
LARRY WALKER (2021)

It is Napa Valley and Sonoma County that make California wine famous. It can be surprising, then, to learn that Napa grows a mere four percent of California's wine, Sonoma around six percent. Both have farmed wine grapes since the early 1800s, and each was important in helping to develop fine wine in California. Even so, their rise to such prominence is relatively recent.

In the late 1800s, they shared the spotlight with regions like Livermore, Saratoga and Santa Clara Valley in the eastern and southern stretches of the San Francisco Bay, while field blends (wines made from mixed vineyards and multiple grape types all harvested together) filled inland parts of the state such as Lodi and the Sierra Foothills.

By the mid-1900s vineyards and family farms dominated these parts of California with the city of San Francisco at their epicentre. But as the population of the northern parts of the state increased, land surrounding the San Francisco Bay was taken over by family homes with little adjacent space for vines.

THE SAN FRANCISCO AND SAN PABLO BAYS

Today, the Livermore AVA remains one of the few hold-outs of wine-growing in the San Francisco Bay area. It didn't get its first vineyards until the 1880s, which meant it was established without the heavy influence of the Spanish Missions: its first vines were not planted for sacramental reasons but specifically with an interest in fine wine.

In 1883, the Wente family established itself in Livermore, soon after developing its eponymous selection of Chardonnay clones that helped transform white wine growing across the state. Today, Wente remains the oldest continuously operating, family-owned winery in the United States and is run by its fourth and fifth generations, still centred in Livermore, while also farming other stretches of the California Central Coast further south.

Also in Livermore, Charles Wetmore established what at the end of the 1800s was one of California's most important vine nurseries importing cuttings from across Europe for both red and white wine grapes. In 1982, Livermore became one of California's first federally recognized AVAs. Today it is primarily known for hearty red wines.

Also in the late 1800s, and just around the corner from Livermore, Contra Costa County was an important foothold for red wine field blends: its persistent cooling winds helped lower disease pressure and keep a vibrant acidity in the wines. Contra Costa survived the phylloxera crisis thanks to its deep granite-based sands, which helped the vines thrive while most of the oldest vineyards in the state fell to the grape louse. Zinfandel as well as Mataro and Carignan were grown but the grapes were regularly trucked out after harvest as there was no local winery to vinify them, or to champion the region. Contra Costa was never formalized as an AVA and merely appears as the county name on a label.

As the pressure of the housing market steadily pushes east, more and more Contra Costa vineyards are disappearing. Those that remain are celebrated by producers such as Bedrock, Turley, Sandlands and others who value old vines.

A little further south, in Saratoga, Paul Masson founded his eponymous winery with cuttings he brought from Burgundy. His inspiration was the work of mentor, Charles LeFranc. LeFranc had founded Almaden winery and improved the quality of viticulture through the Santa Clara Valley with knowledge he brought from France; then in the 1880s he hired Masson as winemaker. Masson's own winery was founded for sparkling wine in 1882 and by the early 1900s he was heralded for his work making 'California Champagne' (*see* page 138). Eventually Masson chose instead to farm on the steep slopes of the neighbouring Santa Cruz Mountains where in the 1940s Martin Ray continued his work by making still Pinot and Chardonnay under the name Mount Eden.

A mere mountain away, and founded in the 1950s, Ridge Vineyards would also help make the Santa Cruz Mountains famous with its focus on Bordeaux varieties and old-vine Zinfandel. In the early 1980s, the Santa Cruz Mountains became the first appellation in the United States to be defined by elevation. More recently, Rhys has established a foothold in the region focused primarily on Pinot Noir in one of the cooler parts of the area.

What these regions surrounding the San Francisco Bay have in common is their shared dependence on the bay itself – on the interaction of the inland Central Valley with the Pacific Ocean. It is this interaction that determines the growing conditions of an enormous portion of the state's wine.

Fog drifting in over the vineyards of Carneros from San Pablo Bay. Carneros is first in line for the fog and the 'Petaluma Express', the brisk wind that hurtles in from the Pacific every afternoon, cooling the vineyards and advantageously prolonging the grape-growing season.

THE CENTRAL VALLEY AND THE DELTA-BAY COMPLEX: CALIFORNIA'S GREAT LUNG

More than half the grapes grown in the state of California are farmed in the Central Valley. It is a region rarely discussed in serious wine circles as its high-yielding vineyards contribute primarily to bulk wines and less expensive bottles at the bottom of liquor stores shelves. Yet its geographical presence proves to be one of the most important in California wine.

Between the Coastal Mountain range in the west and the Sierra Nevada mountains in the east, the Central Valley extends an enormous two-thirds the length of California, running parallel with the Pacific coastline for a full 650 kilometres (400 miles). Set inland, it is largely protected from the wet and cooling influence of the ocean, and is instead dominated by a hot and dry climate through most of its length.

Properly speaking, the Central Valley is actually the merging of two valleys cut by California's two largest rivers – the Sacramento in the northern half and the San Joaquin to the south. They converge to form the California River Delta and pull soil and water down from the Sierra Nevada onto the valley floor, ultimately flowing into the San Francisco and San Pablo Bays (together called the

San Francisco Bays). At their far western boundary, these bays open to the Pacific Ocean through a break in the Coastal Mountains called the Golden Gate. One of California's most famous bridges takes its name from this waterway as it adjoins Marin County (to the north) and the city of San Francisco. Just outside the Golden Gate churns one of the Pacific Ocean's coldest and most powerful currents, the California Current. This is what keeps the northern coast of California cool as it pulls in the chill waters that flow down from Alaska.

The impact of the Sacramento-San Joaquin River Delta and San Francisco Bays on the weather for the rest of the state is profound. As temperatures increase in the Central Valley over the course of a day, hot air rises. The volume of air lifting off such an enormous valley floor every afternoon creates a powerful vacuum effect at ground level. To resolve this vacuum, air is literally pulled in through the only place it can be pulled, the Golden Gate break. As a result, every afternoon, at the hottest part of the day, strong westerly winds rush over the bays and through the delta, cooling the extended region with cold air from the Pacific. As the sun goes down, so does the wind. Air settles and most nights a fog rolls in.

The air currents generated by these daily temperature changes can be thought of as a daily breathing pattern. As temperatures lift and fall in the Central Valley, they act a little like our diaphragm, pulling air through the great lung of the bay and delta complex. In the windiest stretches, enormous turbines generate electricity for the northern parts of the state. Moving east, where the winds are still persistent but not quite as harsh, these currents are known as the Delta Breezes.

These regular breathing motions change the fog and wind patterns of not only the Central Valley but all of the interconnected regions as well. Fog and cooling late-afternoon breezes move into the southernmost parts of Napa Valley and the Sonoma sides of Carneros. Powerful winds blow across Contra Costa, significantly cooling the otherwise warm region. Air currents pick up in Livermore and the entire San Francisco Bay area. Air currents shift in the Santa Cruz Mountains. As winds pick up across the delta, they push directly over Lodi in the Central Valley all the way to the face of the Sierra Foothills.

LODI

Though the Lodi AVA is found around 115 kilometres (70 miles) inland from the ocean, thanks to the opening at the Golden Gate, it can still properly be understood to be coastally influenced. It sits at the intersection of the Central Valley with the Sacramento-San Joaquin River Delta and, as a result, lies directly within the cooling path of the daily winds. This means both that its peak daytime temperatures are significantly lower than the hottest parts of the Central Valley, and that its overall temperature range is narrower.

Lodi's relationship with the delta also means that unlike a lot of the state, it has easy access to water and a naturally high water table. Its soft, sandy, alluvial soils and relatively flat lands were a magnet to family farmers who flocked to the region. The naturally breezy conditions lowered disease pressure by keeping crops comparatively dry, enabling easier farming.

As the Mission era ended in the 1830s, vineyards were either abandoned or slowly upgraded to include newer varieties arriving in California. Many of the vineyards established from the 1850s onwards were planted with field blends, bringing together as great a mix of varieties as the growers could source. Established in the 1870s, Lodi went on to plant the widest range of grape varieties in all California – and its vineyards, today, hold the highest concentration of old and own-rooted vines in the state.

More than 100 different wine grapes are grown here. As in the rest of the state, Chardonnay and Cabernet Sauvignon are the most planted. But the region is famous for Zinfandel and has a high proportion of it. What is likely the oldest Cinsault vineyard in the world, planted in 1886 at the Bechthold Vineyard, can also be found here.

Today, it is the preponderance of fourth-, fifth- and sixth-generation family farmers that has given Lodi its unique character. Glimpses of their investment into its heritage can be found throughout the region not only in their preservation of older vineyards but also in the beautiful, old-growth oak groves and monuments built in the centre of town.

The soft, sandy soils of Lodi, easy to farm, were a magnet for grape growers in the 19th century. Many of the evergreen California live oaks (namely the holm oak *Quercus agrifolia, pictured below*) seen then still dot the vineyards today – these trees can live for 1,000 years and more.

Historically, most growers sold grapes to winery cooperatives and then later to the Gallo brothers. During Prohibition, grapes were packed in grape boxes and carried by train to home winemakers in the east. In the 1970s, Robert Mondavi returned to the region where his parents lived and started Woodbridge Winery. Partnering with Lodi's grape-growing families, Mondavi instigated varietal wine growing and helped increase the quality of grape farming in the region. His efforts ensured that Lodi became known not only for its range of grapes but also for its quality wine, made locally. Even so, it would take until the late 1990s for Lodi-based wineries to truly become established.

While Lodi avoids the heat found in the rest of the Central Valley, it still receives plenty of sun exposure. The combination of sun with the cooling influence of the delta lend to wines both abundant fruit expression and mouthwatering acidity. So, though the region is known for red wines, many of its most exciting wines are crisp, high-acid whites. Grower Markus Bokisch brought in Albariño and other Iberian varieties, which have proven to do very well in Lodi. His Garnacha Blanca is a standout. Before him, Rip Ripken planted an enormous range of varieties from all over the world, citing simple curiosity as his motivation. The Koth family began to establish what seems to be the biggest collection of Austrian and German varieties in the country in the 1990s, and Ron Silva focused his efforts on Portuguese cultivars. Producers such as Acquiesce and Klinker Brick have also shown the Rhône whites do very well here.

THE SIERRA FOOTHILLS

Just beyond Lodi, on the far eastern side of the state, the Sierra Foothills AVA rises up the slopes of the Sierra Nevada Mountains. This growing region includes portions of eight different California counties: Amador, Calaveras, El Dorado, Nevada, Mariposa, Placer, Tuolumne and Yuba. Though the total acreage of the region is enormous, stretching more than 260 kilometres (160 miles) north to south, the planted vineyard acreage is just around 5,700 acres.

The growing conditions in the Sierra Foothills are rugged. The AVA reaches 300–900 metres, thanks to which it is often inundated with winter snow. As spring temperatures rise, the snowpack melts, filling the river system with fresh water from the mountains which becomes part of the state's year-round supply.

The mountain conditions mean soils have very low fertility, slopes tend to be steep, and yields are low. Soil parent materials vary significantly, including a mix of shale, schist, granite and various iron-rich volcanics, and in some areas, limestone can be found beneath the surface. Thanks to the snow-melt much of these mixed parent materials – especially the decomposed granite – are carried downstream into the Central Valley, and along the waterways of Lodi, the

California Delta and the San Francisco Bays. The sandy soils of Contra Costa and the Mokelumne River in the heart of Lodi originate in these Sierra granites.

Most grape growers who have settled in the area have done so appreciating the general sense of remoteness, peace and isolation found throughout the mountains. They have also appreciated the far lower land prices found here compared to the more well-known regions of California.

It was people relocating to chase the Gold Rush that first brought vines to the foothills in the 1840s. Old gold mining towns with their tiny streets and assorted histories can still be found tucked behind the mountain bends and windy roads of the Sierra Foothills. Here, historic sawmills and water wheels are often seen, while street- and shop-names still allude to the original miners. A few ranches are still farmed by the families who first settled them. One example includes the oldest vineyard in North America. The Deaver family still farms the Mission vines they first planted in Amador County in 1854. The oldest Zinfandel in the state, established in the late 1860s, is not far away in Amador's Shenandoah Valley.

With such a low vineyard acreage, there are only a few wineries growing and making wine within the Sierra Foothills. In Amador, Scott Harvey found success with a blend of Chenin Blanc and Viognier, as well as Zinfandel and Barbera. In the far northern stretches of the AVA, Renaissance Winery has focused on Bordeaux and Rhône varieties since the late 1970s. Nearby, its former winemaker, Gideon Beinstock, at Clos Saron, proves that cooler parts of the region can even grow intriguing Pinot Noir. Rhône varieties have made their foothold. Terre Rouge and La Clarine Farm each helped bring attention to Syrah. Further south, in the Calaveras area, Rorick Heritage Vineyard and its associated Forlorn Hope winery grow their own wines and have also sourced varieties such as Tempranillo, Barbera and racy, high-acid white varieties from the French Alps.

Wines from the Foothills across all varieties reflect the rugged and rustic character of the region, while also tending towards layers of earthy, forested flavours rather than merely fruit, always with a strong structural component.

THE FUTURE OF CALIFORNIA

As water levels, warming temperatures and increasing land prices have become an issue in the state of California, both the Sierra Foothills and Lodi have become important alternatives to the Bay area sites being encroached on by housing. Land prices are more affordable in both, and thanks to winter snows, water remains available as well. While the greatest increase of interest and change for wine growing in California has tended to focus on newer coastal regions, the coastal influence in a place like Lodi and the mountain effect of the Sierra Foothills make them distinctive alternatives for growing fine wine.

FINDING NAPA'S TOP TERROIR

Unlike the gravelly Médoc (Bordeaux) or the limestone-based Côte d'Or (Burgundy), the Napa Valley is an area of highly complex soils and intricate climate patterns that are only starting to be understood, so how do we make sense of it all? Elin McCoy gets to the heart of the matter and asks which are better, the 'benchlands' or hillsides?

ELIN McCOY (2021)

On my first visit to the Napa Valley, the sheer beauty of the landscape overwhelmed me: the long verdant valley cupped by two mountain ranges with Mount St Helena at the northern end; the undulating lines of vines on the benchlands and hillsides. It wasn't yet spring, but the land seemed to pop with the colours of soft green grass and the bright, intense yellow of mustard flowers blooming between rows of knobby, twisted, gnarled vines.

In the mornings I woke to vistas of low-lying fog, layers of white that seemed like long feathers from some huge, mythical bird stroking the landscape. The rocky hillsides of the Vaca Range to the east and the dark forested slopes of the Mayacamas Mountains to the west were highlighted in blue light until the sun's rays chased away the fog and revealed a cloudless sky. Only gradually did I come to differentiate what makes up the valley's terroirs – stones and dirt, elevation and exposure, fog and wind, water, temperature and climate.

Now, when I drive from point to point, I'm continually struck by how much geological drama is packed into the 56-kilometre long, six-kilometre-wide viticultural core of this valley. Collisions of huge tectonic plates and violent eruptions over millions of years have formed wrinkles in the earth's crust that became the Mayacamas and the Vaca ranges, leaving fingerprints in bedrock that vary from coarse sandstone to marine conglomerate to volcanic basalt and tuff. And slowly, continuously, all this eroded, transforming into the soils we see in vineyards today – silt and clay, sand and gravel, rounded cobblestones and huge boulders.

For a small, compact valley, Napa is surprisingly diverse, with half the world's soil orders and more than 100 soil variations. 'We're talking about shades of colour that most other wine regions would kill for,' Matt Clifton, the winemaker

Peter Newton's terraced vineyards occupy a fifth of its 490-acre estate, vines interspersed with native forestland. His wines capture the intense berry flavours typical of Napa's hillside vines.

at Chateau Montelena in Calistoga, told me recently. Added to this are variations in climate you might not expect. In a weird reversal of California's normal hot south, cool north, daytime temperatures at the valley's northern end in Calistoga can be 10 degrees higher than in its southernmost appellation, Carneros. Cool maritime air and fog drifting in from the Pacific Ocean through the Golden Gate at San Francisco, and then up through Napa are what cause this.

WHAT'S IN IT FOR THE VINES?

A video on geology and wine in Napa produced in 1990 by geologist Jonathan Swinchatt inspired the Napa Valley Vintners, a trade association of the valley's wineries, to commission the first scientific studies of the region's geologic history, soils and climates. The result was a report in 2002 and a book in 2004, *The Winemaker's Dance: Exploring Terroir in the Napa Valley* co-authored by Swinchatt and geologist David Howell. This was long after the Napa Valley became California's first AVA (American Viticultural Area) in 1981. But back then, the word 'terroir' wasn't on anyone's lips and few even knew what it encompassed. The idea that wines should express a 'sense of place' was barely discussed. And in truth, even now, the boundaries of many of Napa's 16 AVA sub-regions don't reflect the many terroir variations that exist within them.

Vineyard sites in Napa's highest mountain AVAs, for example, sit at widely different elevations, from 120 to more than 800 metres, well above the fog line.

Howell Mountain is the rockiest, with warm mornings and cool evenings. Atlas Peak is cooler, with brick-red soils rich in iron, and yet nothing is as simple as this seems. On Diamond Mountain, Diamond Creek winery's three single vineyards are close to one another but have three distinct soil types – white volcanic ash, shallow gravel and iron-rich red earth.

'Describing the terroir of Mount Veeder,' says winemaker Aaron Pott of Pott Wines, 'is like asking somebody to talk about the colours of the ceiling of the Sistine Chapel. There are so many different sites. Mine, at 488 metres, is one of the weirdest. Schist and sandstone in my vineyards come from a cold-water sea floor that was once off the coast of California. There is not a single volcanic rock on my property and I live on the side of what was once an active volcano!'

Great variability also exists between the east and west sides of AVAs that straddle the valley, according to David Howell, who has been writing geological narratives of vineyards in different parts of the valley for nearly two decades. In west Oakville, known for wineries like Harlan Estate and Opus One, the soil is sedimentary, gravelly. To the east, in the shadow of the Vaca range – where you find Dalla Valle, Backus and Screaming Eagle – it's volcanic in origin. A massive collapse sent iron-rich debris down the slopes and the result is red earth that can glow on a sunny day. The vines that catch the full brunt of this sun yield wines that express their terroir with a highly distinctive, salty mineral tang – a wine-maker once dramatically described it to me as 'the taste of blood'. According to the US Department of Agriculture, Oakville alone has 16 types of soil.

So the complexity of terroir in Napa makes it far more difficult to talk about than, say, Chablis' Grand Cru vineyards on their Kimmeridgian soil, or the lime-stone slopes of Burgundy's Côte d'Or or the gravel terraces of Bordeaux's Médoc. There is simply no way to generalize.

HILLSIDES? OR BENCHLAND?

The most serious Napa terroir debate today concerns which sites make greater wines: vineyards on steep hillsides or those on the gently sloping benchland of the valley floor? There are passionate winemakers and great wines on both sides.

The benchlands are where you find the most historic vineyards, the ones that have their roots in the 19th century – like Oakville's To Kalon – and lie on large alluvial fans. Geneviève Janssens, winemaker at Robert Mondavi Winery, once showed me a detailed geology chart to illustrate how they were formed. 'Rain and floods carried rocks, gravel and silt down the mountain slopes to lower, flatter ground; they deposited the heaviest rock close to the hills – those blocks usually make the best wine,' she explained. 'Lighter-weight gravels, loam, then silt spread out from there in a fan shape.'

In a phone conversation, David Howell outlined how many defined fans there are in Napa, from Oak Knoll to Yountville to Rutherford to St Helena. These are anything but uniform because each has a different source. In west Oakville, for example, there are several large ones; in east Oakville, they are smaller and scattered. Generally, their well-drained soils plus humidity from the foggy mornings give plush-textured, opulent Cabernets with bright cassis fruit, more acidity and finesse, and elegant muscularity.

Among those touting benchlands over hillsides are Pomerol grandee Christian Moueix and winemaker Tod Mostero of Dominus, whose Napanook vineyard, first planted in 1838, sits on one of those classic alluvial fans. Moueix once claimed he slept in the vineyard to get the feeling of the place. The gravelly soil, Mostero says, gives the wines their silky texture. But he raises another idea, that Moueix's devotion to dry-farming (using no irrigation) is essential for greater expression of terroir in the wines. Napanook has plenty of water, in the form of underground springs, that keep vine roots just damp enough.

Hillsides also have many advocates, like Stu Smith, who founded Smith-Madrone winery on Spring Mountain in the early 1970s. As we took in the splendid view over his vineyard at 580 metres elevation, he insisted: 'All things being equal, the best grapes come from the mountains.' Boulder-strewn hillsides have drier, thinner soils, more sun, less humidity, cool days and warm nights, which translate into smaller berries, lower yields and a later harvest. Napa's mountain appellations mean Cabernets with intense berry and mineral flavours, harder, more powerful tannins, big structure. And if you look at where the best wines are based on price, an awful lot of them come from hillsides.

Each mountain is different, though, and for great terroirs to shine you have to plant the right grape variety.

When you walk vineyards on Howell Mountain, you tread on ground packed with white volcanic ash and iron-rich red soil. Sean Capiaux, winemaker at O'Shaughnessy on Howell Mountain, told me the sense of place in his wines is also from elevation as we stood in a steep amphitheatre of vines at 610 metres.

Mountain vineyards are expensive to plant and more difficult to farm. When I lurched around Stagecoach Vineyard on Atlas Peak in a dusty truck with then owner Dr Jan Krupp (it's now owned by the Gallo family), he explained that he'd ripped up half a million tons of bedrock to clear his land for vines; immense boulders were still piled in huge heaps. Winemakers on Howell Mountain, similarly, had to use dynamite to plant their vines.

Some wineries blend the fruit from both hillsides and benchlands in their *cuvées*. Chateau Montelena sits on river rock cobbles in an alluvial fan, but also owns hillside vineyards where the soil is volcanic ash. Ditto Quintessa in western

Rutherford, whose vineyard is a mix of hillside and valley floor, each with its own predominant soil. But as big structure means big prices for Napa Cabernet, it's no wonder many winemakers have taken the plunge and headed for the hills.

THE TOP VINEYARD TERROIRS

When trying to define Napa's complicated terroirs, it often makes more sense to focus on what makes individual vineyards unique rather than focus on their AVAs.

Napa has no official vineyard hierarchy as Burgundy does, but the wine-makers I've spoken to do tend to agree on its 'grands crus': the sites that make distinctive, complex wines that age brilliantly. They toss off names like To Kalon, Eisele, Backus, Dalla Valle, Napanook, J J Cohn, and a few more. Some of these lie on western benchlands in Oakville and Rutherford; others are nestled in eastern Oakville's foothills and middle plateau at about 183 metres, with its famous red dirt; still others are on hillsides.

There will be many more in the future, as vineyards in newer AVAs like Coombsville and Wild Horse Valley and other estates on hillsides produce more great wines, and geologists like Howell work to unravel their secrets.

One of Napa's top terroirs is its most storied vineyard, To Kalon, whose history goes back to 1868 and valley pioneer H W Crabb, who experimented with more than 400 grape varieties there. It is currently at the centre of an on going legal conflict the eventual resolution of which could have serious implications for the future. The name means 'the highest beauty' in ancient Greek, and few spots in California have produced as many acclaimed wines as this one. Documenting the vineyard's historic importance as a place has become the mission of Graeme MacDonald, whose family makes wine from a small piece of it. Over the past few years he's logged hundreds of hours of research.

Its sprawling, 600-plus acres sit on an alluvial fan in west Oakville, spreading towards the valley's centre, where up-valley warmth meets the cooler south. On a map, the vineyard looks like one huge rectangle, stretching from Highway 29 to the Mayacamas Mountains, but it's divided among six owners. The majority share, acquired long ago by Robert Mondavi, now belongs to giant Constellation Brands.

Is To Kalon a place (some owners argue)? Or is it merely a trademark belonging to Constellation Brands?

As mega-grower Andy Beckstoffer, who owns 89 acres of To Kalon, puts it: 'Once places can be trademarked, you violate the integrity of the name, the history and the whole idea of terroir. And that reflects on the entire valley.' When he bought his portion, he recalls, most of the valley's top wines were labelled 'reserve'. Beckstoffer wanted to make the vineyard matter, so he sold grapes to multiple winemakers; if they all made great wines from To Kalon, he reasoned, that proves the terroir is the source of greatness. Because of a lawsuit with Mondavi, buyers of his grapes must use the name 'Beckstoffer To Kalon'. The MacDonalds, however, can't actually put the To Kalon name on the label of their Cabernet, even though the vines are planted on the same terroir as Robert Mondavi's Cabernet.

What all the To Kalon reds share is density, deep, red fruit flavours, a hint of dusty earth, and smooth textures, though some are better balanced and longer-lived than others. 'Not all the vineyard blocks are the same,' observes Tor Kenward of Tor Family Wines. He favours those at the foot of the mountains, with rockier, leaner soil, where afternoon shadows cast by the slopes help preserve the wines' acidity and fruit flavours.

The iconic 38-acre Eisele Vineyard in Calistoga, now owned by billionaire François Pinault, owner of Bordeaux' Château Latour, is another unique spot whose history goes back to the 19th century. 'The vineyard seems to have a special

View eastwards across the rolling benchlands of the Napa Valley at Oakville, with the Robert Mondavi Winery and the To Kalon Vineyard in the foreground. The Vaca Mountain range rises in the backround towards the vineyards of Atlas Peak, where thin hill soils make equally good red.

voice,' Bart Araujo, the former owner told me. What makes its alluvial fan unusual is Simmons Creek, which bisects its heart. Flash floods from two watersheds shaped the soil mix of rough cobbles, volcanic ash, red clay and coarse sand.

NAPA'S NEW TERROIRS

Some of Napa's most interesting terroirs aren't even part of an official appellation. A top example of this is Pritchard Hill, situated on the eastern side of the valley, wedged into the space between east Oakville, Howell Mountain and the Stags Leap District. It's Napa's current cult Cabernet territory, where vineyards were carved out of raw land not so long ago. But while soils are fairly uniform and resemble those in eastern Oakville, different exposures produce dramatically different wines. This isolated, rugged area is home to some of the valley's top producers, like Colgin, Tim Mondavi's Continuum, Chappellet and Ovid. Vineyards lie at elevations from 244 metres above sea level to as high as 610 metres above the fog line. The panoramic views are spectacular. The wines have Oakville sophistication with that extra intensity that comes from hillsides.

There's very little water, and yields are naturally half of what they are at, for example, To Kalon, Tim Mondavi once told me. A vocal convert to mountain vineyards, he says, with passion: 'Altitude changes everything. We're at 488 metres. The vines soak up the sun's heat while the rest of the valley is covered in fog. Warmer nights and cooler days give the wines more nuance and round tannins.' His superb Continuum Estate reds are testaments to a mountain vineyard future.

In a not-that-far-distant past, Napa's winemakers undervalued terroir. No longer. David Howell dug innumerable soil pits at Promontory, a wine project run by Will Harlan, the son of Bill Harlan, the founder of Harlan Estate and Meadowood Resort. The vineyard was carved from a rugged, raw, untamed, 840-acre property in the foothills of the Mayacamas. Promontory, says Howell, is an extraordinary site, one of the most geologically complex of any in the world.

The vineyard is on an old landslide, so just about every vine is planted in a different kind of rock. Howell discovered one pocket between two fault lines that's metamorphic rock, which he says is unique in the Napa Valley.

Now, just to add further complication, the latest research is focussing on discovering the microbiology of terroir, which means including yeasts and other region-specific microbes as part of its definition.

Maybe that's why no one wants to see a grand cru terroir classification system for Napa's vineyards – at least not yet. 'In America,' says Mondavi, 'we don't want to say something is written in stone.'

Parts of this now updated article first appeared in *Club Oenologique* and *Le Pan* magazines.

9

IN A RUSH FOR
NEW GOLD

There's always a new perspective: a new winemaking vision; a new view from the restaurants of San Francisco; or a challenge set by a hypercritical New York sommelier... California wine continues to change, evolve and refine itself in a myriad different ways, ever shifting towards a golden future.

BRIAN ST PIERRE (2021)
California Cuisine...? Why Not!

NATASHA HUGHES MW (2021)
The Melting Pot

VICTORIA JAMES (2021)
Matter Other than Grapes

ESTHER MOBLEY (2019)
California Bright Young Things

MARY MARGARET McCAMIC MW (2021)
Capturing the California Spirit

CALIFORNIA CUISINE...? WHY NOT!

Brian St Pierre explains how, with new-found confidence in its plentiful natural resources, California's sommeliers, winemakers and top female chefs rode the crest of a food and wine wave that impressed even the most cynical New Yorkers and brought 'California Cuisine' to the world.

BRIAN ST PIERRE (2021)

In 1849, after gold was discovered in California, the rest of the world suddenly had a new destination, and eagerly rushed in. Besides the considerable pull of that buried treasure, there were urgent pushes as well right then: Europe was convulsed by wars, civil and otherwise; China was on the downside of an economic slope; Mexico had never been stable anyway; New York was desperately overcrowded by an earlier generation of immigrants; and malcontents who had never adjusted to Australia needed somewhere else to be malcontent in.

A muddy village on the shore of northern California, home to the Mission San Francisco de Asís, a detachment of Mexican troops and a smattering of itinerants, was the new safe haven and the entry to El Dorado. Dozens of ships docked in the harbour of San Francisco Bay, and their crews joined the eager passengers scampering off into the goldfields, leaving the abandoned vessels to become various kinds of shelter for those left behind: hostels, the local jail and restaurants.

San Francisco was awash in wine from the beginning. Missionaries had planted grape vines all along the coast, which thrived where they encircled each settlement. When many of the Italian, French and German immigrants quit the goldfields to go back to what they'd done before, which was often enough growing grapes, making wine and operating restaurants, life improved for all. San Francisco became a marvellous party. When Oscar Wilde passed through, he observed: 'Life is very public. . . the population is very excitable; money is abundant, and of course spent freely.' Jules Verne sent his fictional hero Phileas Fogg there, to break his 80-day, round-the-world trip at the new Palace Hotel, where one of the signature dishes was a breakfast of champagne with oysters and scrambled eggs, better known out in Gold Country as the 'Hangtown Fry'.

As the town boomed and became a city, landfill was needed to shore up the mudflats on the bay, in what became the financial district. No problem: there was a surplus of empty wine bottles available. Wine may be a basis of culture and civilization, but only in San Francisco was it also, literally, part of the foundation.

HITTING A WINE STRIDE...

By 1856, barrels of the local wine were being shipped from San Francisco to England, Germany, Russia, Australia and China. New York was also a market, but it was not so accepting of the California idea – so the wine was bottled and often relabelled as French. Respect wouldn't come until more than a century later; ironically, it began when America was about to celebrate its 200th birthday.

Antipathy between East and West coasts was established early and thrived as time went by; New Yorkers saw the Golden State as 'the granola state – full of flakes and nuts', while westerners thought of Gotham as a cesspool of cynicism, in thrall to France and its wines, especially the occupying army from Bordeaux. Grape vs geography, sunny climes vs characterful struggle, innovation vs history: there were plenty of skirmishes to be fought. French vignerons had plenty of help – in American restaurants. Most white-tablecloth establishments were inclined towards France as the ideal, the mother cuisine; many actually had wine waiters, specialists, sommeliers. They were not in the habit of recommending Zinfandel.

Something had to be done, and finally something was, by two Englishmen, outsiders happy to play spin-the-bottles. Gerald Asher was a former wine merchant in London and New York, who had moved to California to run a new winery, The Monterey Vineyard. A skilled communicator, he brought an outgoing, European-style positive approach that contrasted with the sometimes fragmented and often defensive California wine industry's strategies.

He was also, quietly, a showman, as he proved in March 1976. Inspired by the Burgundian celebration known as the Paulée de Paris held at that city's celebrated Le Taillevent restaurant, he staged the California Vintners Barrel Tasting Dinner at the prestigious Four Seasons restaurant in New York. Seventeen premium wineries presented barrel samples of their 1975 wines alongside older vintages of the same wines (in those days, 'premium' wineries were considered to be the ones that didn't sell large bottles of wine labelled 'Burgundy' or 'Chablis', or have a side-line in punch-like 'coolers'). Asher had negotiated with wineries for months, but not all he approached came aboard. 'They were afraid the New York crowd was lying in wait, eager to put them down,' one vintner recalled.

The holdouts missed a real opportunity. The sold-out dinner, for 200, including press, restaurateurs and members of the wine trade, was noted by *The New York Times* as 'an extraordinary wine tasting and dinner'. The 17 courses served were quite small, and exquisite, but the California wines stole the show, gaining a solid measure of respect. (The annual dinner ran for 10 years, soon becoming 'the wine trade's most glittering social event', averaging 2,000 requests for the 200 seats available every year.)

Then, a few months later, came the celebrated, storied, eventually legendary Judgement of Paris tasting staged by Steven Spurrier. While the Barrel Tasting had given New York something of a wake-up call, this one was more of a fire alarm – Frank Prial wrote two columns on California's shocking success in *The New York Times*, which were syndicated to nearly 200 newspapers around the US, and local wine writers followed suit, jumping aboard what soon became an international roller-coaster. My clipping-service bill at the Wine Institute in San Francisco doubled – California wine was suddenly big news everywhere. Tellingly, much of the new ferment was from restaurants, many on the no-longer-hostile East Coast; it seemed we were beginning to get the attention of those sommeliers, and perhaps Zinfandel might go with *boeuf bourguignon* after all.

THE CUISINE TO GO WITH IT…

Meanwhile, how were things back on home turf? The march towards 'California Cuisine' had already begun, pretty much unnoticed, which was unsurprising, since it started in a small, informal French restaurant. Well, a sort-of French restaurant: Chez Panisse, in Berkeley, the town across the bay from San Francisco that pretty much exemplified the 'nuts and flakes' label, opened in 1971, inspired by films about a café in Marseilles that was home to colourful characters and the cuisine of Provence. Most of the staff in Berkeley were enthusiastic amateurs, as were the owners, led by the demanding, extravagant and high-minded Alice Waters, who was in thrall to France in general and Provence in particular. Disappointed by the quality, freshness and variety of the ingredients available from large-scale purveyors, she became a pioneer of the organic farm-to-table movement. In the beginning, her wine list was eclectic, mostly French, but the logic of 'local' provisions, nudged along by local winemakers, eventually created a balance. Even the house wine, made from grapes bought by the restaurant, was Zinfandel.

In 1986, 10 years after the bicentennial tumult, the California Vintners Barrel Tasting Dinner came home to San Francisco and the elegant Stanford Court Hotel, and Steven Spurrier restaged the Paris tasting at San Francisco's Vintners' Club. Every seat at each event was taken, and both were another triumph for California wine; the major difference was that, this time, it was not a surprise.

The context had also changed over that decade, radically. Chez Panisse had become one of America's most respected and influential restaurants (and often featured dinners with California winemakers, or highlighted California regions and wines; menus were now in English). Julia Child, James Beard and Craig Claiborne, the country's leading food writers, had visited and adored it, as had Richard Olney, Elizabeth David and *Cuisine et Vins de France* magazine. The London Wine Bar – modelled on the classic British version – had opened in San Francisco's financial district as 'America's first wine bar' to yawns of indifference in 1974, but after 1976 you needed a reservation for its lunch-and-wine-tasting menu. Wines by the glass in bars and restaurants had gone from house white or red to Chardonnay or Cabernet Sauvignon. Helped along by California's liberal laws regarding the retailing of wine, delicatessens and other food shops such as The Wine & Cheese Centre's outlets now featured tasting bars. Restaurants held pre-dinner wine tastings and offered flights of wines on their set menus.

The reality of 'California Cuisine' had arrived, in tandem with California wine, swept along together in a full-fledged, tightly bound partnership. Looking back, it seems like an inevitable progression, but back then, it was a series of pleasant shocks, jolts of cheerful discoveries: What'll they think of next?

MAKE IT NEW, KEEP IT COURTEOUS

Cookery everywhere was in flux. A new generation of French chefs had adopted Oriental influences into *nouvelle cuisine*; Indian food was tiptoeing around the edges in search of a way in, and young American chefs in New York integrated the farm-to-table, fresh/organic ethic into what they chose to call 'New American

Cuisine'. Out in California, with the inclusion of vineyard-to-wine cellar, there was no question – it was definitely 'California Cuisine'.

Interviewing local chefs at work back then, I was also struck repeatedly by hearing three words I'd rarely encountered in my time in professional kitchens: 'please' and 'thank you'. They'd had no place in the highly structured hierarchy of restaurant cookery, where before you learned to actually cook, you had to absorb the reality of *la rigeur* – 'the rigour' of the trade, and your place in it (submissive, lowly and on edge). Politeness? *Quel horreur!*

Julia Child was not generally a fan of California Cuisine, calling it 'doleful' and 'chauvinist', and James Beard felt obliged to provide some corrective cooking tips in his reviews, but Craig Claiborne had gotten the essence of the change: 'There is one commodity that is rarer than locally grown truffles or homemade foie gras. That is a chef of international repute who was born in the United States. Even rarer is a celebrated chef who is a woman.' He was writing approvingly about Alice Waters. Her freewheeling approach and lack of rigour in almost everything but sensory engagement with food was already being adopted by a small army of cooks who had learned their trade – and that unregimented working method – at Chez Panisse, and were now opening their own restaurants and inspiring a new generation of other cooks to move to San Francisco and follow suit. Their kitchens were communal, tasks were shared rather than rigidly stratified. They were dedicated and determined, but polite. They were also, mostly, women; the subsidence of testosterone appeared to create a new openness.

EQUALITY, CONGENIALITY AND GLORIOUS INEVITABILITY

To chefs in Lyon or Paris, this sort of equality, not to mention congeniality, was heresy, even anarchy. At Greens, in San Francisco, where Deborah Madison and then Annie Somerville linked vegetarian cooking with fine dining, the wine list evolved by committee at weekly wine-tasting staff 'seminars'. At Fog City Diner – where chef Cindy Pawlcyn posted a sign at the front door meant to guarantee a good time inside that read 'No cry-babies', and the chilli con carne was made with top sirloin steak – the California list included at least one version of every varietal wine made in the state (her restaurant in the Napa Valley, Mustards, had its own vegetable and herb garden just outside and was known by locals as 'a wine geek's paradise').

Judy Rodgers took over San Francisco's Zuni Café and brought collaboration to the kitchen: she could often be found wandering around and pitching in, all cooks together. The same applied to wine: one night at dinner there, two British wine writers were amazed when a young waiter ventured to recommend a relatively inexpensive California wine he'd discovered after his shift had ended the night before, when staff got to drink up the remainders from the by-the-glass list.

That was the other new aspect – suddenly, every restaurant had to have an array of different wines by the glass, most often Californian; 'choice' was the operative principle, in every sense of the word, and that notion completed the new way of dining out. The new player in the game was the wine waiter, occasionally known as the sommelier, and the list he or she compiled mattered. And it was competitive; in 1973, 21 wineries in Napa and Sonoma (including Stag's Leap, Clos du Val, Chateau Montelena and other now-famous names) were less than a year old, but after 1976, the roller-coaster never slowed. New players burst on the scene from across the Central Coast and Santa Cruz; new wines from Randall Grahm and other Rhône Rangers (Le Cigare Volant, Clos du Gilroy, Qupé Syrah) jostled with Pinot Noir from cool Carneros (from Acacia, Carneros Creek and Saintsbury); Johannisberg Riesling from Firestone, down in Santa Barbara county, was hot, and so was Ridge Zinfandel from all over the state.

You suddenly had to be nimble to keep up; it helped that the new sommeliers were young, just like a lot of the winemakers. Joyce Goldstein's son Evan, at Square One, and Nunzio Alioto, whose family helped make Fishermen's Wharf a tourist destination in San Francisco, were typical: when they weren't working, they were hanging out with other sommeliers and winemakers. It wasn't so much a wine culture as it was a wine circus, entertaining, arduous and ultimately rewarding. Goofy, yes, but glorious fun for all – and home-grown!

Thus it went, onward and upward. Whatever it was called (and it was called many things, but 'California Cuisine' finally won out), this quirky communal culinary partnership was here to stay. Wineries hosted cookery classes, restaurants staged wine tastings; the goat's cheese was from Sonoma, the vegetables from the Zen Center in Sausalito, the mesquite wood for grilling from the southern California desert, fennel grew wild in the Italian district of North Beach in San Francisco and artichokes thrived on Monterey's foggy coast. Oysters were still easily found. We had our own variety of salmon. Farmers' markets were cornucopias, and featured artisanal, offbeat wines. What cook could resist the bounty, as well as the camaraderie? It would take a heart of stone, or some other form of *la rigeur*. Luckily, battalions of cooks were happy to show up and be seduced: diversity, balance, adventure and… courtesy? Right this way – take the first turning to the west.

Near the end of this tumultuous time, I staged a California wine tasting in Tokyo. The choice of venue seemed obvious: the new branch of Spago, where Wolfgang Puck had reinvented pizza with a wildly imaginative variety of home-grown toppings. Some of those who attended were nervous about this radically new food, but in the end the event lasted until we ran out of wine. One slightly tipsy local journalist called me over saying he would like to know if this is what they call 'California Cuisine'? There was only one possible answer, and it still holds: Why not?

THE MELTING POT

Master of Wine and food adventurer, Natasha Hughes, dives into California's 21st-century culinary scene. Eschewing deep-dish pizza and embracing everything from huevos rancheros to teriyaki-spiced bowl-food, she finds no shortage of wines to match.

NATASHA HUGHES MW (2021)

American food usually gets a bad rap. The country's culinary efforts seem to be focused on cheap takeaways, burgers, fries and deep-dish pizzas – a cuisine in which the only things that really count are the calories. Dig a little deeper, though, and you'll find both variety and excellence – just think of Louisiana's Cajun cuisine; the complex barbecue culture of the Sout, and the clambakes and lobster rolls that form such an integral part of the seafood Shangri-la of the eastern seaboard.

But it's the most ethnically diverse state of all, California, that offers the greatest culinary range, with an astonishing smorgasbord of dishes that pays tribute to the waves of immigrants to its shores. People whose roots lie in Asia, western and eastern Europe, the Mediterranean basin and central and southern America have, quite literally, created a culinary melting pot. California cuisine – like that of the other great centre of Pacific immigration, Australia – is renowned for its fusion of flavours and its profusion of high-quality ingredients. And, to cap it all, California is a source of viticultural variance, creating the opportunity for some astounding harmonies between its wines and its wealth of dishes.

BEST FOR BRUNCH

If you start the day – as many Californians do – with brunch, sparkling wine is the drink of choice. Eggs are notoriously tricky to pair with wine, but scrambled eggs (especially when served with smoked salmon on the side) seem to rub along quite happily with a glass or two of elegant Californian fizz from the state's coolest sites (unfortunately these are seldom mentioned by name on the label, so there's no go-to area specifically associated with the very best sparkling wines). These wines also work well should you eschew the eggs and load your lox onto a toasted, buttered bagel and top with a refreshing squeeze of lemon. If you opt instead for a richer dish of Eggs Benedict, look for a boldly flavoured, richly oaked Chardonnay from Napa, especially one with the buttery hit from malolactic fermentation.

If you happen to be brunching on spicy huevos rancheros, though, you should be looking for a juicy, unoaked red wine: something based on Gamay would do the trick nicely. This fruity red grape is not one you'd normally associate with California, but an increasing number of producers are looking to Gamay – and grapes like Trousseau and Dolcetto – in an attempt to make refreshing wines that pair well with a range of foods. The best Gamays are grown on the granite soils near Camino in the Sierra Foothills (an echo of the grape's French homeland, where it thrives on the ancient granite slopes of Beaujolais), while the North Coast is the source of what little Trousseau is being grown. These varieties generally show modest alcohol, good acidity and little or no oak – all characters that allow them to take on spice without creating an unpleasant chilli burn.

RAMPING UP THE SPICE

Mexican dishes are very much part of the Californian repertoire, and you don't have to save them for the brunch table. Some of the best tacos and burritos are served from road-side trucks at lunchtime, or you can enjoy Mexican flavours in salads and long-cooked stews at home at any point during the day. While wine might not be the first thing you might think of when choosing a drink to accompany a central American meal – beers, horchatas and aguas frescas all come into play, as do tequila- or mezcal-based cocktails – supple reds and refreshing rosés cope well with the demanding flavour profiles of these dishes.

And here's the bit where wine snobs should look away... California makes rosés of most denominations, from delicate Provençal-style pinks and robustly flavoured *clairets* to bubblegum-hued sweeties, incidentally creating a surprisingly versatile range of food wines. Some of the best of the drier styles are made along the Central Coast, and these bring out the best in dishes based on Mediterranean flavours while off-dry rosés (usually from the broader California designation), as long as they're not toothachingly sweet, partner well with all kinds of spice (try them with tortillas as well as with Thai curries).

Asian flavours of all kinds are very much on the Californian menu. The Chinese first flocked to California during the Gold Rush of the mid-19th century, and were followed over the course of the next 150 years by immigrants from Japan, Korea, the Indian sub-continent, Vietnam and Thailand. Each of these groups brought new ingredients and techniques to their American homeland.

Typically, Asian meals consist of a competing array of dishes, so precise food pairing is a challenge. However, some general rules of thumb apply. Brightly flavoured salads and stir fries – especially those enlivened with an abundance of herbs and lemongrass – benefit from pairing with bright white wines. Sauvignon Blanc should be a good call here, but Napa's fumé styles are sometimes a little too rich for these delicate flavours – save these wines for barbecued lobsters or shrimp, where their richness and smoky oak pay dividends. If you can find an unoaked Sauvignon, that will do the job nicely, but bear in mind that a handful of Californian producers are now making zesty Grüner Veltliners, wines whose brisk acidity and herbaceous notes should also work well. These wines also marry harmoniously with dishes based on raw fish, whether sashimis, crudos or South American ceviches and tirados. When it comes to sushi, though, look for richer wines made along the Central Coast and based on the white grapes of the Rhône – Viognier, Marsanne and Roussanne, whether singly or in blends – as the additional weight helps to offset the sweetness of the rice and the sting of the wasabi.

BRING OUT THE REDS

Reds have a part to play in Asian meals, too. Japanese yakitori skewers – usually based on bits of chicken, glazed with a tare sauce that combines the savoury, salty taste of miso with the gentle sweetness of mirin – respond well to the silky tannins and red-berry flavours of Pinot Noir, especially the delicate versions grown in the southern AVAs of Santa Barbara and the Sta Rita Hills. Rich, rounded Napa Merlots, with their deep plum flavours, on the other hand, are better used to offset the umami richness of Chinese stir-fries containing beef or lamb, and Korean barbecues, as can bold Zinfandels and field blends based on this richly fruited grape.

Zinfandel is also very much at home with grilled meats, especially when you're cooking simple meaty dishes like burgers or ribs drenched in the sweet molasses-based sauces of the southwest USA. If you're experimenting with slow-cooked brisket with a typically Texan dry rub, on the other hand, you might fare better with a peppery Syrah from the Sta Rita Hills. Sprinkle your barbecued meats with the flavours of the Middle East, though, and you should probably reach for the spicy Grenache-based reds of the Central Coast.

Barbecues offer an opportunity to bring out your big Napa Cabernet Sauvignons – just as long as you're cooking nothing more complex than a simply grilled steak or some lamb chops. These big, glossy wines are not the most versatile food partners (their bold tannins, generous alcohol levels and rich oaking struggle with spice, and their rich flavours overwhelm chicken or pork) and as a result benefit from being partnered by grilled or griddled red meats.

You might well consider Pinot Noir to be Cabernet Sauvignon's polar opposite when it comes to culinary marriages. While Cabernet is a finicky food partner, Pinot is the Swiss Army knife of pairing. Chill a bottle for half an hour or so before opening and its light body and silky structure will allow it to harmonize with tuna, salmon, halibut and other relatively robust fish as well as chicken or pork dishes. The bright acidity typical of Pinot grown in southern California handles the rich flavour and fattiness of duck with ease, while the more robust Pinots typical of Sonoma and Russian River can comfortably handle red meats. Age your Pinot for a bit and it will develop subtle earthy flavours that chime nicely with mushroom dishes and game – and we've already seen that Pinot partners the blend of umami and sweetness typical of Japanese cuisine (and this ultra-versatile grape will take on the challenge of the multiple flavours of a Chinese feast with ease).

THERE'S CHARDONNAY, SANGIOVESE AND NEBBIOLO...

It almost goes without saying that Chardonnay is a great match for California's abundance of seafood, but the growing diversity of styles being made in the sunshine state allows for a wider variety of pairings. Take the now near-ubiquitous bowl-meals. Increasingly part of California's food scene, these layered flavour bombs combine a protein element – tofu, seafood or chicken, most typically – with a generous variety of vegetables, with weight and substance coming from the addition of beans, rice, quinoa or other grains. These basic elements are spiked with seasonings – pickled vegetables, soy or teriyaki sauces and a host of spices.

The zesty, citrusy Chardonnays being made in the cool highlands of southern California sit incredibly well with the bright flavours of these complex vegetable-focused dishes. The riper, more generous Chardonnays typical of northern California, on the other hand, are probably better suited to dishes based on white meats. Plain roast chicken is a good starting point, but when enhanced by the addition of wild mushrooms the combination of flavours can be quite startling. Perhaps the zenith of pairings for richer Chardonnays comes with roast pork, particularly when boosted by the fennel and garlic so integral to a slow-cooked porchetta.

Porchetta is, of course, an Italian specialty, and the strong history of Italian migration to California has resulted not only in a strong Italianate flavour to many menus, but has also contributed to the growth of interest in Italian grape varieties in the state. Look to juicy Barberas or Sangioveses when tucking into pizzas with red sauce, while the richer, cheese-based white pizza toppings need the burst of acidity typical of Vermentino. Creamy pasta sauces might benefit from the richness of a Malvasia, while rich, meaty ragus or mushroom-based pastas benefit from the depth of savoury flavour you find in the best Nebbiolos.

Sometimes, though, the simplest matches are the best. As far as I'm concerned, there are few pleasures in life that surpass that of washing down a platter of mixed briny Pacific oysters and tiny, creamy Kumamotos with a glass of Californian fizz – especially if you're enjoying the pairing from a harbourside table with a view out over San Francisco's Golden Gate Bridge.

MATTER OTHER THAN GRAPES

New York-based sommelier Victoria James wasn't bargaining for a near-death experience when she went to work in Sonoma one harvest. She found the real world of wine and winemaking tougher than many would guess…

VICTORIA JAMES (2021)

For sommeliers, working a harvest is a rite of passage. I would even describe it as essential to fully understanding and appreciating wine. So off I went to Sonoma to work a harvest at a small winery called Tricycle Wine Company (TWC).

The sunshine warmed my tired New York City bones. It was thrilling to drive past vineyards I recognized from my studies. I followed along on my wine map of California, amazed that I was in the region. Californians seemed so relaxed in comparison to New Yorkers. Complete strangers would ask me how my day was going.

For lodging, the winemaker at TWC had a friend who had just renovated a house. He had a second bedroom and kindly offered it to me at no cost. When I arrived, I realized that the 'house' was a chicken coop. As in, it was actually a chicken coop before it was renovated. Its history accounted for the smell that seemed infused into the walls and the low ceilings that I crouched below. 'Beggars can't be choosers' had never rung so true.

On a Monday morning at the start of October, I biked to TWC for the first time. The sun had not yet risen. I pedalled past fields of cows and over rolling hills, and the aroma of sweet manure and freshly cut grass seeped into my nostrils. There was no litter, no cigarette butts, no horns honking. The only noise for miles must have been my wheels humming against the dirt roads.

TWC was not exactly a grand château but rather a shared warehouse space. It wasn't the romantic setting I'd originally had in mind, but I figured it would do. I biked around a massive parking lot and peeked into the different garage-like wineries. It was like a strip mall of grape juice. Kamen, Enkidu, Talisman, Tin Barn . . . Tricycle Wine Company!

I parked my bike underneath the TWC sign. With all of my strength, I swung open the garage door that separated TWC from the parking lot. A group of faces met mine, startled by the loud *slam* the door made as it hit the ceiling.

'I . . . um. . . I am . . . the harvest intern. Is this Tricycle Wine Company?' A man with a friendly face and goatee smiled. 'Welcome, Victoria. We are excited to have you learn with us.' This man was a winemaker named Alex. There was another gentleman named Casey, the cellar manager, who always wore a baseball cap. Although their relaxed nature should have put me at ease, it made me more nervous. I wasn't sure how to respond to calm; I only knew stress.

Before this, I'd thought I couldn't have possibly found a lowlier job than cellar rat, but here I was as a cellar hand. No longer even a living animal but rather a body part. My job title essentially meant copious amounts of physical labour and mopping – I would spend hours on the sorting table, picking bugs off grapes as they tried to wiggle up my arms and cleaning out tanks full of skins and seeds.

There was another intern as well, Ana, from Argentina, and this was her third harvest internship. Third! She had worked harvests before in Germany and France. I was definitely at the bottom of the totem pole. Ana just nodded when Casey yelled: 'Okay, three punch-downs. One on tank two in 15 minutes, the other on tank six in an hour, and the last on tank eight in 90 minutes. And hand me three two-inch camlocks, a Perlick valve and a cross TC.' Meanwhile, I would rush to find a notepad, and by the time I had, it would be too late. Casey would let out an exasperated sigh and then look to Ana, who nodded with understanding.

Safety was another concern. A punch-down was when the top of the tank, full of juice and grape skins, had to be stirred up and literally punched down with a big stick. Grape skins naturally float upwards, so many winemakers will push them downward so all of the juice is continuously in contact with the skins. When I was asked to do a punch-down, I think Casey forgot I had never done it before. Scared to confess, I just looked around for a stick and decided to go ahead with it. Before travelling to Sonoma, I had read all about winery procedures, and a punch-down seemed the simplest thing. What could go wrong?

To get to the top of the tank, I climbed up a ladder that led to a catwalk, an elevated metal platform that ran along the tops of the tanks. Once on the catwalk with my long stick, I began to panic. High above the concrete floors, I was sure that even the slightest misstep would lead to my head cracking open below. I timidly made my way to the tank that needed punching down. Then I rested the stick on the catwalk and grabbed the lid of the container. I unhinged a metal clamp and swung open the top. The next thing I remember is waking up on the floor of the catwalk, the stick resting behind my crumpled knees.

If I had paid closer attention during my studies, I would have recalled that carbon dioxide (CO_2) is a by-product of fermentation. The gas was trapped in the tank, with nowhere to go – until I lifted the lid. All at once it hit me like a poisonous cloud. I was lucky that I'd only passed out and hadn't fallen to my death.

Casey shouted and asked if I was taking a nap. 'And what is that stick for? Use the wine-cap punch-down tool. It's hovering right above you!' He pointed to a metal rod above the tank with a flat and circular bottom, like the base of a lamp. Ah, that would make more sense. Absolutely humiliated that I had just huffed an entire tank's worth of CO_2, I shuffled to my feet. I shook away the woozy feeling in my head and grabbed the punch-down tool.

Every morning I would wake up to an aching body. I thought that working in the restaurant industry was harsh manual labour, but being a cellar hand showed me how spoiled I had been. I barely saw the daylight, trapped in the garage from sunrise until well after sunset. It continued like this for days.

'You think this is hard, try picking grapes,' Casey would chuckle. To prove to him that I was tough stuff, I decided to volunteer to pick grapes with their morning crew. After one row of grapes, my entire back was on fire. The hovering in a crouched position was wreaking havoc on my body. '*Qué chica tan tonta!*' (silly girl!) the crew would laugh when I stumbled.

'Get low, girl . . . and get your legs strong!' one worker said, and slapped his thick thigh, glistening with sweat, and flexed his enormous muscles. Bees would land on the grapes, and my fingers tensed in fear that they would sting me. The worker who had slapped his thigh earlier saw me cower in horror when I came upon a whole cluster covered in bees. In one swift move, he grabbed the bunch with his sausage-like fingers and tossed it into the bucket. This guy was a badass.

I barely lasted the day. The workers ran circles around me, cutting grapes off vines and placing them in bins with such grace and speed, it looked like I was working backwards. After that attempt, I swore off grape picking altogether. Instead, I stayed in the winery and stuck to following Casey's orders. Before the grapes arrived, my job was to check tanks and barrels for progress. In a tiny little notebook, I would write down the sugar level of each wine. As the yeast would convert the sugar to alcohol, the Brix (sugar content) reading would lower.

Next was cleaning the hopper (the destemming and grape-crushing machine) to get it ready for use, setting up the sorting table (a conveyor belt not too dissimilar to one found in a grocery store), transferring finished wine from tanks to barrels, cleaning out tanks, hosing out the bladder press, etc.

Essentially, I would get everything ready for new grapes to come into the winery. Once they arrived, chilled and sticky from the vineyards, the clock was ticking. We had to get the bunches sorted, destemmed and crushed immediately. The grapes could not get too warm.

On the sorting table, my fingers would fly in constant panic. Casey would drive a forklift, grabbing huge containers of grapes and dumping them into the sorting machine. 'Don't let any rotten bunches get in the hopper and look out for MOG!' he screamed over the loud machines.

MOG? What is a MOG? I looked over the sorting table at Ana and tried to ask her, but it was too loud. Instead, I just tried to follow her lead. She seemed to pick out anything that wasn't perfect. A mouldy grape, a rotten grape, an underripe grape – they all went off the table and into a bucket by her feet. What if I missed one of these? Would I ruin the whole batch of wine? The conveyor belt moved quickly, and my tiny fingers struggled to keep up as the grapes marched into the hopper. Bugs crawled up my arm, and an earwig somehow managed to get under my shirt. I screamed and shook my top until Casey stopped the machines in dread. He was worried I had lost a finger or something.

Instead, Ana just made a bug-like gesture to him, and he laughed. 'It's just MOG!' Apparently, that stood for 'matter other than grapes'.

I was quickly kicked off the sorting table and given the lowliest of jobs, raking grape stems. Ashamed, I kept my head down for the rest of the day. Raking stems was easy and not at all scary. This I could manage.

After the grapes had all been sorted and crushed, we transferred them to a tank for fermentation. Throughout the day I ran to fetch hoses, tubes, connecting tools and fancy-looking wrenches. By sunset, the winery was sparkling. I had flushed out each pesky grape skin into a compost pile and scrubbed every tank clean.

Casey handed me a beer as a peace offering. I had never enjoyed the taste of beer before. Where was all of the fancy wine we were supposed to be sipping? I popped open the can, not wanting to offend Casey, and took a sip. He watched me as I glugged down the whole lot. It was terrific. There was something about a hard day's work that made beer taste so much more delicious. It was like the tiny bite of New York strip steak I was afforded as a child if we had balanced our grocery budget cunningly. For the rest of harvest, I drank only beer. And lots of it.

Excerpt from *Wine Girl* (2020) by Victoria James reproduced here with kind permission of the author and publishers, Fleet, an imprint of the Little, Brown Book Group and HarperCollins.

CALIFORNIA BRIGHT YOUNG THINGS

Game-changers, shape-shifters and Beaujolais revolutionaries, Esther Mobley discovers a new world of bright, juicy, translucent reds that are bringing a striking change to the way we think about California wines – it's no longer all about the blockbuster…

ESTHER MOBLEY (2019)

Every once in a while in wine there is a paradigm shift. The reference points move. New heroes emerge. With the polarizing force of a swinging pendulum, the measurements of quality transform. One decade, we might prize opulent fruit flavours in a wine; the next, we fetishize high acidity.

Right now, within a certain subset of California wine, a realignment is under way. Chances are, you've tasted it. Have you noticed that some red wines are creeping lighter and lighter, to the point of translucence? Fruit flavours in these wines are bright, crunchy, tart and often red-hued – more pomegranate and raspberry, less blackberry and fig. Whole-cluster fermentation, in which stems are not removed from grapes, is increasingly common. Extraction is gentle. Aroma is privileged. Weight is not.

The model for these wines is not, as has been the case for many of California's great Cabernet Sauvignons, Bordeaux. It's not even really burgundy. To the extent that there is a French corollary for these – the new translucent reds of California – it's a region much sleepier and far less prestigious: Beaujolais.

If burgundy is the older sibling who had a successful career on Wall Street, Beaujolais is the freewheeling, quirky younger brother who decided to go to art school. Located at the southern end of Burgundy, the Beaujolais region is home to Gamay, a grape that recalls a simpler version of Pinot Noir. Many Americans know Beaujolais for its *nouveau* wines, released just after harvest each November, but recent years have seen a surge in popularity – and quality – for the more serious, age-worthy Cru Beaujolais.

Just how influential is Beaujolais for some of California's boundary-pushing producers today? Here's a sampling of sentiments that winemakers have recently offered to me. (I didn't put them up to it, I swear.)

'I love Beaujolais,' says Kristie Tacey, who makes Tessier Wines. 'It's what I'm inspired by and what I want to do.'

Creeping towards translucence... The pendulum is swinging away from deeply flavoured, rich, dark reds towards lighter, fresher, pomegranate- and raspberry-scented wines.

'We make Pinot Noir, but we found ourselves not drinking much Pinot Noir,' says Mikey Giugni, who makes the Scar of the Sea label. 'We found ourselves drinking Beaujolais.'

'Beaujolais is what we drink the most,' says Matt Naumann, who makes Newfound Wines with his wife, Audra Chapman. 'We took our Counoise' – a grape from France's Rhône Valley – 'and said: "Let's make this like Gamay."'

I barely have to explain myself to Abe Schoener, of the Scholium Project, before he interjects. 'Oh, new-school Beaujolais?' he says. 'Yeah. That has become the paradigm. The paradigm.'

Let's be clear. This is by no means to say that every winery in California is doing this, nor (crucially) that they should be. But the rise of these translucent reds, these California Cru Beaujolais wines, has taken hold among a group of winemakers here in a very strong way. To those of us paying attention, the movement has become impossible to ignore.

Hardy Wallace, of Dirty & Rowdy Family Wines, deserves credit for this.

When Wallace began making wine, in 2010, he set out to look for Gamay. But there was – still is – very little of the grape planted in California. (Edmunds St John in Berkeley was getting most of the state's haul.) What Wallace could find, though, was Mourvèdre, which in the southern Rhône produces a meaty, rich style of wine. A wine not at all like Beaujolais.

Wallace wasn't deterred. 'We thought: what if we took this Beaujolais-like approach – whole cluster, whole berry, minimal crushing but not full carbonic,' he says, 'with a grape variety that is not normally produced in this way?' Colleagues told him he was crazy, but he loved the results. 'We were blown away by how expressive the wine was aromatically, and how crystal-clear it showed the soils where it grew,' he says.

Dirty & Rowdy has since evolved into a Mourvèdre-as-Beaujolais specialist, working with nine Mourvèdre vineyards and treating them all in a relatively similar way, with 100-percent whole-cluster fermentations and gentle extractions. If you get caught up on whether Wallace's wines taste like Mourvèdre 'should' taste, you won't get very far. His have little in common with the classic Mourvèdres of Domaine Tempier or Château Beaucastel or even California's Tablas Creek.

'I don't think about varietal correctness at all,' says Wallace.

But you'd have to be an ascetic to not find his wines delicious. The Dirty & Rowdy reds smell juicy, energetically fruity, their aromas sometimes verging on candied apple or raspberry preserves. They feel tactile, grippy, raw against the mouth. They sacrifice not a bit of complexity for their translucence and feather-light weight. They go down easy.

How did we get here? None of this happened out of the blue. We have witnessed a gradual lightening of wines in California over the last decade. Groups like In Pursuit of Balance preached, almost literally, the gospel of lower alcohol levels. The burgeoning natural wine movement celebrates 'glou glou' – wine meant for quick guzzling. Chillable reds are in. Carbonic maceration, including for *nouveau* wines, is now a standard tool in the California winemaker's kit.

Consider the European wines that are now in vogue with wine's hipster elite: Mencía from Bierzo, Spain. Frappato and Nerello Mascalese from Sicily. Mission from Chile and the Canary Islands. Trousseau and Poulsard from France's Jura region. (Gamay from Beaujolais — that goes without saying.) All these wines cut a similar profile: light-bodied, yet structured.

'Those are the wines that we're drinking,' says Jessica Stolpman, whose family owns Stolpman Vineyards in Santa Barbara County. 'We started wondering: why aren't we making wines like that?' In addition to their long-standing line of more traditional, meant-to-age Syrahs and Roussannes, Stolpman Vineyards has now introduced a line they call So Fresh, which includes a vibrant Gamay and a carbonic-maceration Sangiovese, plus a spicy Trousseau under the new Combe label.

'I hadn't seen a lot of stuff like this when we started in 2010,' Wallace says. 'Now you're starting to see this movement really go places.'

Does this strong stylistic vision – to make a wine like Beaujolais – conflict with the idea of expressing terroir? Maybe. But Wallace truly believes that his method is the best way he can express a vineyard's personality, even if all his Beaujolais-inspired Mourvèdres seem to have a distinctive Dirty & Rowdy personality, too.

Or maybe California terroir can rewrite our understanding of what varietal correctness is. Take the Bechthold Vineyard in Lodi, for example. 'The closest analog for Bechthold Cinsault is definitely Cru Beaujolais,' says John Locke, winemaker at Birichino in Santa Cruz. Do Bechthold's Cinsaults taste like French Cinsault? No, but they certainly convey a sense of place. In the hands of a dozen different winemakers, the wines unfailingly taste like Bechthold.

Like Wallace, Locke has a strong style that permeates his lineup of wines. He makes varieties as disparate as Carignan and Pinot Noir, and all wear a Birichino signature of light extraction, crunchy fruit and intense savoury qualities. (Interestingly, for a small portion of his Besson Vineyard Grenache, Locke performs *appassimento*, a process of drying grapes commonly used for Amarone.) 'I've moved from thinking that the process creates flavour,' says Locke, 'to thinking that these processes reveal flavour.'

If you grew up on the California classics, an appreciation of these pale red wines requires a palate recalibration. You might wonder: Where's the oomph? Where's the concentration? Will these wines age like the best California Cabernets? We don't really know yet. Birichino, Dirty & Rowdy and their cohort have been around for only about a decade.

It helps that the wines are getting better and better. While it would be easy to make a low-extraction red wine in a style that ends up feeling anaemic, stingy, flavour-depleted, the best of the California translucent reds are generous: explosively aromatic, richly textured and plenty fruity. A wine like Scar of the Sea's Santa Barbara Pinot Noir might look weedy alongside your prototypical concentrated, dark-fruited Russian River Valley Pinot, but to my palate it's far more flavourful.

Still, I have concerns. None of the components that make these new Cru Beaujolais wines successful – the whole-cluster fermentations, the soft extractions, the low alcohol levels – should be taken to their extremes. Too many light-bodied wines for the sake of light-bodied wines, too many bubblegum-laden carbonic experiments – it all threatens to levy the same result as overripe grapes and excessive oak-barrel use, the qualities that many of today's progressive winemakers decry: homogenization. That's the beautiful thing about wine's swinging pendulum. It never stops moving.

This article was written by Esther Mobley, wine critic for the *San Francisco Chronicle*, in March 2019. Reproduced here with kind permission of the author and publishers, Hearst Communications.

CAPTURING THE CALIFORNIA SPIRIT

Napa Valley wine consultant Mary Margaret McCamic
asks what the future holds for this great wine state.

MARY MARGARET McCAMIC MW (2021)

California is a state with an unapologetic, pioneering spirit. It encapsulates the best of 'Americana': there are few restrictions to inhibit innovation and no limits to the wines its best estates can produce. They are the result – through necessity and out of natural curiosity – of constant experimentation in vine-growing, winemaking, blending and bottling.

With so many regions, grape varieties, climates and oenological perspectives in play, California's wines are not necessarily stylistically predictable. For those unable to hop in a car and speed down the Pacific Coast, they might even appear monochromatic. Sine Qua Non, Ridge, Kistler, Robert Mondavi Winery, Schramsberg, Stony Hill, Domaine de la Côte and Screaming Eagle. This handful of names alone represents a diverse range of styles, price points, interpretations and expressions in terms of place, and varieties spanning Chardonnay to Zinfandel, Riesling to the Rhône. The Napa Valley offers frontier aesthetics paired with science, ample investment and the quest for excellence. Its valley floor fruit produces vastly different wines to the more firmly structured, burly wines one can find atop Howell Mountain or Atlas Peak. The whistling winds and high peaks of the Sta Rita Hills produce Pinot Noir, Chardonnay and Syrah with a tension that belies the more concentrated styles from the Russian River Valley. California is a land of contrasts aplenty. One must accept that there is and never was a 'California style' but without question, there is a California spirit.

And how to capture this? Globally, California wine remains underappreciated in terms of its ageability. And both the trade and the consumer tend to scrutinize the concept of terroir in such a young winemaking region. Yet both elements – longevity and the ability to express a distinct sense of place – provide clear ways in which the 'soul' of California can reveal itself through its wines, and promise to benefit wine growers, winemakers and wine lovers alike for decades to come.

THE 'SOUL' OVER TIME...

In a relatively short period of time, the wines of California have evolved in terms of style and global perception. While it is no secret that the great classic California wines have the potential to improve over decades – just open a bottle of Heitz Martha's Vineyard from the 1970s for proof – the idea of longevity in California still strikes many as a relatively new concept. Sharing wines among collectors with a self-declared preference for claret, the greatest wines of California have been praised, but simultaneously derided as young upstarts, the freckle-faced teenagers who simply got lucky with an ideal climate perfect for ripening grapes but who lack the experience to express real depth beyond fruit. But vintages like 1975, 1999 and 2013 in Napa change all that; the response can no longer be 'just wait'. These are wines with sophistication, complexity and alluring intensity in both the short and long term; attributes that few classic regions can boast.

Cabernet Sauvignon from Napa's top AVAs arguably appeals best to those looking for a European comparison, and producers in California have emulated Bordeaux icons for this very reason. Yet part of what has limited the appreciation and understanding of Napa's finest on a global scale, at least, is that the wines are so enjoyable young. In the minds of drinkers who will not touch their First Growths for decades, it seems impossible that a wine capable of delivering hedonistic pleasure in its infancy could also bring joy 30 years later. For those who know California intimately, this concept is a given. That said, as styles evolved in California from the more European-inspired refinement of the 1960s and 1970s to the more robust wines of the 1990s and early 2000s, critics and producers alike questioned whether some possessed the structural integrity to improve long term.

What time has revealed is that the best Napa Valley Cabernet can and does age with grace, whether it is a bottle of 1998 Dunn from Howell Mountain, 1994 Harlan Estate from Oakville or 1977 Diamond Creek from Calistoga (the list goes on). And vintage variation in California is far less dramatic than it is in Bordeaux, a fact that gives the region even greater appeal for consumers. In fact, blind-tasting older California Cabernet Sauvignons against the wines of Saint Julien or Pauillac is an education for the palate – the latter simply fall short.

Added to these, a diverse range of wines from beyond Napa also continue to prove their long-term merits. Zinfandel, Merlot, Chardonnay, Syrah and Pinot Noir (to name a few) from Santa Barbara, Santa Cruz and Sonoma show exceptional quality, and exciting opportunities for long-term enjoyment.

Longevity is important for the future of California wine as it will enable it to reach a broader audience. Collectors can buy wines to drink in the short term and – if they have the patience – the long term too. Availability of an increasing number of 'long-term' wines also broadens California's range in terms of 'future classics'. Wines like Ridge Vineyards' Monte Bello have long since been established as benchmarks, but there are newer projects, too, that also benefit from historical wisdom, improved technology and innovation – and not all of them are synonymous with microscopic production and sky-high prices. Bedrock Wine Company based in Sonoma is making some of the freshest, liveliest, well-structured Zinfandel blends in California. Further south, high-altitude expressions of Pinot Noir from producers like The Hilt in the Sta Rita Hills prove captivating with all of their wild and savoury fruit, bright acidity and firm structure. With fresh, bright styles and new structures, these emerging classics hold the potential to age in a way that is perhaps even more exciting than the traditionally expected bottlings.

If there is a thread that links the success of wines with longevity in California, it is a keen appreciation for the land coupled with a focus on balance in the winery. Whether one buys into the notion of terroir or not, the pursuit to find it within California will continue to be a positive force forward for its identity.

THE SPIRIT OF THE LAND

Some argue that terroir reveals itself – it is not found. This is a hard argument to disagree with in a region where there are no legal regulations in place to create a controlled lens through which one can see place or typicity. Would a vineyard or region express itself more authentically if planted with a different variety or root-stock, or farmed with less intervention? There has simply not been enough time in California's winemaking history to know with full certainty, so it seems more appropriate to define terroir in California as a 'pursuit' rather than a destination.

I recently reflected on the idolization of the pre-1990s era with Julia van der Vink of Harlan Estate, Oakville. Her question for winemakers crafting wine from the valley's best sites was: 'Have the best wines from this site already been pro-duced?' If the answer was yes, then the future of Napa – and California as a whole – would look bleak. Luckily, the answer is a resounding 'No'. We can be inspired by the fortunes of the past while moving forwards with even more precision, determination and understanding. One of the aspects that has allowed California to progress so quickly is that it is a region willing to adapt and start afresh for the better rather than cling to tradition.

As in any region, a particular microclimate will determine the way a vine functions – its health, yield and the quality of the fruit it produces. Again, without a particular set of consistent practices across producers, it is difficult to distin-guish what defines a quality wine. Ask 10 different producers on the Napa Valley benchlands when their grapes are truly ripe, and you'll get just as many answers; each batch of wine they make, while different in its unique way, will equally be reflective of the Napa Valley style as a whole. A Master of Wine panel conver-sation hosted in San Francisco in 2017 revealed that this was one of the most compelling points of conversation among winemakers Cathy Corison (Corison), Chris Carpenter (Lokoya), Andy Erickson (Favia) and Geneviève Janssens (Robert

Mondavi Winery). Pick times vary from site to site, not just because of a philosophical preference, but because of distinct microclimates within individual AVAs. Something so critical – ripeness – is arguably more subjective than objective.

And yet, California producers need not feel alone. One must ask why estates with vines mere metres apart in Grand Cru Corton-Charlemagne express themselves so differently, even with the same legal parameters. The answer: terroir in any region is a moving target. Some places have simply had more time to determine what it could be.

THE EVOLUTION OF CALIFORNIA WINEMAKING

Renowned Napa Valley winemaker Andy Erickson believes in listening to specific sites rather than allowing a stylistic trend to drive decisions in the vineyard and in the winery. 'There's a re-focus on the land,' he says. And while we both agreed that certain areas have the potential to showcase their 'sense of place' in the bottle because of a combination of factors unique to that site year after year, we conceded that this expression depends on whether or not a wine grower or winemaker chooses to prioritize this identity throughout the production process.

Take the concept of single vineyards: bottles of Napa Valley Cabernet Sauvignon have been labelled as 'To Kalon' or 'Martha's Vineyard' for decades. Each, arguably, shows a consistent expression of place. Others would emulate the success of this single-vineyard expression and a plethora of vineyard-labeled bottlings are emerging from vineyards and regions across the state – many with far less track record. Vineyards from 'Bentrock' to 'Radian' in Sta Rita, 'Occidental Ridge' in the Sonoma Coast and 'Ritchie' in Russian River enter the fray. Vineyard labelling allows producers who have intimate relationships with their sites to explore potential, highlight unique qualities and communicate a sense of place to the consumer. The challenge, however, is to present this account of terroir in earnest without it being perceived as a marketing strategy. Integrity is paramount in a world where listing a vineyard site could come across as forced differentiation without any real meaning.

BREAKING AWAY FROM COMPARISON

Historically, producers in California have always compared their wines to European counterparts. Ten years ago, a winemaker could hardly introduce a cool-climate Sonoma Coast Chardonnay without some reference to Burgundy. Any California Cabernet Sauvignon showing a hint of green bell pepper 'must surely be reminiscent of Bordeaux'. Investment in California from notable Champagne houses – Taittinger and Mumm, specifically – makes it nearly impossible to discuss California sparkling wine without comparing it to champagne, despite these wine styles differing so obviously in fruit style and autolytic interplay.

Comparisons with French classics seem natural enough when trying to sum up a particular style or place for a global audience. The strength to this strategy is that it has made both the trade and consumer more comfortable with their new California choices. The weakness, however, is that the comparative approach fails to accurately differentiate distinct stylistic elements: a Santa Barbara Chardonnay never should taste like Puligny-Montrachet – it should proudly display its firm core of fruit alongside racy acidity. California's regions have arrived at a point where they can stand confidently on their own feet, and more clearly define what makes their wines distinctive without comparison beyond themselves.

What remains in question is how this quest for regional terroir will reveal California's distinct spirit. And while this quest for quality and greatness is spurred on by inherent curiosity it is driven, too, by necessity: climate change has forced winemakers to seek more suitable vineyards for production and to experiment with new varieties that better suit the evolving conditions. Coombsville AVA in Napa was deemed, some 20 years ago, as too cool to ripen Cabernet Sauvignon grapes; now it is home to some of the most vibrant and promising Bordeaux blends. Producers like Steve Matthiasson challenge the conventional notions of what 'belongs' in Napa by championing more obscure varieties like Friulano and Ribolla Gialla. In a world so accustomed to Cabernet Sauvignon and Merlot it takes real guts to make this transition, but results showcase what happens when producers consider land over style – and convenience. Cabernet Sauvignon might be king in Napa and Pinot Noir might have put the Russian River Valley on the map, but they are not the only varieties that grow best.

A CAPTIVATING SPIRIT

There is a tendency to romanticize the past, especially in times when the future feels uncertain. As this chapter is penned, the world finds itself amid a global pandemic; we are at a critical moment for action on climate change, and wildfires and drought are consistent concerns for growers in California. Simultaneously, the promise of what California wine can deliver in future has never seemed so exciting.

With cellars full of well-aged wines under its belt, California can now declare the propensity of its wines for longevity, both at home and abroad, from established estates and newcomers alike. Terroir may seem a more elusive concept, but its pursuit continues to lead to new perspectives, and most importantly, delicious, inspiring wines. As producers continue to seek it out, California wines gain in expression through style and quality, and transform into unique new reference points. What seems to lie ahead for California wine is an even grander awakening, one with riveting explorations and discoveries, and even more creative ways to express its captivating spirit in a bottle.

ON CALIFORNIA, THE CAST

JANE ANSON, British journalist and award-winning author, is an authority on the wines of Bordeaux. She has lived in the region since 2003 and comments regularly on its wines for *Decanter* magazine and for her own website janeanson. com. Jane is well placed to follow the path of Cabernet Sauvignon through the wine world – she charts its epic journey to California on these pages – having brought this grape's trajectory to life in her book, *Inside Bordeaux* (2020).

GERALD ASHER After introducing to London wines from then lesser-known regions of France, British-born Gerald Asher moved to New York in 1971 to join Austin, Nichols, at the time the leading importer of Bordeaux classed growths. Simultaneously, he began his writing career as wine editor of Condé Nast's *Gourmet* magazine. Later he transferred to California to manage the launch of a winery in a newly developed region and soon after was appointed the first chairman of the California Wine Institute's geographic appellations committee. His work in support of California wine led to a formal resolution of recognition from the California State Assembly in March 2009.

JON BONNÉ With his clear, easy-going writing style, Jon is one of America's leading voices on wine and food. He served for nearly a decade as chief wine critic and wine editor at *The San Francisco Chronicle*, part of his quarter-century as a working journalist, and continues to cover wine and drinks in a range of top publications, including his award-winning books *The New California Wine* (2013) and *The New Wine Rules* (2017).

STEPHEN BROOK's motto as a wine writer is 'Do the work!' By which he means go to the regions, wander the vineyards, meet the people, taste the wines. And this he does with incomparable energy, piecing together his findings in an impressive portfolio of nearly 40 books. California is one of Stephen's specialties (alongside Burgundy, Bordeaux, Austria and Germany). Steven was born in London and educated at Trinity College, Cambridge.

ELAINE CHUKAN BROWN Although multi-talented Elaine has spent part of her working life training camels and fishing for wild Alaskan salmon (she is a native Alaskan), her main motivation is wine. She is a passionate wine writer, speaker and educator and in 2020 was named Wine Communicator of the Year by the International Wine & Sprit Competition (IWSC) for her contributions to wine literature. Elaine lives in Sonoma.

OZ CLARKE OBE has championed California wine ever since he was an impoverished young actor discovering (quite by accident) the joys of its Schramsberg sparkling wine – it was cheaper than champagne: 'The wine was so good, it reduced a bunch of stargazery actors to silence.' He went back to Europe still an actor but not for much longer: 'Something thrilling was happening in the world of wine far away from the tired old continent of Europe. And I wanted to be part of it…'

PAUL DRAPER is one of the most important figures in the history of California wine, not only for the success of his Monte Bello Cabernet Sauvignon at the Judgement of Paris (where it ranked fifth in 1976 and first in 2006 at the 30-year repeat tasting) but for his demonstration that Zinfandel can be counted as one of the state's most serious wines. Paul has been at Ridge Vineyards since 1969, and, though he was trained neither as a winemaker or writer, practises both these skills with immeasurable eloquence.

HARRY EYRES Critic, essayist, wine communicator and poet, Harry's career as a writer has spanned everything from the 'Slow Lane' – his *Financial Times* column encouraging thoughtful savouring of the day – to the memoir *Horace and Me: Life Lessons from an Ancient Poet* and co-authorship of *Johnson's Brexit Dictionary* (2018). He is well versed in the vacillations of Cabernet Sauvignon (having written a book on the grape in 1991) and comments wisely for us on its Napa manifestations.

PATRICIA GASTAUD-GALLAGHER As an aspiring American journalist living in Paris in the 1970s, Patricia was thrilled to discover an equally young Englishman successfully selling wine to the French! The story got even better when Steven Spurrier named her 'director' of his Académie du Vin and they created together (it was Patricia's bright idea) the Judgement of Paris…

RANDALL GRAHM started out as a Beverly Hills floor sweeper, but the wine merchant he worked at allowed him to taste enough *cru classé* to turn him into a 'complete and insufferable wine fanatic' (his words). He completed a degree in Plant Sciences at UC Davis and was then lucky enough to purchase a property in the Santa Cruz Mountains, at which his mission to produce great American Pinot Noir met instead with highly successful Rhône varietals. The rest, as they say…

NATASHA HUGHES MW, wine consultant, judge and writer, became a Master of Wine in 2014. She has long been involved in the food and wine scene, initially as a professional cook, and offers insights and sound counsel to those in need of advice on menus, wine lists and the interaction between the two. Natasha's great skill is food and wine pairing; she can always be relied upon to team her favourite champagnes, Australian or California wines with pinpoint gastronomic accuracy.

VICTORIA JAMES To become a top sommelier in New York, Victoria surmounted many difficulties to gain her wine schooling – not the least of which was the great expense involved – but she was determined to succeed. She became the US's youngest qualified sommelier at the age of only 21. Of course, learning about wine means having some knowledge of the winemaking process too. For this, Victoria ventured west to Sonoma…

HUGH JOHNSON OBE needs very little introduction except to say that he is the world's best-selling wine writer. His easy, eloquent prose is as distinctive as it is spellbinding – there is truly no other writer like him for gently enticing a reader to his subject – and we are lucky to have his words grace these pages.

DR WILLIAM KELLEY has reviewed the wines of California for *Decanter* magazine and *The Wine Advocate*. As well as writing about wine, he produces some of his own, in Clarksburg, California, and Chambolle-Musigny, Burgundy. Making wine informs the way he writes about it.

ADAM LECHMERE is a wine journalist and consultant editor for Club Oenologique, which he launched in 2018. He was launch editor for the *Decanter.com* website in 2000, editing the site for 11 years. He is one of only a handful of journalists to have visited Screaming Eagle.

MARY MARGARET McCAMIC MW California-based Mary Margaret earned the prestigious Master of Wine qualification in 2016. When not selling, teaching or talking about wine, you can find her happily drinking it. Her work in the Napa Valley makes Mary Margaret ideally situated to comment on the way California wines are evolving, and what we might expect of them in the future.

KAREN MacNEIL first sat down, unpaid, to write *The Wine Bible* without expectation that anyone would buy it. She just wanted to write the book that she'd have liked when she started learning about wine. It took 10 years – and sold over one million copies. This masterpiece of writing has not only won every major wine award given in the English language, it has taken Karen's career on a magical trajectory of wine travel and tastings. She is a wine educator, author and consultant. We know her as the 'Queen of Napa Valley'.

ELIN McCOY is an award-winning journalist and wine author. A skilled communicator, she also serves as a wine judge in American and international competitions, appears on radio and television, and is a frequent speaker at wine festivals and industry events. Her book, *The Emperor of Wine: The Rise of Robert M Parker Jr and the Reign of American Taste* (2005) has been published in five languages.

ESTHER MOBLEY *The San Francisco Chronicle's* wine critic since 2015, Esther has reported on all aspects of California's $40-billion wine industry, from the natural wine movement to undocumented vineyard workers to wildfires and climate change. Her work has been recognized by the Louis Roederer International Wine Writers' Awards and other awards programmes for feature writing, criticism and agricultural reporting.

FIONA MORRISON MW is an acclaimed writer, author, merchant and négociant with a 30-year wine career spanning both sides of the Atlantic. She is managing director of Thienpont Wine and with her husband, Jacques Thienpont, runs their three Bordeaux estates, Le Pin in Pomerol, L'IF in St Emilion and L'Hêtre in Castillon. Fiona's long love affair with California wine began in the 1980s when she visited the state as a young wine student.

LISA PERROTTI-BROWN MW has spent more than 25 years working in the wine trade, living in London, Tokyo, Singapore and now Napa, California. A Master of Wine since 2008, she is currently the editor-in-chief for *Robert Parker's Wine Advocate* and website RobertParker.com, as well as the publication's critic for the wines of Bordeaux, Napa Valley and Sonoma County. Lisa's first book, *Taste Like a Wine Critic: A Guide to Understanding Wine Quality*, was published in 2015.

REX PICKETT is a California-born novelist, screenwriter, playwright and filmmaker best known for his novel *Sideways*, which features 'Miles' (Rex's alter-ego) and 'Jack' on a week-long wine-tasting sojourn in the Santa Ynez Valley. *Sideways* was adapted into the multiple award-winning film of 2004, which was credited with dramatically increasing Pinot Noir sales in the US and UK. Rex is currently involved in *Sideways: the Musical* and his own *Sideways* wine brand from Chile and New Zealand.

MARGARET RAND is an award-winning author, wine writer and journalist. Her whip-smart interviewing skills ensure that her copy always delivers the most informative quotes and insightful character portrayals. Margaret is general editor of the annual *Hugh Johnson's Pocket Wine Book*.

NORM ROBY is a California-based writer, blogger and wine judge. His written work includes regular contributions to the *Wine Spectator, Decanter*, *winereviewonline* and *Vinosity*. He is co-author of *Connoisseurs Guide to California Wines* (four editions). Norm pieces together the tesserae of California's complicated phylloxera story on these pages.

BRIAN ST PIERRE has been writing about food and wine since 1974, when he joined the Wine Institute in San Francisco; later, he became a contributing editor for *Decanter* magazine in London. He now lives in rural Scotland. He is author of 12 books, a contributor to or editor of a dozen more, and still journalistically inclined.

STEVEN SPURRIER (1941–2021), founder and mentor of the Académie du Vin Library, is remembered and revered for his passionate communication on all aspects of wine. Here, in one of his last interviews, Steven shares his memories of the landmark tasting on May 24th 1976 that became known as the Judgement of Paris and changed the future of California wine forever.

JOHN SZABO MS was the first Canadian to add the 'Master Sommelier' title after his name, in 2004. In his career, he has seen the wine business from all angles, and today spends his time tasting and writing about wines, people and places for multiple publications, co-hosts the *Wine Thieves* podcast, selects wines for the MarQuee Wine Club, and consults on designing and filling one-of-a-kind wine spaces with CellArt.

LIZ THACH MW was the first woman in California (and the seventh in the US) to become a Master of Wine. She has visited most of the major wine regions of the world – and more than 50 countries – but she will always call the Golden State home. Liz charts the history of California sparkling wine here on these pages.

GEORGE M TABER's introduction to wine happened somewhat incidentally to his life and work as a journalist and editor for *Time* magazine. An American in Paris, he was invited to attend a modest blind tasting being held to commemorate his country's 200th year of independence. He was busy that day and nearly didn't make it, but his subsequent report (and book) of the event opened the world's eyes…

BOB THOMPSON, the 'Sage of St Helena', is one of California's most respected wine commentators. His involvement with wine began in the 1960s; he worked for the Wine Institute in San Francisco and took Hugh Johnson on his first Napa winery visits. He has been wine editor of the *San Francisco Chronicle* and often collaborated with Hugh, notably on *The California Wine Book* in 1976. Hugh describes him as his 'oldest and best CA friend'.

CLARE TOOLEY MW Clare says: 'I enjoy wine, drink it, share it, talk about it (a lot, according to my family). I am even fortunate enough to make a living from it.' She began her wine life in London, spent eight years in Bordeaux, and now lives, works and writes in California, where – she was delighted to announce – she passed her Master of Wine exam in 2021.

LARRY WALKER is a food, wine and travel writer. He is passionate about the wines of the Napa Valley (his book on the subject, published in 2005, met with critical acclaim), in particular the Cabernet Sauvignons of Frog's Leap Winery. For this book, Larry leaves his comfort zone and seeks out the wines of California's new cool-climate 'terroir'…

HARRY WAUGH MBE Writer, merchant and wine connoisseur, Harry was born in 1904. He deserves singular recognition for his contribution to the modern California wine story as he was one of the first British champions of Napa wines. Harry was a gifted taster and a prolific writer. In praise of his nine books, one commentator wrote: 'He writes with such high spirits that one is never bogged down by the encyclopedic nature of his subject.' A much-loved member of the wine trade, he died in 2004; he was 97.

KELLI WHITE is director of education for Napa Valley's Meadowood Estate. Prior to that, she worked as a sommelier in New York City and in Napa. She published *Napa Valley, Then & Now* in 2015 and has won two Roederer Awards for her articles. She is a celebrated speaker and educator, and has contributed to several books, including the eighth edition of the *World Atlas of Wine*.

WARREN WINIARSKI Perhaps it is no small coincidence that 'wine' is the root word of the Polish name 'Winiarski'. Warren seemed destined for an academic career until 1964 when he made the fateful decision to leave his post as lecturer at the University of Chicago and move with his family to the Napa Valley. His first commercial wine release, Stag's Leap's 1973 Cabernet Sauvignon, was the highest-ranked wine in the famous '1976 Judgment of Paris', France vs California, blind tasting. This year, 2021, marks his 57th harvest as a winemaker and grapegrower.

INDEX

Page numbers in **bold** refer to main entries; *italic* numbers refer to the illustrations

wildfires 118, 123
  Zinfandel 26
Napa Valley Vintners 233
Napanook vineyard 235, 236
natural wine movement 34–5, 97, 256
Navarro Vineyards 110
Nebbiolo grape 14, **209**, 249
Neibaum, Gustave 24
Nerath, Fritz 78
Newton, Peter *233*
Newton Vineyard 194
Niven, Jack and Catherine 44–8
noble rot 50–1
North Coast 12–14, *13*, 78, 112–13, 145

oak barrels 84
Oak Knoll 235
Oakville 88, 114, 116, 199, 234–8, *237*,
  259, 260
Occidental Vineyard 26
Oliver, Raymond 66, 68, *69*
Olmo, Dr Harold 145, 156, *157*, 160–1,
  162
Opus One 90, 108, 110, 201, **209**, 234
Oregon 62–4, 114, 117, 126
organic viticulture **30–6**
Ortman, Charles 48, 49
Osborne, J W 150
Ovid 223, 238

Pacific Ocean **38–42**, 205, 207, 227–8, 233
Paragon Vineyard Company 46, 48
Parducci 26
Parellada grape 78
Parker, Robert 103, 104, 106–8, 196, 197,
  203
Parr, Rajat 62–3
Parrott, Tiburcio 24
Paso Robles 212
Pejić, Ivan 146–7
Peju Province 110
Penedès 77
Pennsylvania Railroad 96
Pennsylvania Vine Company 21
Perkins, Samuel 148
Perrin family 115
Petaluma Gap 184, 207, 217, 219
Peterson, Austin 223
Peterson, Richard 101
Petit Verdot grape 40, 115
Petite Sirah grape 41, 152, 184
Peynaud, Emile 102
Phelps, Chris 203–4, 205
Phelps, Joseph 89, 195
Phillips, Jean 104, 197–8, *198*
phylloxera 90, 103, **109–16**, *111*, 156–7,
  158, 226

Pickett, Rex, *Sideways* **52–6**
Picpoul grape 41
Pierce's disease 32, 207
Pinot Grigio grape 40
Pinot Meunier grape 138
Pinot Noir grape 26, 40, 55–6, 77, 113,
  167, *172*, 175, 176, 259, 260
  clonal trials 114
  food and 248–9
  Sonoma 14, **57–64**, 184–5
  sparkling wines 138
Piper-Heidsieck 139
Plavac Mali grape 146
Popelouchum 168, 171–3, *172*
Portet, Bernard 100
Pott, Aaron 196, 234
Pott Wines 234
Pouilly-sur-Loire 143
Price Mountain 223
Primitivo grape 146, 147
Prince, William 148–9
Pritchard Hill 222–3, 238
Prohibition 46, 82, 85, 89, **94–7**, 131,
  158–9, 175, 178–9, 183, 190, 230
Promontory 238

Quintessa 235–6
Quivera 34

Rack & Riddle 141
Ramey, David 64, 87–8, 130, 216
Rattlesnake Acres *149*
Ray, Martin 99, 138, 174–5, 226
red wines, translucence **254–7**, *255*
Refosco grape 184, 205
regenerative organic agriculture 35–6,
  127
Renaissance Winery 231
Repris Wines 218
restaurants, 'California cuisine' **242–5**
Rhodes, Belle & Barney **206**
Rhône Rangers **210**
Rhys 62, 226
Ridge Vineyards 26, 68, **79–86**, *81*, *83*,
  100, 147, 226, 258, 259
Riesling grape 14, 40, 75, 115, 137, 138,
  176
ripeness 87–8, 260–1
Rochioli, Joe 57–8, 216
Rodale, J I 30–1, 32
Rodgers, Judy 244
Roederer 62, 139–40, *139*
Rolland, Michel 106, 200
Roosevelt, Franklin D. 96
rootstocks 90, 103, 109–16
Rorick Heritage Vineyard 231
rosé wines 247

Rossese grape 168
Rossi, Edmund and Robert 97
Rossi Ranch 33
Rothschild, Baron Philippe de 108, 209
Roussanne grape 115, 248, 256
Russian River Valley 57, 105, 116, 137,
  140–1, 185, 216, 258, 261, 262
Rutherford 110, 212, 235, 236

St Clement 48, 114
Saint-Emilion 74
St Helena 88, 99, 204–5, 223, 235
Saintsbury, George 57, 174, 176
San Andreas Fault 79, 184, 214–16
San Diego 17
San Francisco 17–18, 39, 117, 158, 207,
  210, 214, 216, 225, 240–1
San Francisco Bay 40, 217, **225–6**, 227–8,
  231
San Gabriel Winery 136
San Joaquin Valley 160
San Luis Obispo 33, 43–6, *44–5*, 51, 175
San Pablo Bay 225, 227–8, *227*
Sandlands 226
Sanford, Richard 32–3, 53–6
Sanford & Benedict 58, 61
Sangiovese grape 249, 256
Santa Barbara 32–3, 40, 57, 119, 126, 175,
  207, 248, 259, 262
Santa Clara Valley 225, 226
Santa Cruz Mountains 210, 226, 228, 259
Santa Lucia Highlands 41
Santa Maria Valley 207, 209
Santa (Sta) Rita Hills *59*, 60, 61, 63, 198,
  248, 258, 260, 261
Santa Rosa 50
Santa Ynez Valley 52–6, 57, 198, 207
Saratoga 225, 226
Sauternes 50–1, 142–3
Sauvignon Blanc grape 22, 23–4, 55, 116,
  142–4, 146, 175, 176
Sauvignon Musque grape 116
Savagnin de Jura grape 143
Scharffenberger Cellars 139, 140
Schioppettino grape 205
Schoonmaker, Frank 24, 102
Schramsberg 103, 138, *139*, 155, 224, 258
scoring wines **178–80**
Screaming Eagle 104, 106, 107, *107*,
  197–201, 197–8, *200*, 223, 234, 258
Scribe Winery 188
Sea Smoke 61
sélection massale **132–4**, 135, 167
self-crosses, grapes 168–70
Sémillon grape 116, 143
Sérine grape 168, 169, 170
Serra, Junípero 45

PICTURE CREDITS